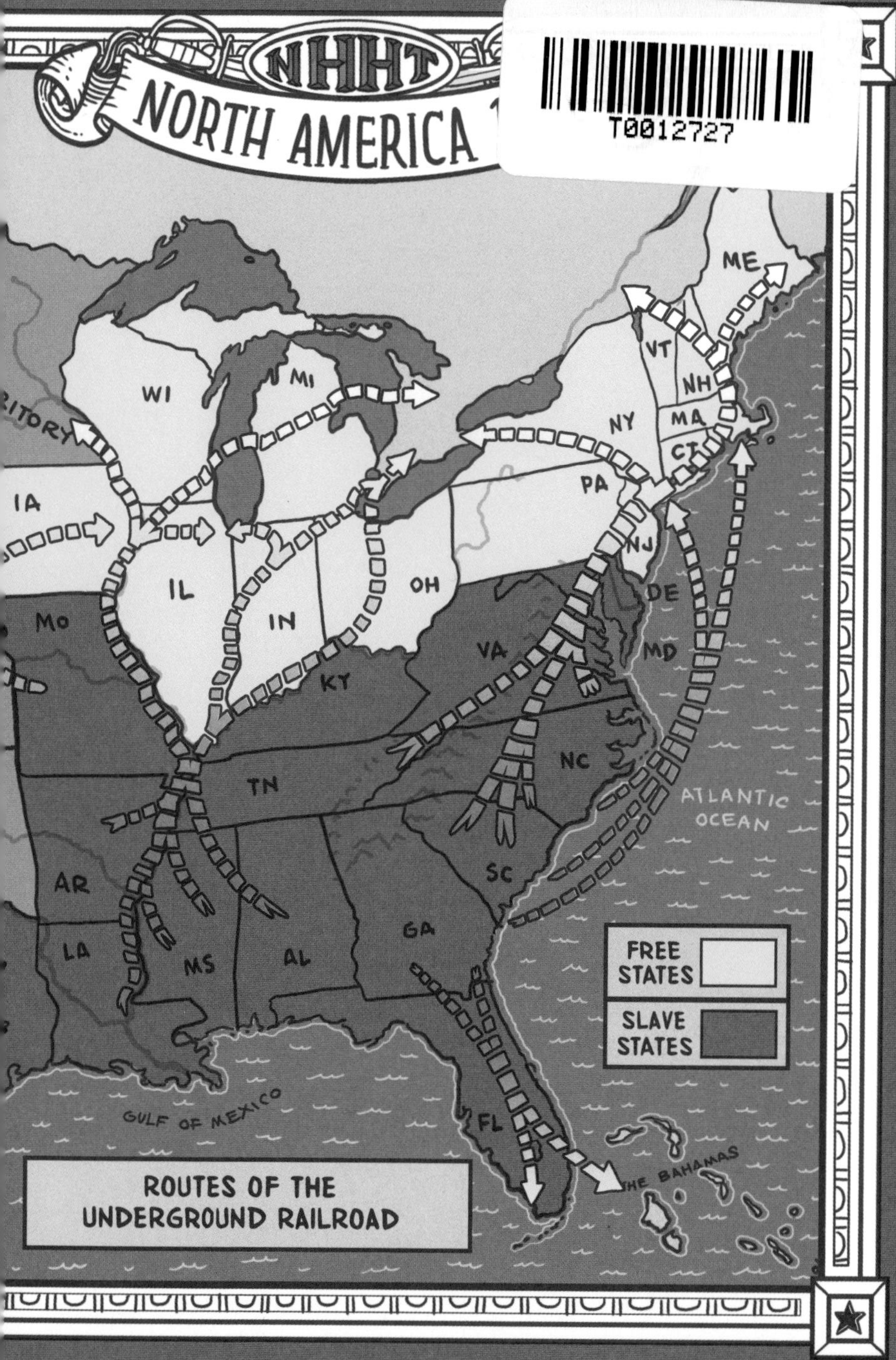
NHHT
NORTH AMERICA
ROUTES OF THE UNDERGROUND RAILROAD
FREE STATES
SLAVE STATES
WI
MI
IA
IL
IN
OH
PA
NY
VT
NH
ME
MA
CT
NJ
DE
MD
VA
KY
MO
TN
NC
SC
GA
AL
MS
AR
LA
FL
ATLANTIC OCEAN
GULF OF MEXICO
THE BAHAMAS

THE UNDERGROUND ABDUCTOR

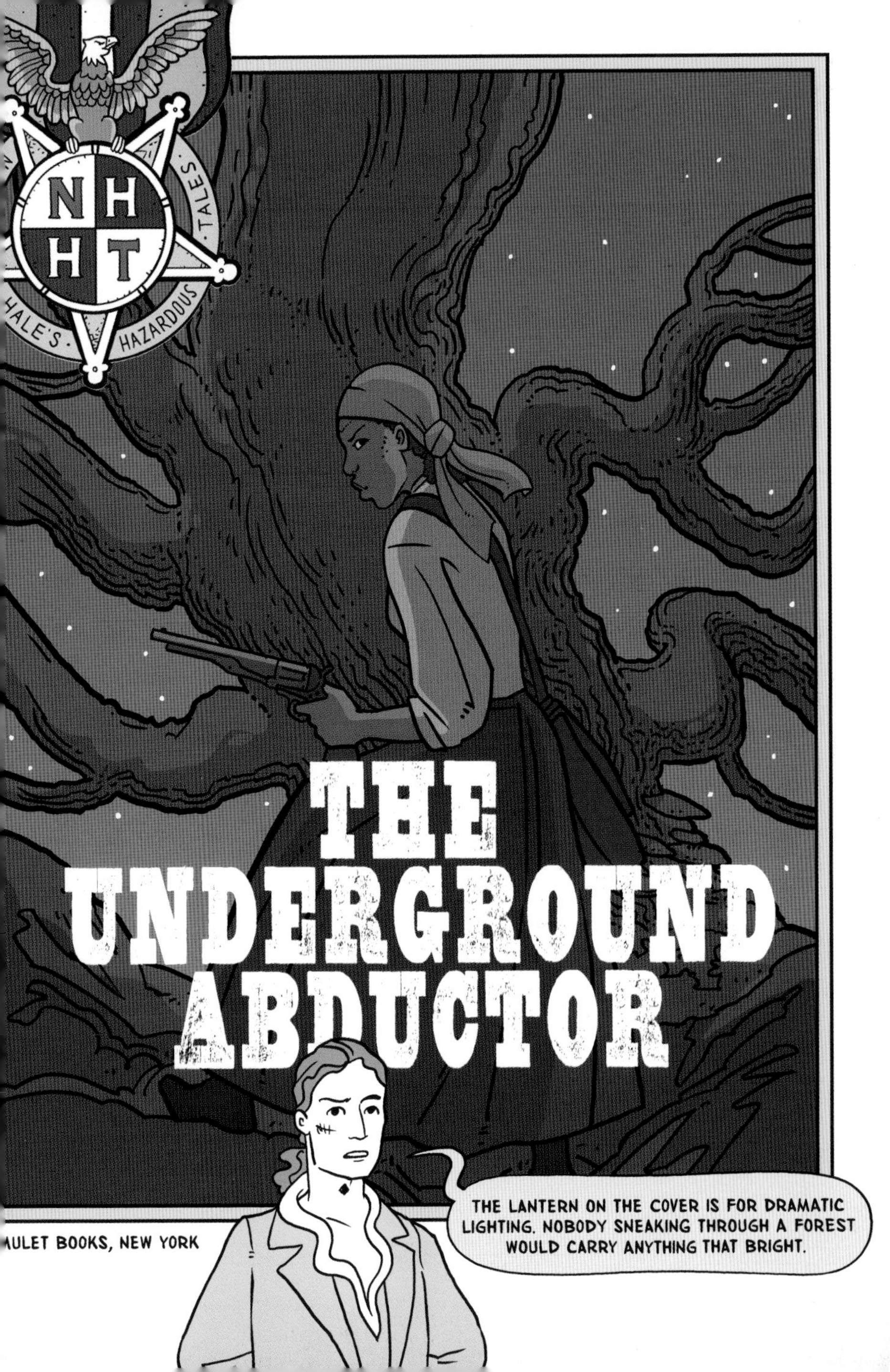
NATHAN HALE'S HAZARDOUS TALES
NHHT
THE UNDERGROUND ABDUCTOR
THE LANTERN ON THE COVER IS FOR DRAMATIC LIGHTING. NOBODY SNEAKING THROUGH A FOREST WOULD CARRY ANYTHING THAT BRIGHT.

AMULET BOOKS, NEW YORK

CATALOGING—IN—PUBLICATION DATA HAS BEEN APPLIED FOR
AND MAY BE OBTAINED FROM THE LIBRARY OF CONGRESS.

LIBRARY OF CONGRESS CONTROL NUMBER 2016297698
ISBN: 978-1-4197-1536-5

PRINTED AND BOUND IN CHINA
16

AMULET BOOKS ARE AVAILABLE AT SPECIAL DISCOUNTS WHEN
PURCHASED IN QUANTITY FOR PREMIUMS AND PROMOTIONS
AS WELL AS FUNDRAISING OR EDUCATIONAL USE. SPECIAL
EDITIONS CAN ALSO BE CREATED TO SPECIFICATION. FOR
DETAILS, CONTACT SPECIALSALES@ABRAMSBOOKS.COM OR
THE ADDRESS BELOW.

ABRAMS The Art of Books
195 Broadway, New York, NY 10007
abramsbooks.com

TO MY MOM

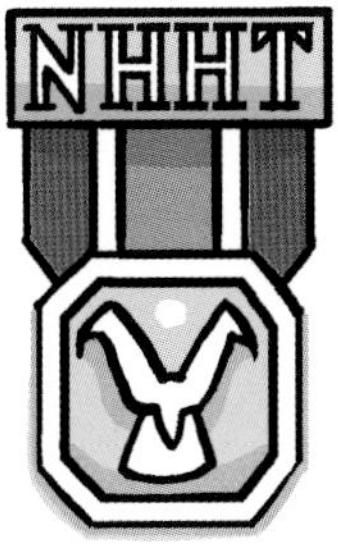
NHHT

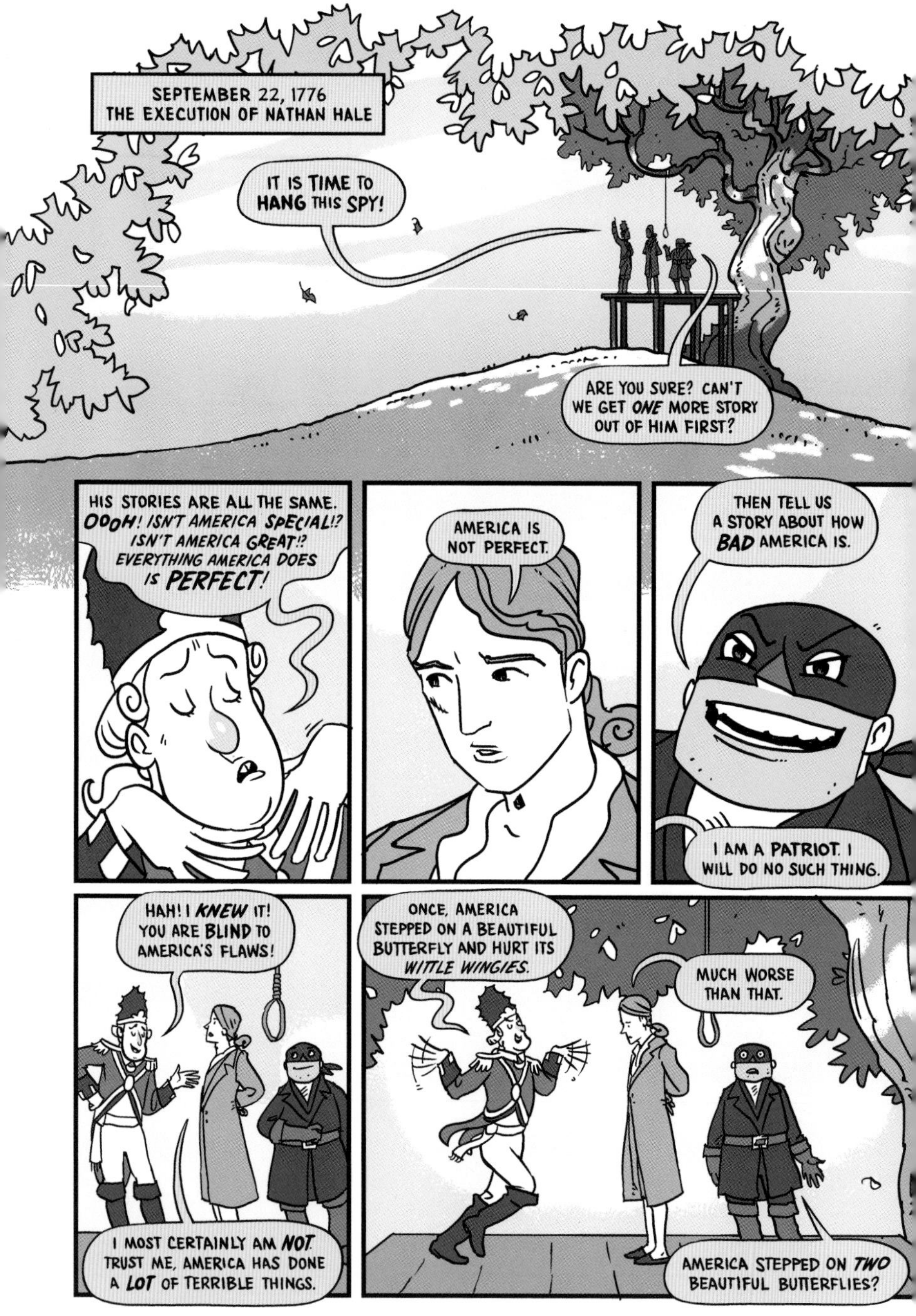
SEPTEMBER 22, 1776
THE EXECUTION OF NATHAN HALE
IT IS TIME TO HANG THIS SPY!
ARE YOU SURE? CAN'T WE GET ONE MORE STORY OUT OF HIM FIRST?
HIS STORIES ARE ALL THE SAME. OOOH! ISN'T AMERICA SPECIAL!? ISN'T AMERICA GREAT!? EVERYTHING AMERICA DOES IS PERFECT!
AMERICA IS NOT PERFECT.
THEN TELL US A STORY ABOUT HOW BAD AMERICA IS.
I AM A PATRIOT. I WILL DO NO SUCH THING.
HAH! I KNEW IT! YOU ARE BLIND TO AMERICA'S FLAWS!
I MOST CERTAINLY AM NOT. TRUST ME, AMERICA HAS DONE A LOT OF TERRIBLE THINGS.
ONCE, AMERICA STEPPED ON A BEAUTIFUL BUTTERFLY AND HURT ITS WITTLE WINGIES.
MUCH WORSE THAN THAT.
AMERICA STEPPED ON TWO BEAUTIFUL BUTTERFLIES?

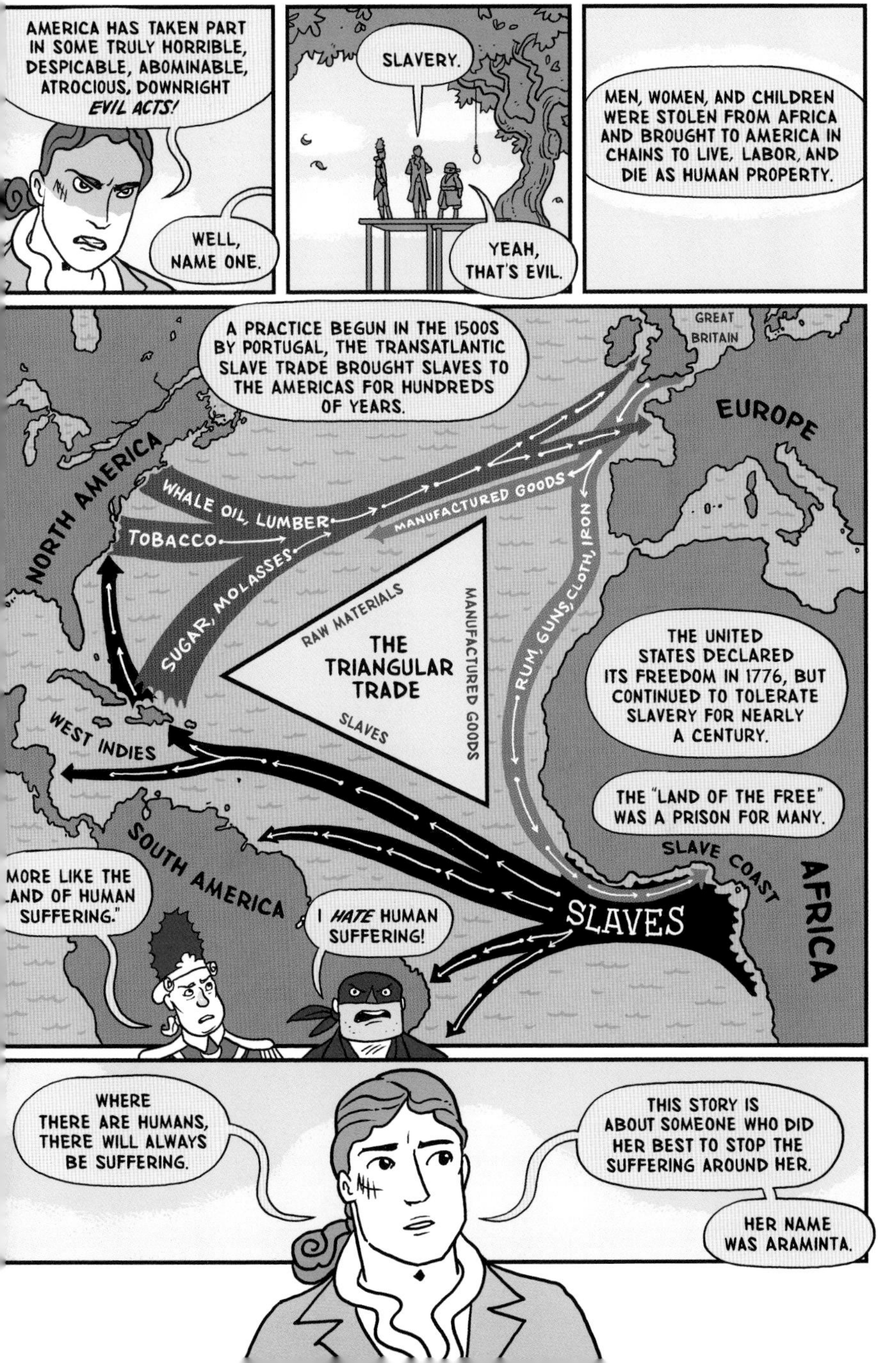
AMERICA HAS TAKEN PART IN SOME TRULY HORRIBLE, DESPICABLE, ABOMINABLE, ATROCIOUS, DOWNRIGHT *EVIL ACTS!*
WELL, NAME ONE.
SLAVERY.
YEAH, THAT'S EVIL.
MEN, WOMEN, AND CHILDREN WERE STOLEN FROM AFRICA AND BROUGHT TO AMERICA IN CHAINS TO LIVE, LABOR, AND DIE AS HUMAN PROPERTY.
A PRACTICE BEGUN IN THE 1500S BY PORTUGAL, THE TRANSATLANTIC SLAVE TRADE BROUGHT SLAVES TO THE AMERICAS FOR HUNDREDS OF YEARS.
GREAT BRITAIN
EUROPE
NORTH AMERICA
WHALE OIL, LUMBER
TOBACCO
SUGAR, MOLASSES
MANUFACTURED GOODS
RUM, GUNS, CLOTH, IRON
RAW MATERIALS
THE TRIANGULAR TRADE
MANUFACTURED GOODS
SLAVES
WEST INDIES
SOUTH AMERICA
SLAVE COAST
AFRICA
SLAVES
THE UNITED STATES DECLARED ITS FREEDOM IN 1776, BUT CONTINUED TO TOLERATE SLAVERY FOR NEARLY A CENTURY.
THE "LAND OF THE FREE" WAS A PRISON FOR MANY.
MORE LIKE THE LAND OF HUMAN SUFFERING."
I *HATE* HUMAN SUFFERING!
WHERE THERE ARE HUMANS, THERE WILL ALWAYS BE SUFFERING.
THIS STORY IS ABOUT SOMEONE WHO DID HER BEST TO STOP THE SUFFERING AROUND HER.
HER NAME WAS ARAMINTA.

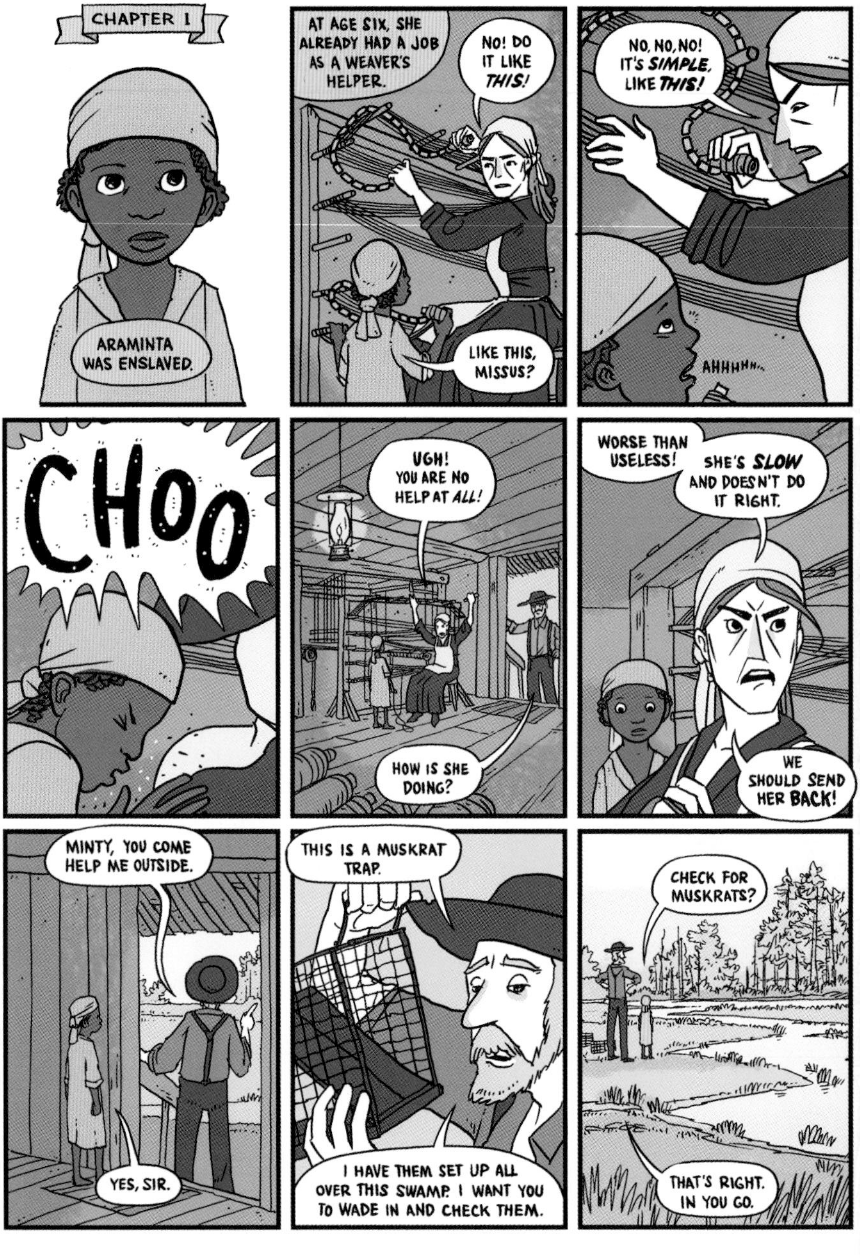
CHAPTER 1
ARAMINTA WAS ENSLAVED.
AT AGE SIX, SHE ALREADY HAD A JOB AS A WEAVER'S HELPER.
NO! DO IT LIKE *THIS!*
LIKE THIS, MISSUS?
NO, NO, NO! IT'S *SIMPLE*, LIKE *THIS!*
AHHHHH...
CHOO
UGH! YOU ARE NO HELP AT *ALL!*
HOW IS SHE DOING?
WORSE THAN USELESS!
SHE'S *SLOW* AND DOESN'T DO IT RIGHT.
WE SHOULD SEND HER **BACK!**
MINTY, YOU COME HELP ME OUTSIDE.
YES, SIR.
THIS IS A MUSKRAT TRAP.
I HAVE THEM SET UP ALL OVER THIS SWAMP. I WANT YOU TO WADE IN AND CHECK THEM.
CHECK FOR MUSKRATS?
THAT'S RIGHT. IN YOU GO.

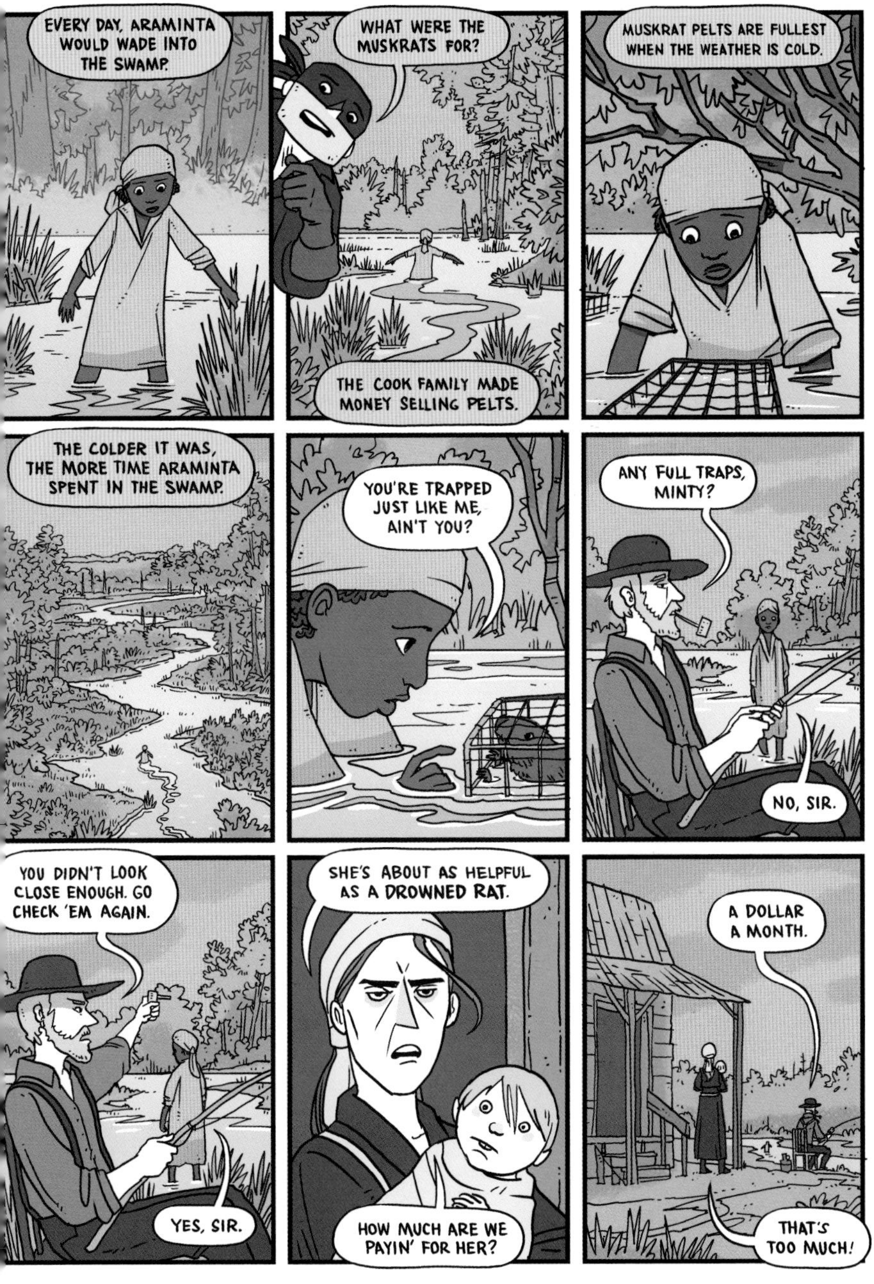
EVERY DAY, ARAMINTA WOULD WADE INTO THE SWAMP.
WHAT WERE THE MUSKRATS FOR?
THE COOK FAMILY MADE MONEY SELLING PELTS.
MUSKRAT PELTS ARE FULLEST WHEN THE WEATHER IS COLD.
THE COLDER IT WAS, THE MORE TIME ARAMINTA SPENT IN THE SWAMP.
YOU'RE TRAPPED JUST LIKE ME, AIN'T YOU?
ANY FULL TRAPS, MINTY?
NO, SIR.
YOU DIDN'T LOOK CLOSE ENOUGH. GO CHECK 'EM AGAIN.
YES, SIR.
SHE'S ABOUT AS HELPFUL AS A DROWNED RAT.
HOW MUCH ARE WE PAYIN' FOR HER?
A DOLLAR A MONTH.
THAT'S TOO MUCH!

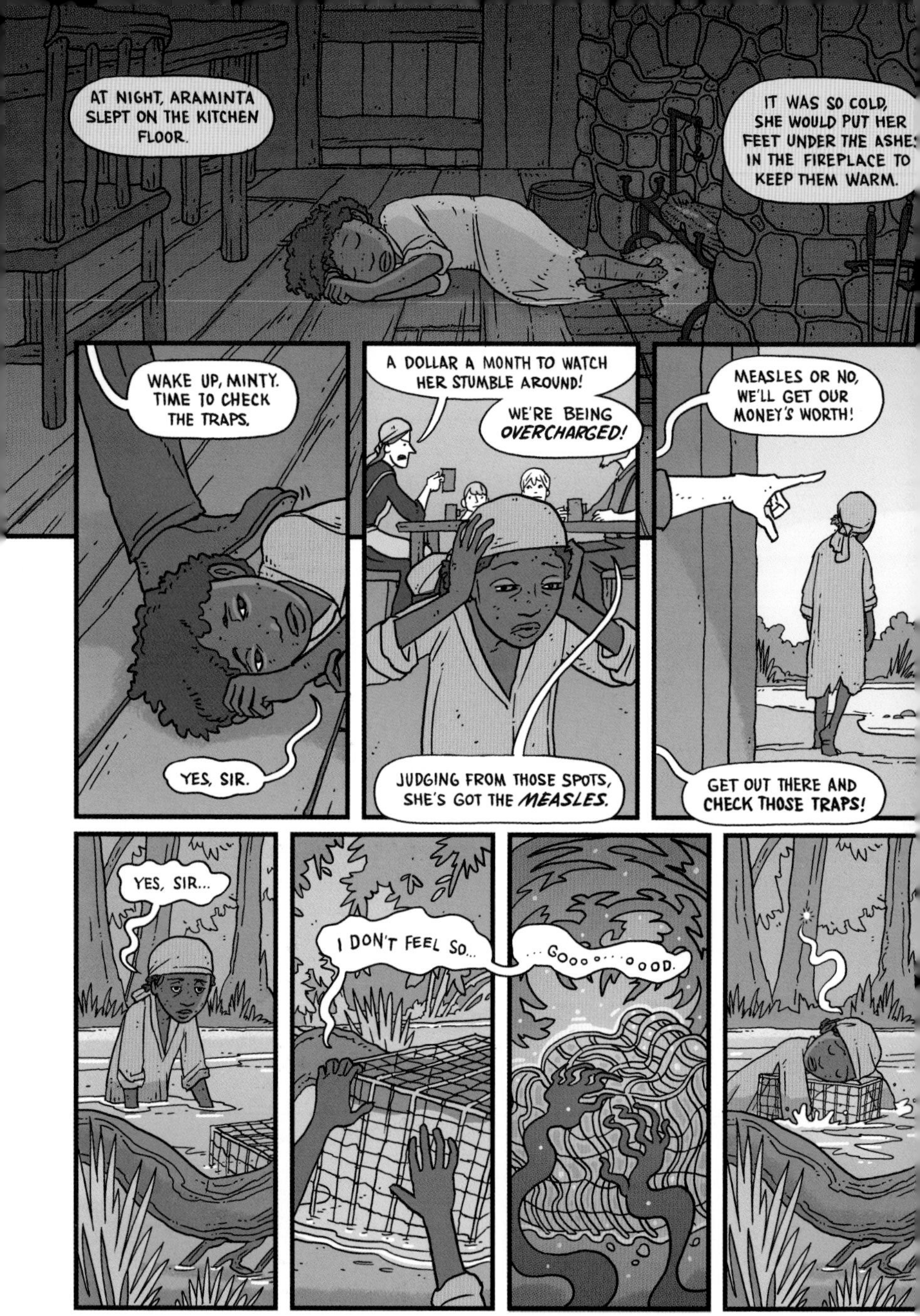
AT NIGHT, ARAMINTA SLEPT ON THE KITCHEN FLOOR.
IT WAS SO COLD, SHE WOULD PUT HER FEET UNDER THE ASHES IN THE FIREPLACE TO KEEP THEM WARM.
WAKE UP, MINTY. TIME TO CHECK THE TRAPS.
YES, SIR.
A DOLLAR A MONTH TO WATCH HER STUMBLE AROUND!
WE'RE BEING OVERCHARGED!
JUDGING FROM THOSE SPOTS, SHE'S GOT THE MEASLES.
MEASLES OR NO, WE'LL GET OUR MONEY'S WORTH!
GET OUT THERE AND CHECK THOSE TRAPS!
YES, SIR...
I DON'T FEEL SO...
...GOOo o...o OOD.

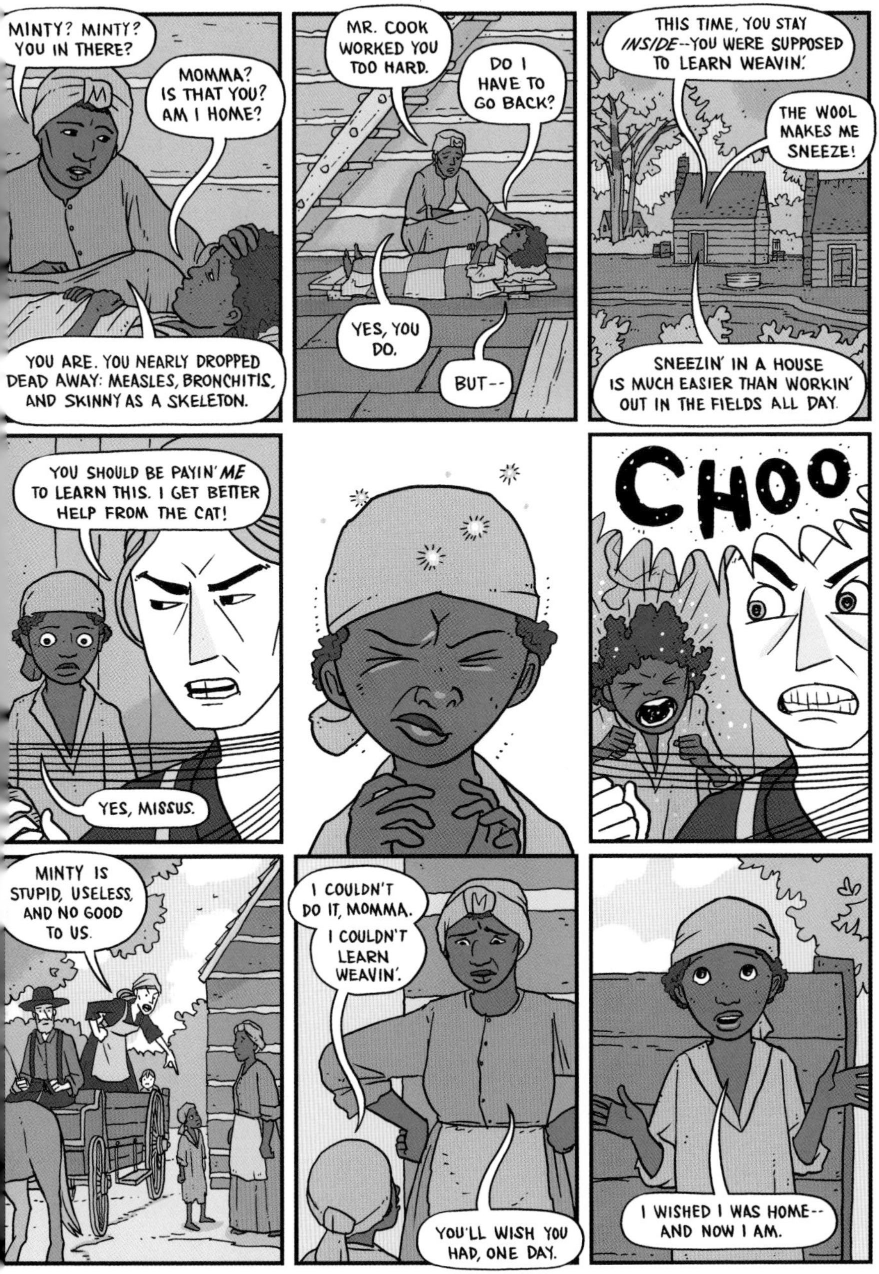
MINTY? MINTY? YOU IN THERE?
MOMMA? IS THAT YOU? AM I HOME?
YOU ARE. YOU NEARLY DROPPED DEAD AWAY: MEASLES, BRONCHITIS, AND SKINNY AS A SKELETON.
MR. COOK WORKED YOU TOO HARD.
DO I HAVE TO GO BACK?
YES, YOU DO.
BUT--
THIS TIME, YOU STAY *INSIDE*--YOU WERE SUPPOSED TO LEARN WEAVIN'.
THE WOOL MAKES ME SNEEZE!
SNEEZIN' IN A HOUSE IS MUCH EASIER THAN WORKIN' OUT IN THE FIELDS ALL DAY.
YOU SHOULD BE PAYIN' *ME* TO LEARN THIS. I GET BETTER HELP FROM THE CAT!
YES, MISSUS.
CHOO
MINTY IS STUPID, USELESS, AND NO GOOD TO US.
I COULDN'T DO IT, MOMMA.
I COULDN'T LEARN WEAVIN'.
YOU'LL WISH YOU HAD, ONE DAY.
I WISHED I WAS HOME-- AND NOW I AM.

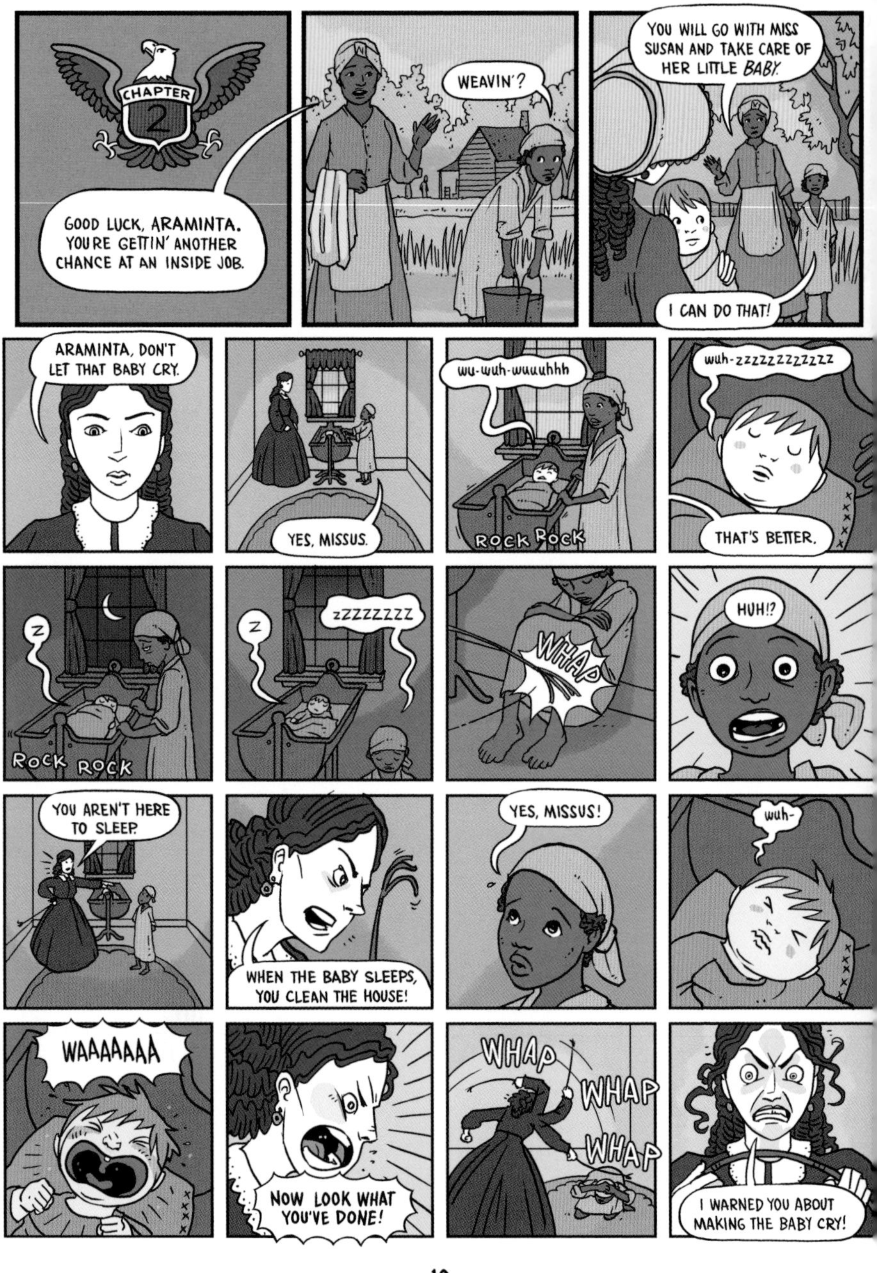
CHAPTER
2
GOOD LUCK, ARAMINTA. YOU'RE GETTIN' ANOTHER CHANCE AT AN INSIDE JOB.
WEAVIN'?
YOU WILL GO WITH MISS SUSAN AND TAKE CARE OF HER LITTLE BABY.
I CAN DO THAT!
ARAMINTA, DON'T LET THAT BABY CRY.
YES, MISSUS.
wu-wuh-wuuuhhh
ROCK ROCK
wuh-zzzzzzzzzzz
THAT'S BETTER.
Z
ROCK ROCK
Z
zZZZZZZZ
WHAP
HUH!?
YOU AREN'T HERE TO SLEEP.
WHEN THE BABY SLEEPS, YOU CLEAN THE HOUSE!
YES, MISSUS!
wuh-
WAAAAAAA
NOW LOOK WHAT YOU'VE DONE!
WHAP
WHAP
WHAP
I WARNED YOU ABOUT MAKING THE BABY CRY!

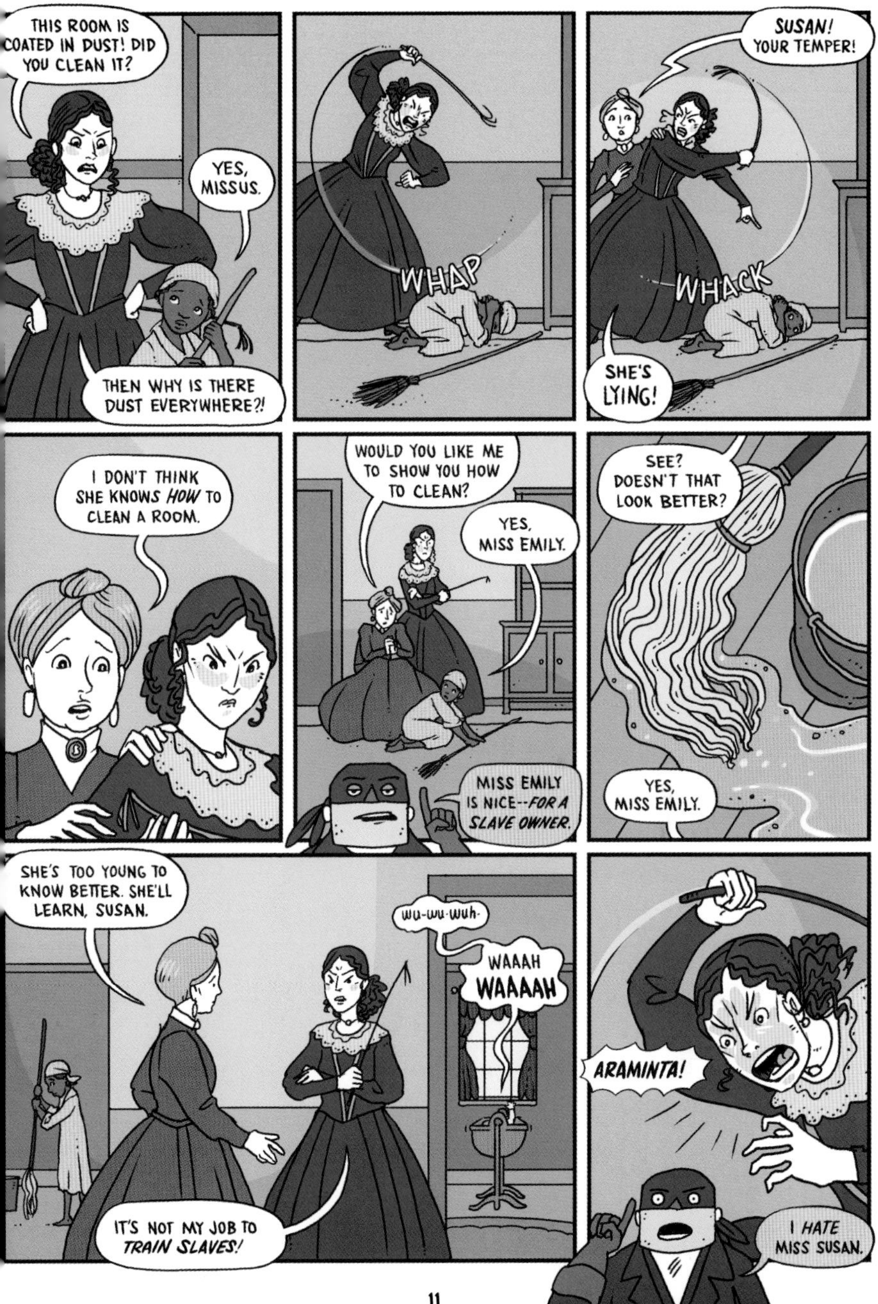
THIS ROOM IS COATED IN DUST! DID YOU CLEAN IT?
YES, MISSUS.
THEN WHY IS THERE DUST EVERYWHERE?!
WHAP
SUSAN! YOUR TEMPER!
WHACK
SHE'S LYING!
I DON'T THINK SHE KNOWS *HOW* TO CLEAN A ROOM.
WOULD YOU LIKE ME TO SHOW YOU HOW TO CLEAN?
YES, MISS EMILY.
MISS EMILY IS NICE--*FOR A SLAVE OWNER.*
SEE? DOESN'T THAT LOOK BETTER?
YES, MISS EMILY.
SHE'S TOO YOUNG TO KNOW BETTER. SHE'LL LEARN, SUSAN.
wu-wu-wuh-
WAAAH WAAAAH
IT'S NOT MY JOB TO *TRAIN SLAVES!*
ARAMINTA!
I *HATE* MISS SUSAN.

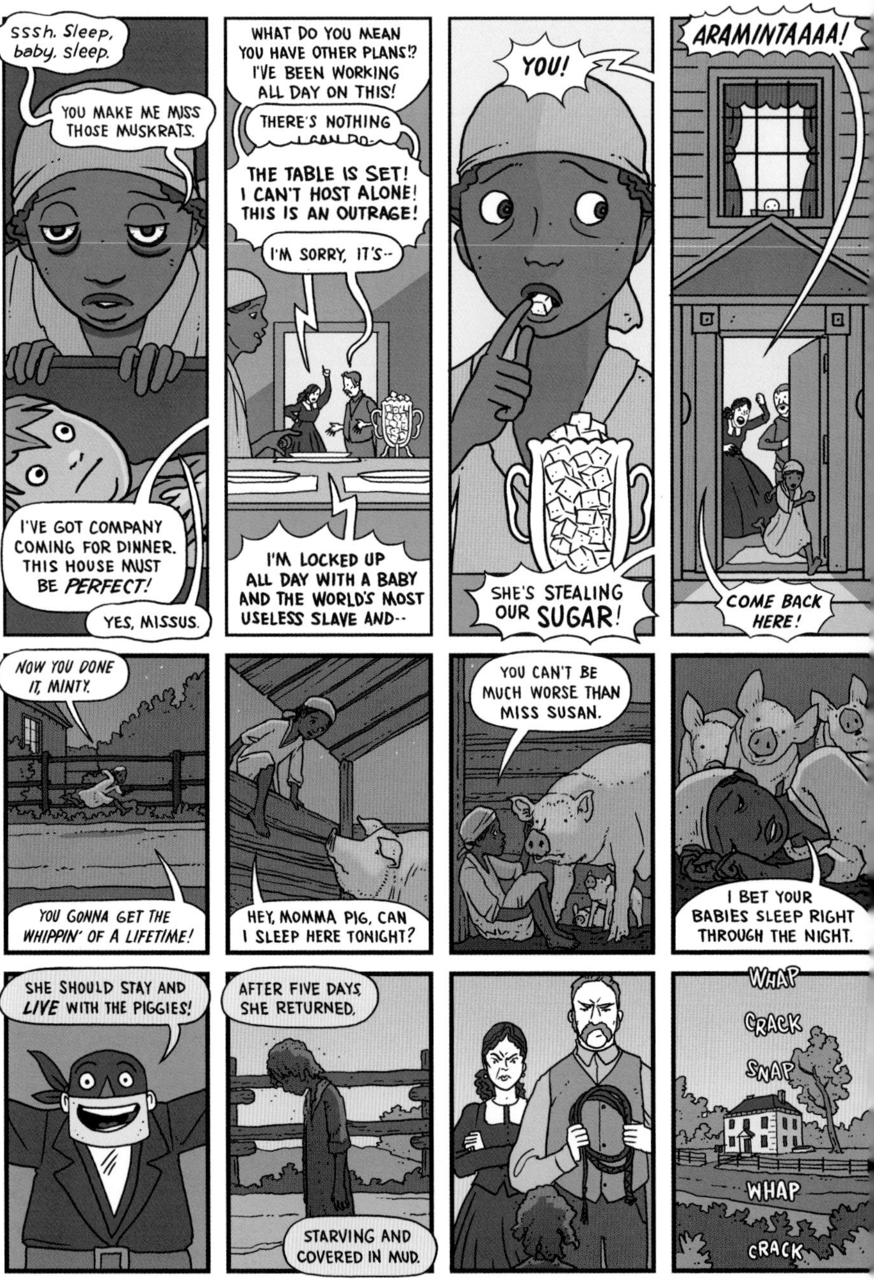
sssh. Sleep, baby, sleep.
YOU MAKE ME MISS THOSE MUSKRATS.
I'VE GOT COMPANY COMING FOR DINNER. THIS HOUSE MUST BE PERFECT!
YES, MISSUS.
WHAT DO YOU MEAN YOU HAVE OTHER PLANS!? I'VE BEEN WORKING ALL DAY ON THIS!
THERE'S NOTHING
THE TABLE IS SET! I CAN'T HOST ALONE! THIS IS AN OUTRAGE!
I'M SORRY, IT'S--
I'M LOCKED UP ALL DAY WITH A BABY AND THE WORLD'S MOST USELESS SLAVE AND--
YOU!
SHE'S STEALING OUR SUGAR!
ARAMINTAAAA!
COME BACK HERE!
NOW YOU DONE IT, MINTY.
YOU GONNA GET THE WHIPPIN' OF A LIFETIME!
HEY, MOMMA PIG, CAN I SLEEP HERE TONIGHT?
YOU CAN'T BE MUCH WORSE THAN MISS SUSAN.
I BET YOUR BABIES SLEEP RIGHT THROUGH THE NIGHT.
SHE SHOULD STAY AND LIVE WITH THE PIGGIES!
AFTER FIVE DAYS, SHE RETURNED,
STARVING AND COVERED IN MUD.
WHAP
CRACK
SNAP
WHAP
CRACK

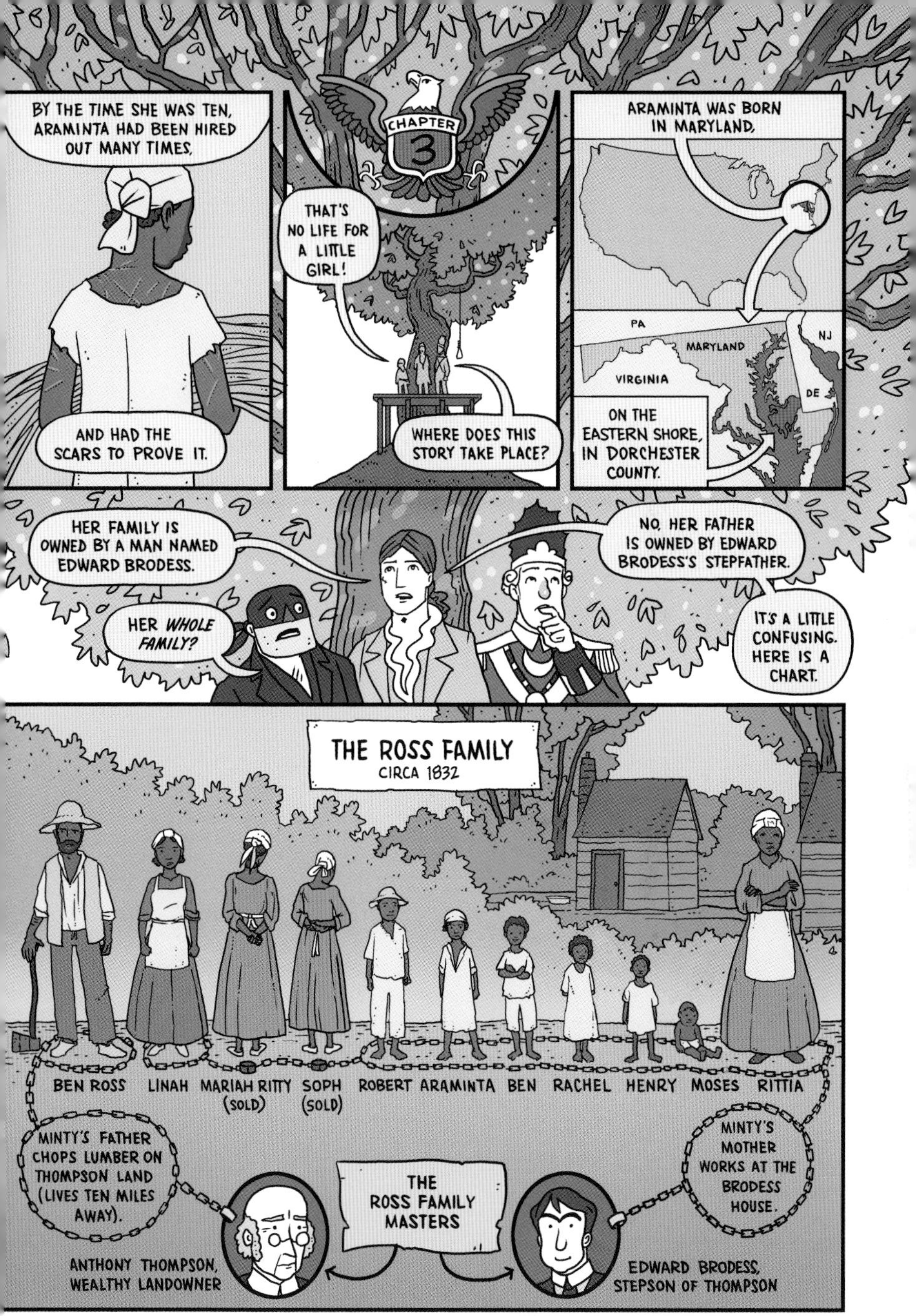
BY THE TIME SHE WAS TEN, ARAMINTA HAD BEEN HIRED OUT MANY TIMES,
AND HAD THE SCARS TO PROVE IT.
CHAPTER 3
THAT'S NO LIFE FOR A LITTLE GIRL!
WHERE DOES THIS STORY TAKE PLACE?
ARAMINTA WAS BORN IN MARYLAND,
PA
MARYLAND
NJ
VIRGINIA
DE
ON THE EASTERN SHORE, IN DORCHESTER COUNTY.
HER FAMILY IS OWNED BY A MAN NAMED EDWARD BRODESS.
NO, HER FATHER IS OWNED BY EDWARD BRODESS'S STEPFATHER.
HER *WHOLE FAMILY?*
IT'S A LITTLE CONFUSING. HERE IS A CHART.
THE ROSS FAMILY
CIRCA 1832
BEN ROSS
LINAH
MARIAH RITTY (SOLD)
SOPH (SOLD)
ROBERT
ARAMINTA
BEN
RACHEL
HENRY
MOSES
RITTIA
MINTY'S FATHER CHOPS LUMBER ON THOMPSON LAND (LIVES TEN MILES AWAY).
MINTY'S MOTHER WORKS AT THE BRODESS HOUSE.
THE ROSS FAMILY MASTERS
ANTHONY THOMPSON, WEALTHY LANDOWNER
EDWARD BRODESS, STEPSON OF THOMPSON

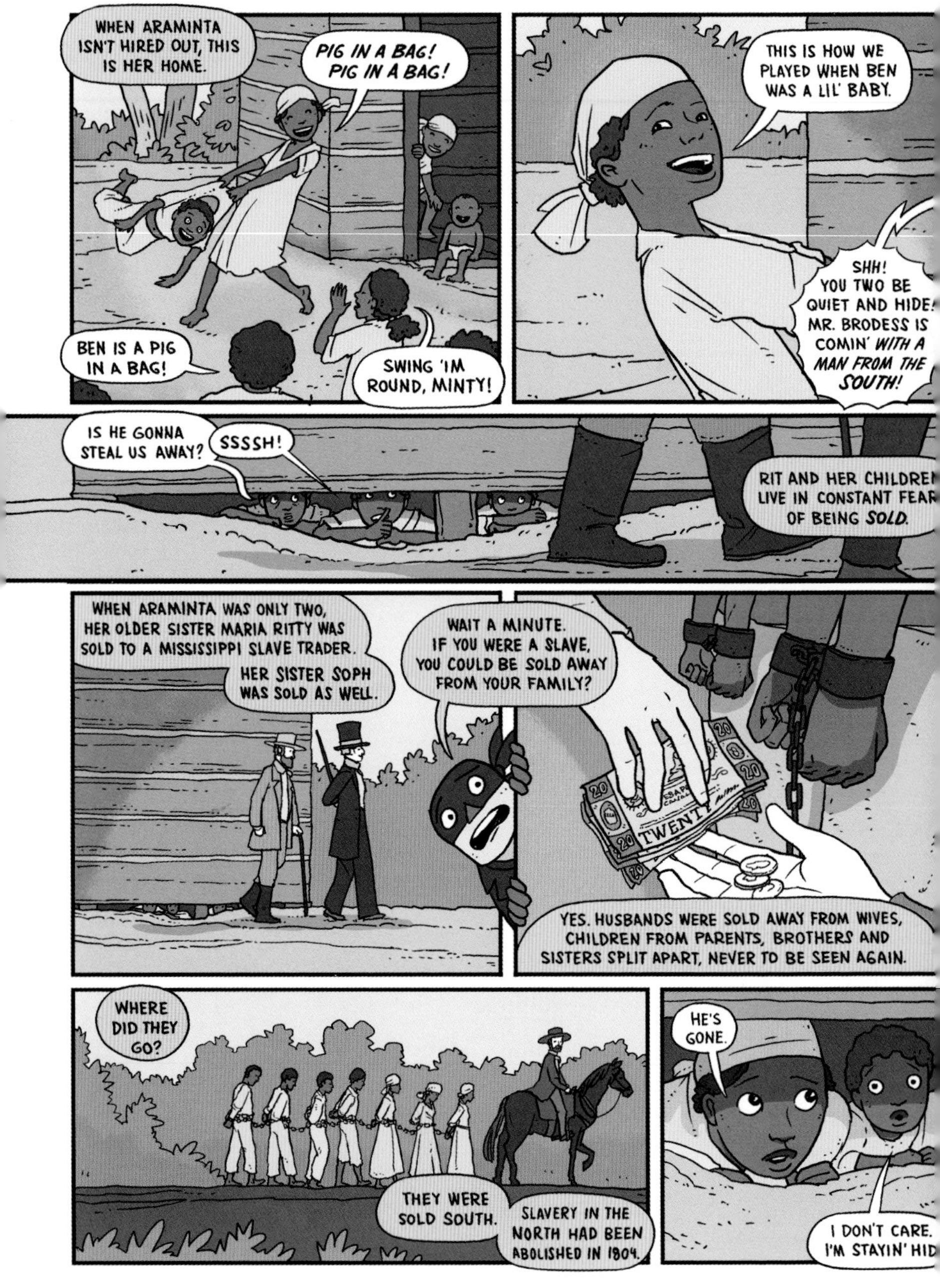

WHEN ARAMINTA ISN'T HIRED OUT, THIS IS HER HOME.
PIG IN A BAG! PIG IN A BAG!
BEN IS A PIG IN A BAG!
SWING 'IM ROUND, MINTY!
THIS IS HOW WE PLAYED WHEN BEN WAS A LIL' BABY.
SHH! YOU TWO BE QUIET AND HIDE! MR. BRODESS IS COMIN' WITH A MAN FROM THE SOUTH!
IS HE GONNA STEAL US AWAY?
SSSSH!
RIT AND HER CHILDREN LIVE IN CONSTANT FEAR OF BEING SOLD.
WHEN ARAMINTA WAS ONLY TWO, HER OLDER SISTER MARIA RITTY WAS SOLD TO A MISSISSIPPI SLAVE TRADER.
HER SISTER SOPH WAS SOLD AS WELL.
WAIT A MINUTE. IF YOU WERE A SLAVE, YOU COULD BE SOLD AWAY FROM YOUR FAMILY?
YES. HUSBANDS WERE SOLD AWAY FROM WIVES, CHILDREN FROM PARENTS, BROTHERS AND SISTERS SPLIT APART, NEVER TO BE SEEN AGAIN.
WHERE DID THEY GO?
THEY WERE SOLD SOUTH.
SLAVERY IN THE NORTH HAD BEEN ABOLISHED IN 1804.
HE'S GONE.
I DON'T CARE. I'M STAYIN' HID

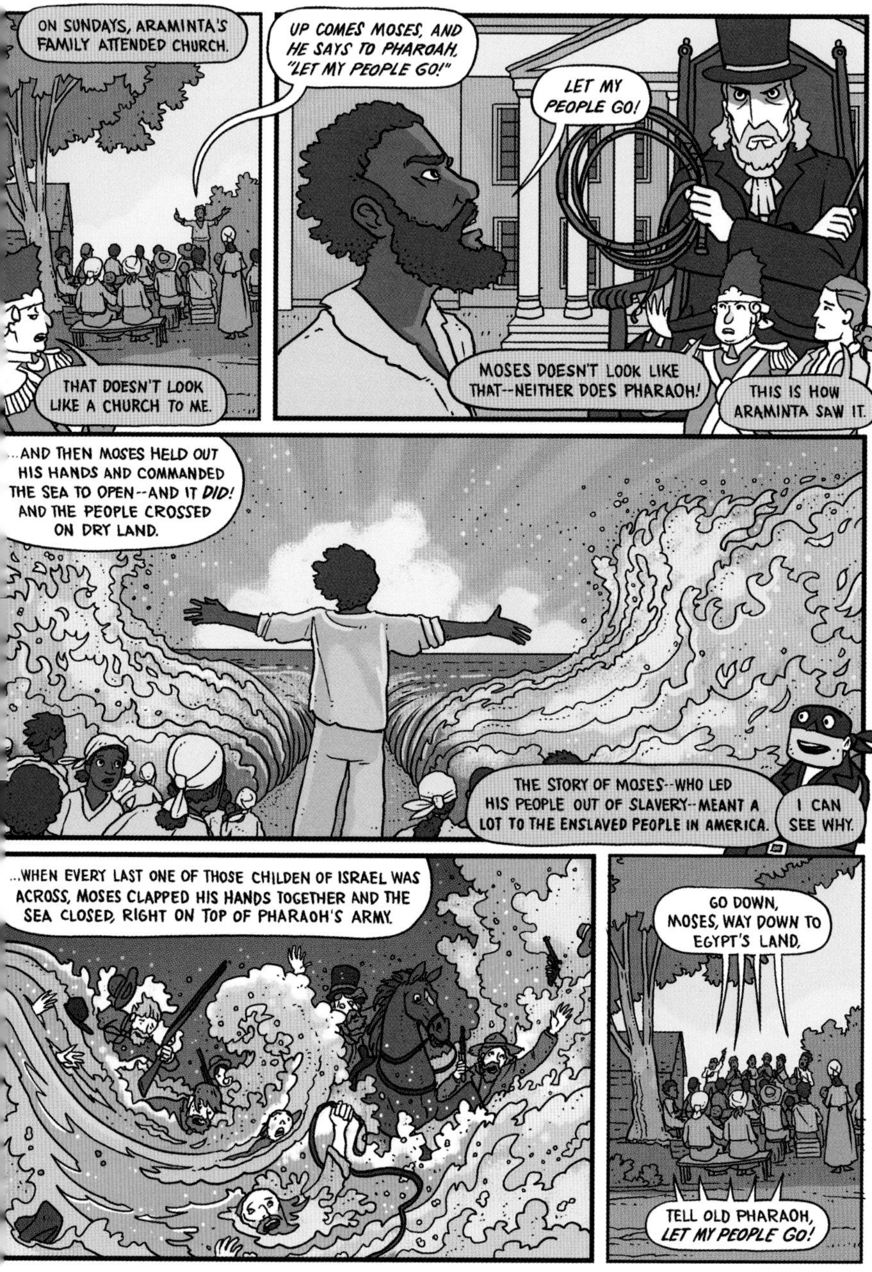
ON SUNDAYS, ARAMINTA'S FAMILY ATTENDED CHURCH.
THAT DOESN'T LOOK LIKE A CHURCH TO ME.
UP COMES MOSES, AND HE SAYS TO PHAROAH, "LET MY PEOPLE GO!"
LET MY PEOPLE GO!
MOSES DOESN'T LOOK LIKE THAT--NEITHER DOES PHARAOH!
THIS IS HOW ARAMINTA SAW IT.
...AND THEN MOSES HELD OUT HIS HANDS AND COMMANDED THE SEA TO OPEN--AND IT DID! AND THE PEOPLE CROSSED ON DRY LAND.
THE STORY OF MOSES--WHO LED HIS PEOPLE OUT OF SLAVERY--MEANT A LOT TO THE ENSLAVED PEOPLE IN AMERICA.
I CAN SEE WHY.
...WHEN EVERY LAST ONE OF THOSE CHILDEN OF ISRAEL WAS ACROSS, MOSES CLAPPED HIS HANDS TOGETHER AND THE SEA CLOSED, RIGHT ON TOP OF PHARAOH'S ARMY.
GO DOWN, MOSES, WAY DOWN TO EGYPT'S LAND,
TELL OLD PHARAOH, LET MY PEOPLE GO!

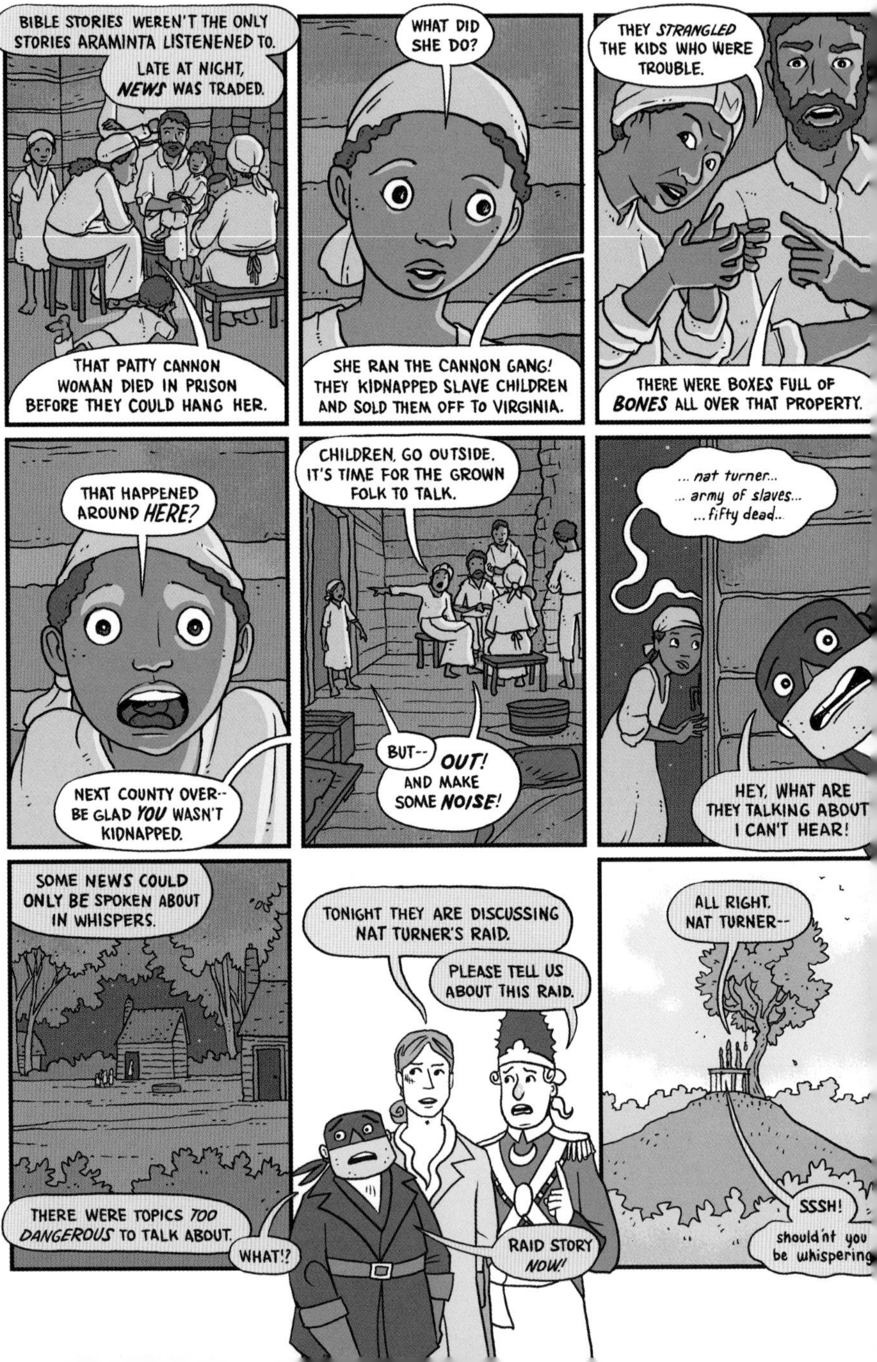
BIBLE STORIES WEREN'T THE ONLY STORIES ARAMINTA LISTENENED TO.
LATE AT NIGHT, NEWS WAS TRADED.
THAT PATTY CANNON WOMAN DIED IN PRISON BEFORE THEY COULD HANG HER.
WHAT DID SHE DO?
SHE RAN THE CANNON GANG! THEY KIDNAPPED SLAVE CHILDREN AND SOLD THEM OFF TO VIRGINIA.
THEY STRANGLED THE KIDS WHO WERE TROUBLE.
THERE WERE BOXES FULL OF BONES ALL OVER THAT PROPERTY.
THAT HAPPENED AROUND HERE?
NEXT COUNTY OVER-- BE GLAD YOU WASN'T KIDNAPPED.
CHILDREN, GO OUTSIDE. IT'S TIME FOR THE GROWN FOLK TO TALK.
BUT--
OUT! AND MAKE SOME NOISE!
... nat turner... ... army of slaves... ...fifty dead...
HEY, WHAT ARE THEY TALKING ABOUT I CAN'T HEAR!
SOME NEWS COULD ONLY BE SPOKEN ABOUT IN WHISPERS.
THERE WERE TOPICS TOO DANGEROUS TO TALK ABOUT.
TONIGHT THEY ARE DISCUSSING NAT TURNER'S RAID.
PLEASE TELL US ABOUT THIS RAID.
WHAT!?
RAID STORY NOW!
ALL RIGHT. NAT TURNER--
SSSH!
should'nt you be whispering

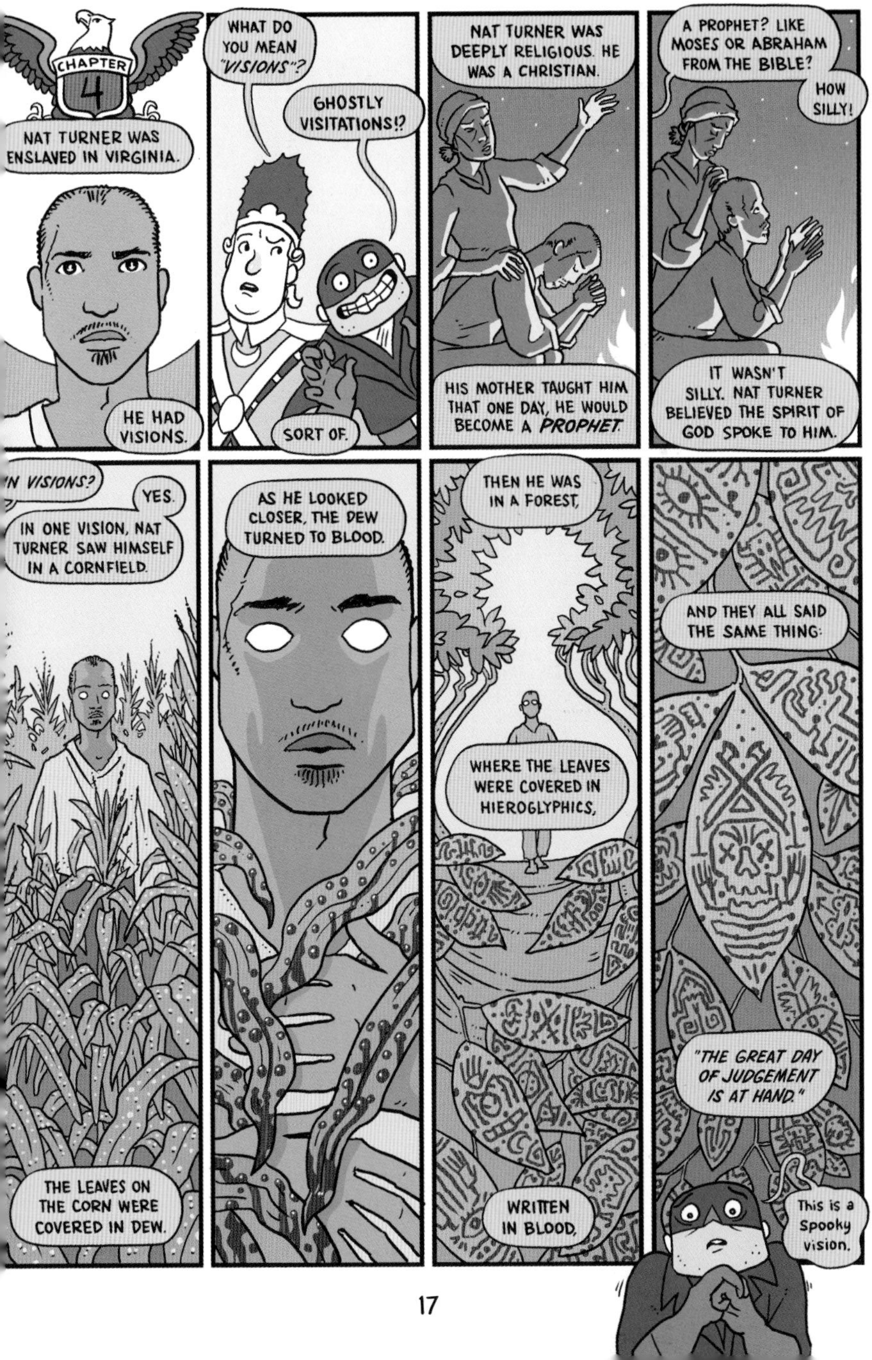
CHAPTER 4
NAT TURNER WAS ENSLAVED IN VIRGINIA.
HE HAD VISIONS.
WHAT DO YOU MEAN "VISIONS"?
GHOSTLY VISITATIONS!?
SORT OF.
NAT TURNER WAS DEEPLY RELIGIOUS. HE WAS A CHRISTIAN.
HIS MOTHER TAUGHT HIM THAT ONE DAY, HE WOULD BECOME A PROPHET.
A PROPHET? LIKE MOSES OR ABRAHAM FROM THE BIBLE?
HOW SILLY!
IT WASN'T SILLY. NAT TURNER BELIEVED THE SPIRIT OF GOD SPOKE TO HIM.
YES.
IN ONE VISION, NAT TURNER SAW HIMSELF IN A CORNFIELD.
THE LEAVES ON THE CORN WERE COVERED IN DEW.
AS HE LOOKED CLOSER, THE DEW TURNED TO BLOOD.
THEN HE WAS IN A FOREST,
WHERE THE LEAVES WERE COVERED IN HIEROGLYPHICS,
WRITTEN IN BLOOD,
AND THEY ALL SAID THE SAME THING:
"THE GREAT DAY OF JUDGEMENT IS AT HAND."
This is a Spooky vision.

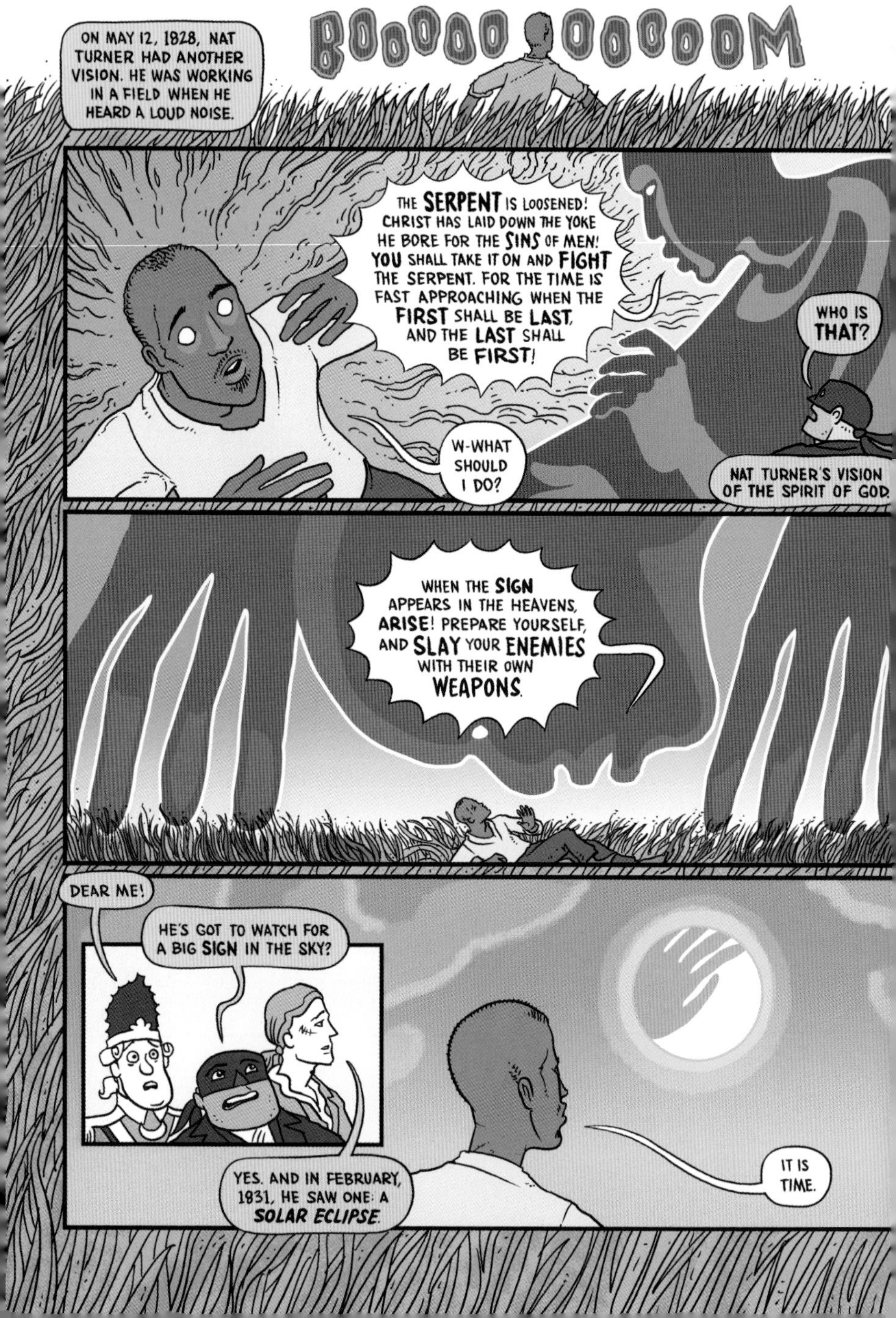
ON MAY 12, 1828, NAT TURNER HAD ANOTHER VISION. HE WAS WORKING IN A FIELD WHEN HE HEARD A LOUD NOISE.
BOOOOOOOOOOOOOM
THE SERPENT IS LOOSENED! CHRIST HAS LAID DOWN THE YOKE HE BORE FOR THE SINS OF MEN! YOU SHALL TAKE IT ON AND FIGHT THE SERPENT. FOR THE TIME IS FAST APPROACHING WHEN THE FIRST SHALL BE LAST, AND THE LAST SHALL BE FIRST!
WHO IS THAT?
W-WHAT SHOULD I DO?
NAT TURNER'S VISION OF THE SPIRIT OF GOD.
WHEN THE SIGN APPEARS IN THE HEAVENS, ARISE! PREPARE YOURSELF, AND SLAY YOUR ENEMIES WITH THEIR OWN WEAPONS.
DEAR ME!
HE'S GOT TO WATCH FOR A BIG SIGN IN THE SKY?
YES. AND IN FEBRUARY, 1831, HE SAW ONE: A SOLAR ECLIPSE.
IT IS TIME.

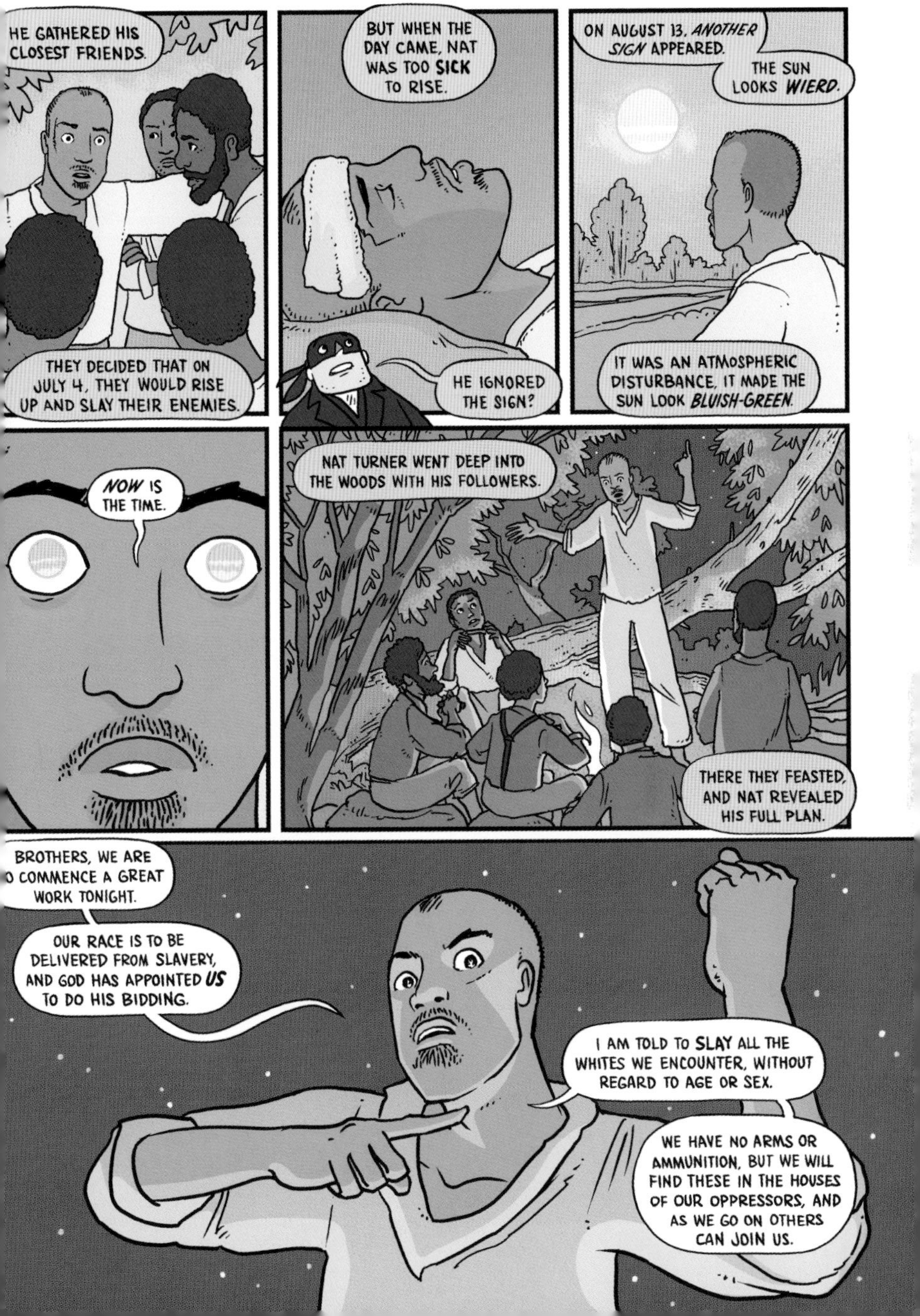
HE GATHERED HIS CLOSEST FRIENDS.
THEY DECIDED THAT ON JULY 4, THEY WOULD RISE UP AND SLAY THEIR ENEMIES.
BUT WHEN THE DAY CAME, NAT WAS TOO SICK TO RISE.
HE IGNORED THE SIGN?
ON AUGUST 13, ANOTHER SIGN APPEARED.
THE SUN LOOKS WIERD.
IT WAS AN ATMOSPHERIC DISTURBANCE, IT MADE THE SUN LOOK BLUISH-GREEN.
NOW IS THE TIME.
NAT TURNER WENT DEEP INTO THE WOODS WITH HIS FOLLOWERS.
THERE THEY FEASTED, AND NAT REVEALED HIS FULL PLAN.
BROTHERS, WE ARE O COMMENCE A GREAT WORK TONIGHT.
OUR RACE IS TO BE DELIVERED FROM SLAVERY, AND GOD HAS APPOINTED US TO DO HIS BIDDING.
I AM TOLD TO SLAY ALL THE WHITES WE ENCOUNTER, WITHOUT REGARD TO AGE OR SEX.
WE HAVE NO ARMS OR AMMUNITION, BUT WE WILL FIND THESE IN THE HOUSES OF OUR OPPRESSORS, AND AS WE GO ON OTHERS CAN JOIN US.

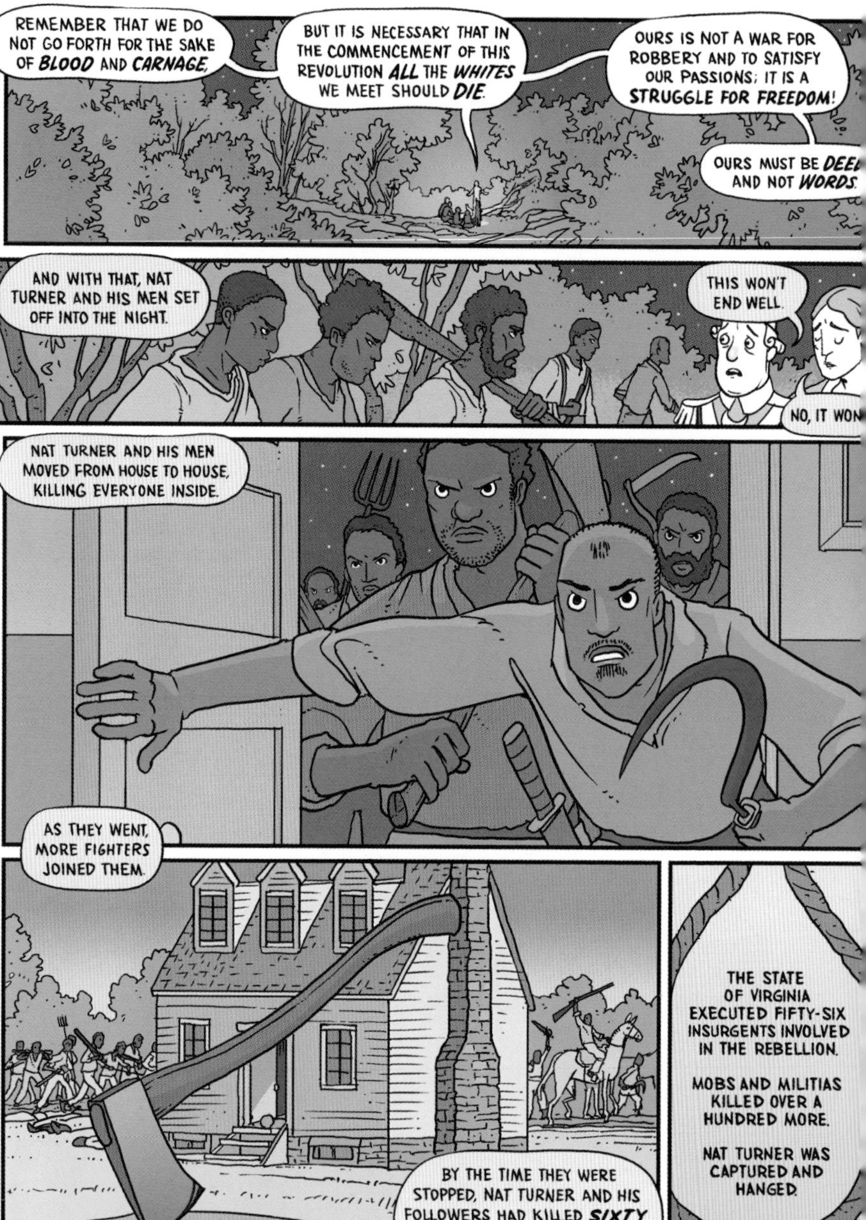
REMEMBER THAT WE DO NOT GO FORTH FOR THE SAKE OF BLOOD AND CARNAGE,
BUT IT IS NECESSARY THAT IN THE COMMENCEMENT OF THIS REVOLUTION ALL THE WHITES WE MEET SHOULD DIE.
OURS IS NOT A WAR FOR ROBBERY AND TO SATISFY OUR PASSIONS; IT IS A STRUGGLE FOR FREEDOM!
OURS MUST BE DEE
AND NOT WORDS.
AND WITH THAT, NAT TURNER AND HIS MEN SET OFF INTO THE NIGHT.
THIS WON'T END WELL.
NO, IT WON
NAT TURNER AND HIS MEN MOVED FROM HOUSE TO HOUSE, KILLING EVERYONE INSIDE.
AS THEY WENT, MORE FIGHTERS JOINED THEM.
BY THE TIME THEY WERE STOPPED, NAT TURNER AND HIS FOLLOWERS HAD KILLED SIXTY PEOPLE, MEN, WOMEN, AND CHILDREN.
THE STATE OF VIRGINIA EXECUTED FIFTY-SIX INSURGENTS INVOLVED IN THE REBELLION.
MOBS AND MILITIAS KILLED OVER A HUNDRED MORE.
NAT TURNER WAS CAPTURED AND HANGED.

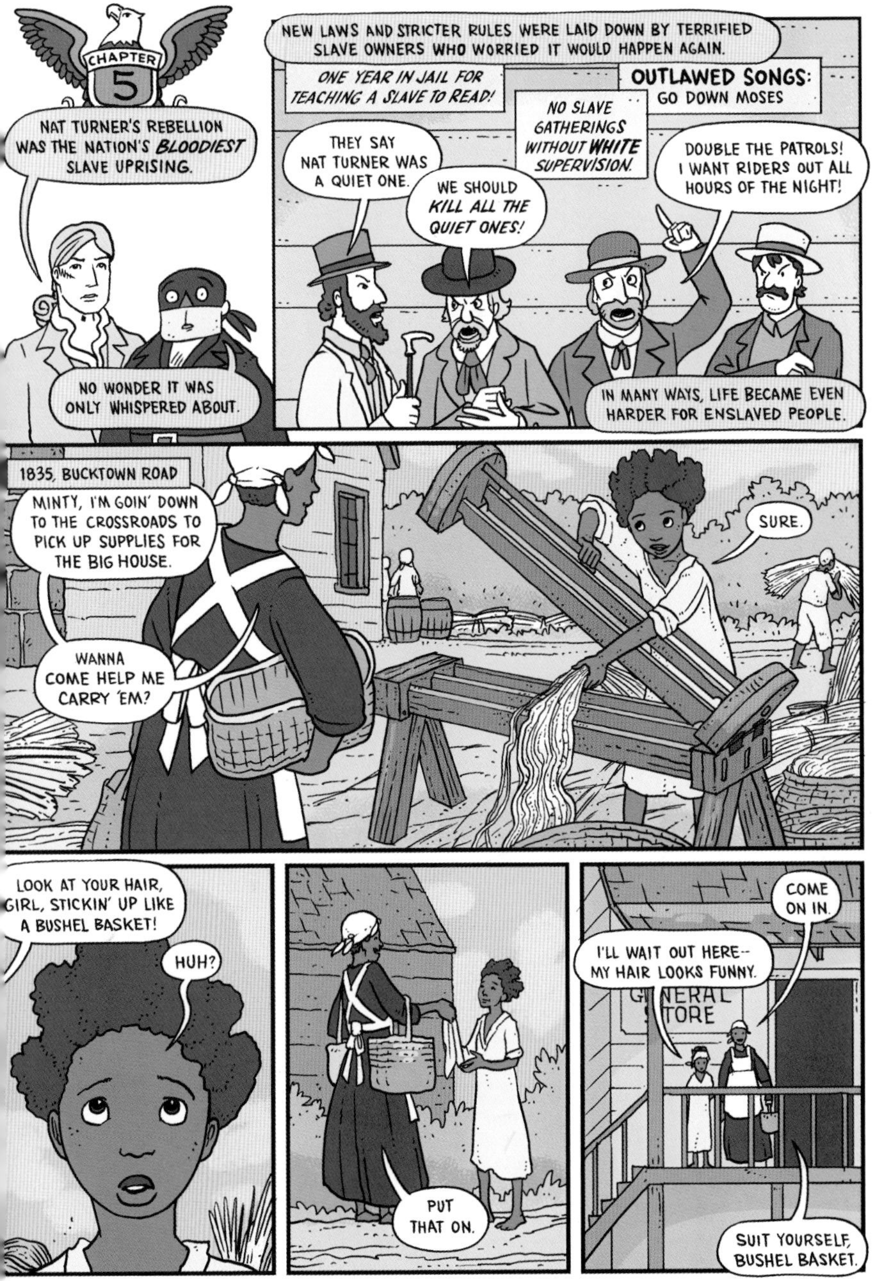
CHAPTER
5
NAT TURNER'S REBELLION WAS THE NATION'S *BLOODIEST* SLAVE UPRISING.
NO WONDER IT WAS ONLY WHISPERED ABOUT.
NEW LAWS AND STRICTER RULES WERE LAID DOWN BY TERRIFIED SLAVE OWNERS WHO WORRIED IT WOULD HAPPEN AGAIN.
ONE YEAR IN JAIL FOR TEACHING A SLAVE TO READ!
NO SLAVE GATHERINGS WITHOUT ***WHITE*** *SUPERVISION.*
OUTLAWED SONGS: GO DOWN MOSES
THEY SAY NAT TURNER WAS A QUIET ONE.
WE SHOULD *KILL ALL THE QUIET ONES!*
DOUBLE THE PATROLS! I WANT RIDERS OUT ALL HOURS OF THE NIGHT!
IN MANY WAYS, LIFE BECAME EVEN HARDER FOR ENSLAVED PEOPLE.
1835, BUCKTOWN ROAD
MINTY, I'M GOIN' DOWN TO THE CROSSROADS TO PICK UP SUPPLIES FOR THE BIG HOUSE.
WANNA COME HELP ME CARRY 'EM?
SURE.
LOOK AT YOUR HAIR, GIRL, STICKIN' UP LIKE A BUSHEL BASKET!
HUH?
PUT THAT ON.
COME ON IN.
I'LL WAIT OUT HERE-- MY HAIR LOOKS FUNNY.
GENERAL STORE
SUIT YOURSELF, BUSHEL BASKET.

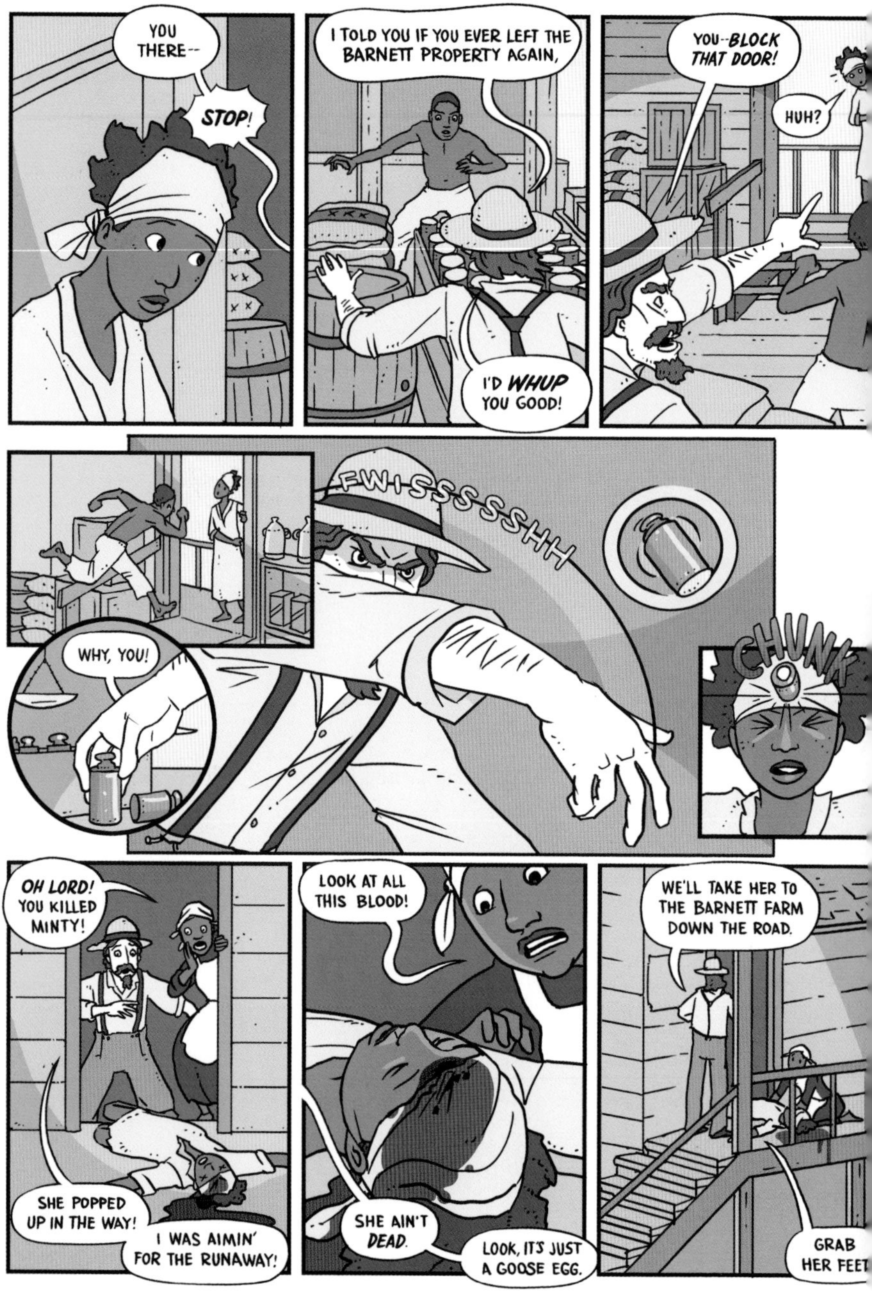
YOU THERE--
STOP!
I TOLD YOU IF YOU EVER LEFT THE BARNETT PROPERTY AGAIN,
I'D WHUP YOU GOOD!
YOU--BLOCK THAT DOOR!
HUH?
FWISSSSSSHH
WHY, YOU!
CHUNK
OH LORD! YOU KILLED MINTY!
SHE POPPED UP IN THE WAY!
I WAS AIMIN' FOR THE RUNAWAY!
LOOK AT ALL THIS BLOOD!
SHE AIN'T DEAD.
LOOK, IT'S JUST A GOOSE EGG.
WE'LL TAKE HER TO THE BARNETT FARM DOWN THE ROAD.
GRAB HER FEET

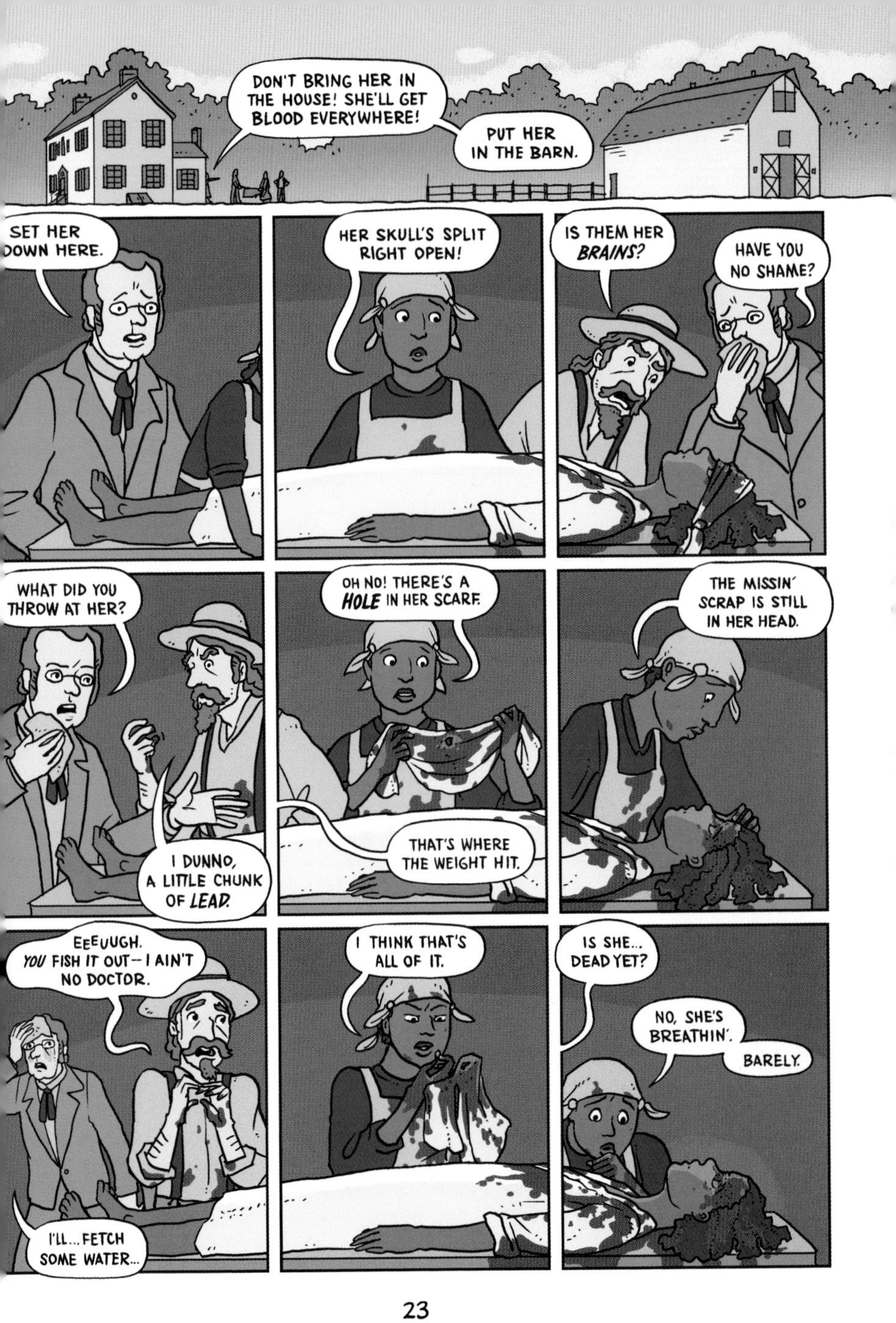
DON'T BRING HER IN THE HOUSE! SHE'LL GET BLOOD EVERYWHERE!
PUT HER IN THE BARN.
SET HER DOWN HERE.
HER SKULL'S SPLIT RIGHT OPEN!
IS THEM HER *BRAINS?*
HAVE YOU NO SHAME?
WHAT DID YOU THROW AT HER?
I DUNNO, A LITTLE CHUNK OF *LEAD.*
OH NO! THERE'S A *HOLE* IN HER SCARF.
THAT'S WHERE THE WEIGHT HIT.
THE MISSIN' SCRAP IS STILL IN HER HEAD.
EEEUUGH. *YOU* FISH IT OUT-- I AIN'T NO DOCTOR.
I'LL... FETCH SOME WATER...
I THINK THAT'S ALL OF IT.
IS SHE... DEAD YET?
NO, SHE'S BREATHIN'.
BARELY.

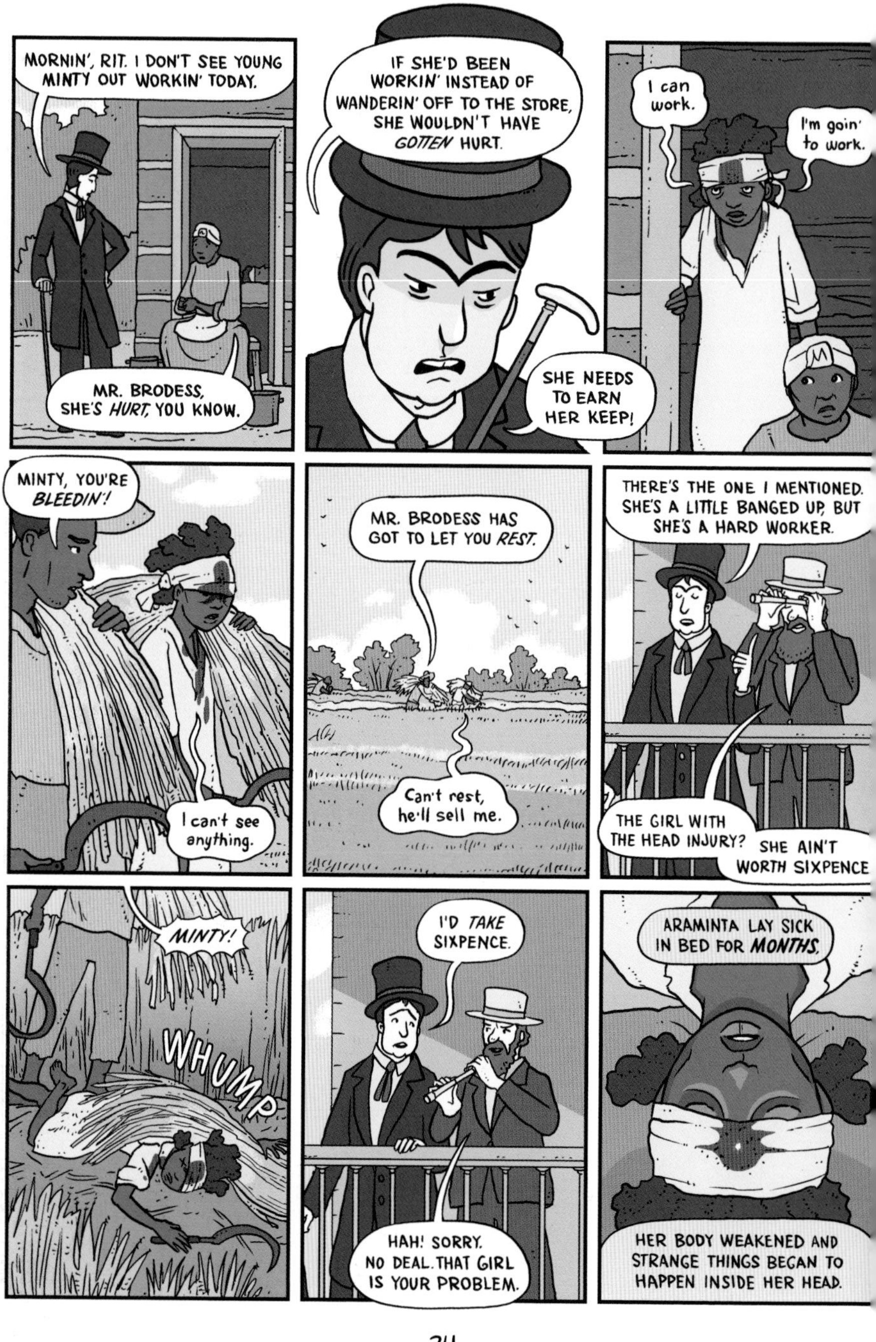
MORNIN', RIT. I DON'T SEE YOUNG MINTY OUT WORKIN' TODAY.
MR. BRODESS, SHE'S *HURT,* YOU KNOW.
IF SHE'D BEEN WORKIN' INSTEAD OF WANDERIN' OFF TO THE STORE, SHE WOULDN'T HAVE *GOTTEN* HURT.
SHE NEEDS TO EARN HER KEEP!
I can work.
I'm goin' to work.
MINTY, YOU'RE *BLEEDIN'!*
I can't see anything.
MR. BRODESS HAS GOT TO LET YOU *REST.*
Can't rest, he'll sell me.
THERE'S THE ONE I MENTIONED. SHE'S A LITTLE BANGED UP, BUT SHE'S A HARD WORKER.
THE GIRL WITH THE HEAD INJURY?
SHE AIN'T WORTH SIXPENCE
MINTY!
WHUMP
I'D *TAKE* SIXPENCE.
HAH! SORRY. NO DEAL. THAT GIRL IS YOUR PROBLEM.
ARAMINTA LAY SICK IN BED FOR *MONTHS.*
HER BODY WEAKENED AND STRANGE THINGS BEGAN TO HAPPEN INSIDE HER HEAD.

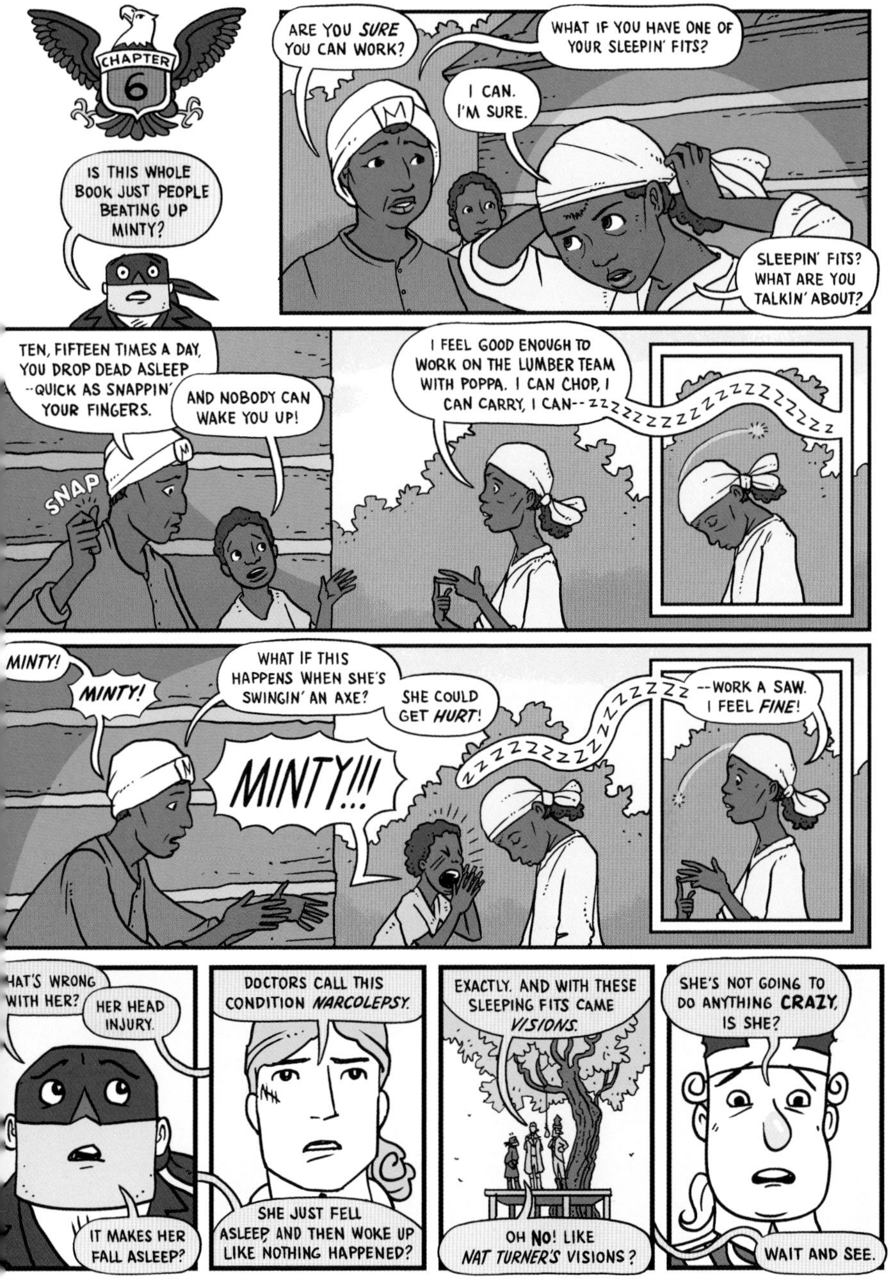
CHAPTER 6
IS THIS WHOLE BOOK JUST PEOPLE BEATING UP MINTY?
ARE YOU *SURE* YOU CAN WORK?
WHAT IF YOU HAVE ONE OF YOUR SLEEPIN' FITS?
I CAN. I'M SURE.
SLEEPIN' FITS? WHAT ARE YOU TALKIN' ABOUT?
TEN, FIFTEEN TIMES A DAY, YOU DROP DEAD ASLEEP --QUICK AS SNAPPIN' YOUR FINGERS.
SNAP
AND NOBODY CAN WAKE YOU UP!
I FEEL GOOD ENOUGH TO WORK ON THE LUMBER TEAM WITH POPPA. I CAN CHOP, I CAN CARRY, I CAN-- zzzzzzzzzzzzzzzzzzzz
MINTY!
MINTY!
WHAT IF THIS HAPPENS WHEN SHE'S SWINGIN' AN AXE?
SHE COULD GET *HURT*!
MINTY!!!
zzzzzzzzzzzzzzzzzz
--WORK A SAW. I FEEL *FINE*!
HAT'S WRONG WITH HER?
HER HEAD INJURY.
IT MAKES HER FALL ASLEEP?
DOCTORS CALL THIS CONDITION *NARCOLEPSY*.
SHE JUST FELL ASLEEP, AND THEN WOKE UP LIKE NOTHING HAPPENED?
EXACTLY. AND WITH THESE SLEEPING FITS CAME *VISIONS*.
OH **NO**! LIKE *NAT TURNER'S* VISIONS?
SHE'S NOT GOING TO DO ANYTHING **CRAZY**, IS SHE?
WAIT AND SEE.

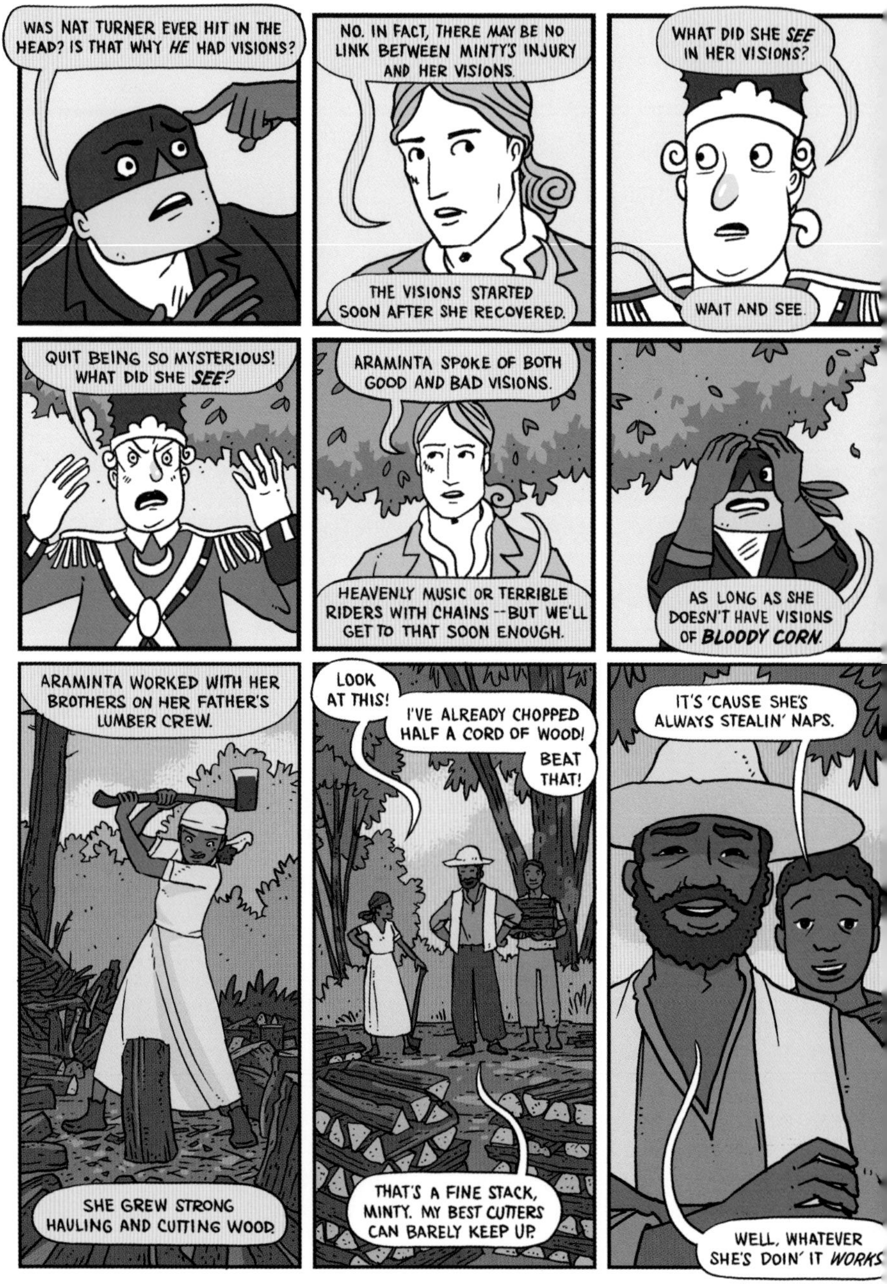
WAS NAT TURNER EVER HIT IN THE HEAD? IS THAT WHY HE HAD VISIONS?
NO. IN FACT, THERE MAY BE NO LINK BETWEEN MINTY'S INJURY AND HER VISIONS.
THE VISIONS STARTED SOON AFTER SHE RECOVERED.
WHAT DID SHE SEE IN HER VISIONS?
WAIT AND SEE.
QUIT BEING SO MYSTERIOUS! WHAT DID SHE SEE?
ARAMINTA SPOKE OF BOTH GOOD AND BAD VISIONS.
HEAVENLY MUSIC OR TERRIBLE RIDERS WITH CHAINS--BUT WE'LL GET TO THAT SOON ENOUGH.
AS LONG AS SHE DOESN'T HAVE VISIONS OF BLOODY CORN.
ARAMINTA WORKED WITH HER BROTHERS ON HER FATHER'S LUMBER CREW.
SHE GREW STRONG HAULING AND CUTTING WOOD.
LOOK AT THIS!
I'VE ALREADY CHOPPED HALF A CORD OF WOOD!
BEAT THAT!
THAT'S A FINE STACK, MINTY. MY BEST CUTTERS CAN BARELY KEEP UP.
IT'S 'CAUSE SHE'S ALWAYS STEALIN' NAPS.
WELL, WHATEVER SHE'S DOIN' IT WORKS.

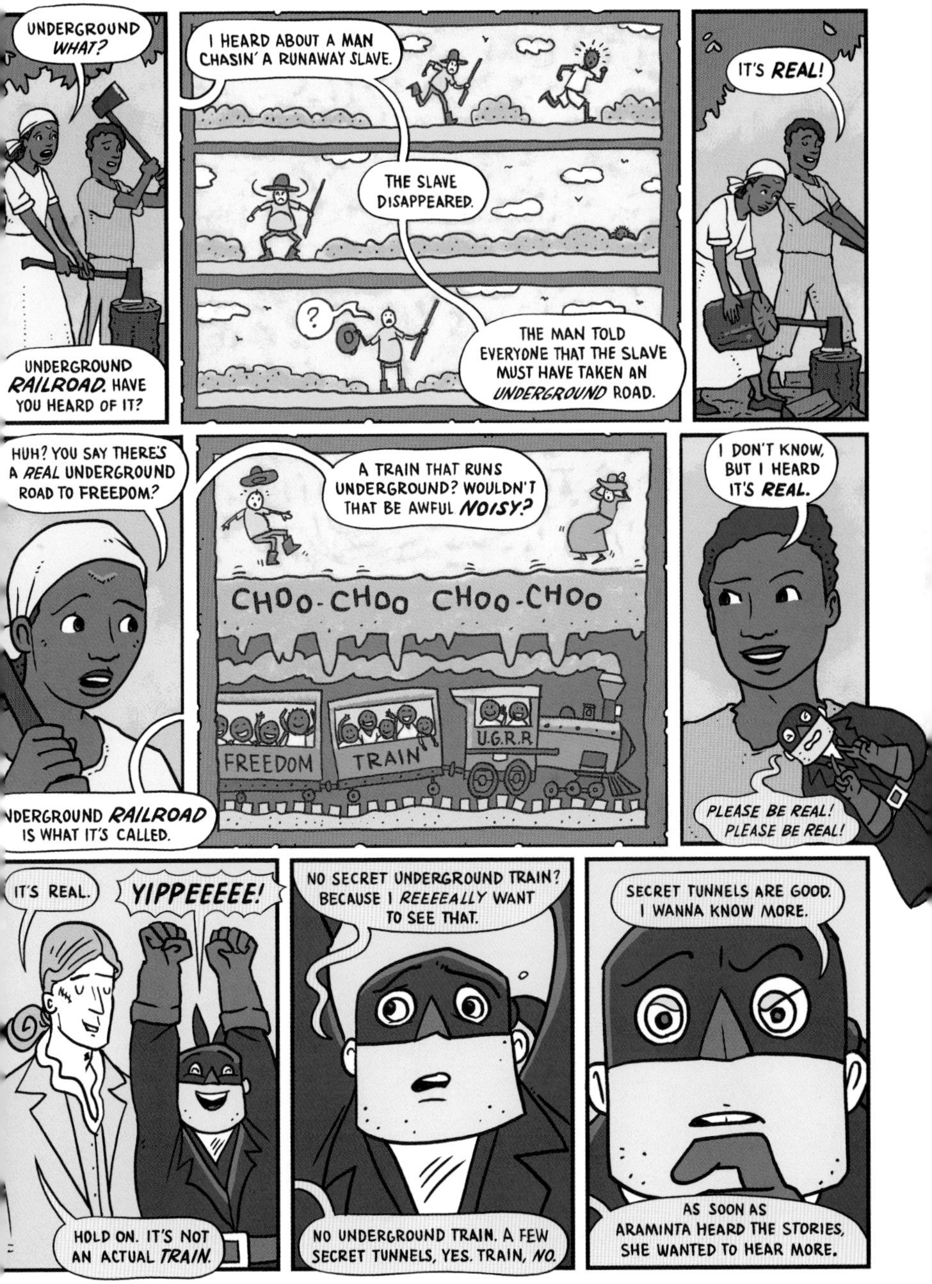

UNDERGROUND WHAT?
UNDERGROUND RAILROAD. HAVE YOU HEARD OF IT?
I HEARD ABOUT A MAN CHASIN' A RUNAWAY SLAVE.
THE SLAVE DISAPPEARED.
?
THE MAN TOLD EVERYONE THAT THE SLAVE MUST HAVE TAKEN AN UNDERGROUND ROAD.
IT'S REAL!
HUH? YOU SAY THERE'S A REAL UNDERGROUND ROAD TO FREEDOM?
A TRAIN THAT RUNS UNDERGROUND? WOULDN'T THAT BE AWFUL NOISY?
CHOO-CHOO CHOO-CHOO
FREEDOM
TRAIN
U.G.R.R
NDERGROUND RAILROAD IS WHAT IT'S CALLED.
I DON'T KNOW, BUT I HEARD IT'S REAL.
PLEASE BE REAL! PLEASE BE REAL!
IT'S REAL.
YIPPEEEEE!
HOLD ON. IT'S NOT AN ACTUAL TRAIN.
NO SECRET UNDERGROUND TRAIN? BECAUSE I REEEEALLY WANT TO SEE THAT.
NO UNDERGROUND TRAIN. A FEW SECRET TUNNELS, YES. TRAIN, NO.
SECRET TUNNELS ARE GOOD. I WANNA KNOW MORE.
AS SOON AS ARAMINTA HEARD THE STORIES, SHE WANTED TO HEAR MORE.

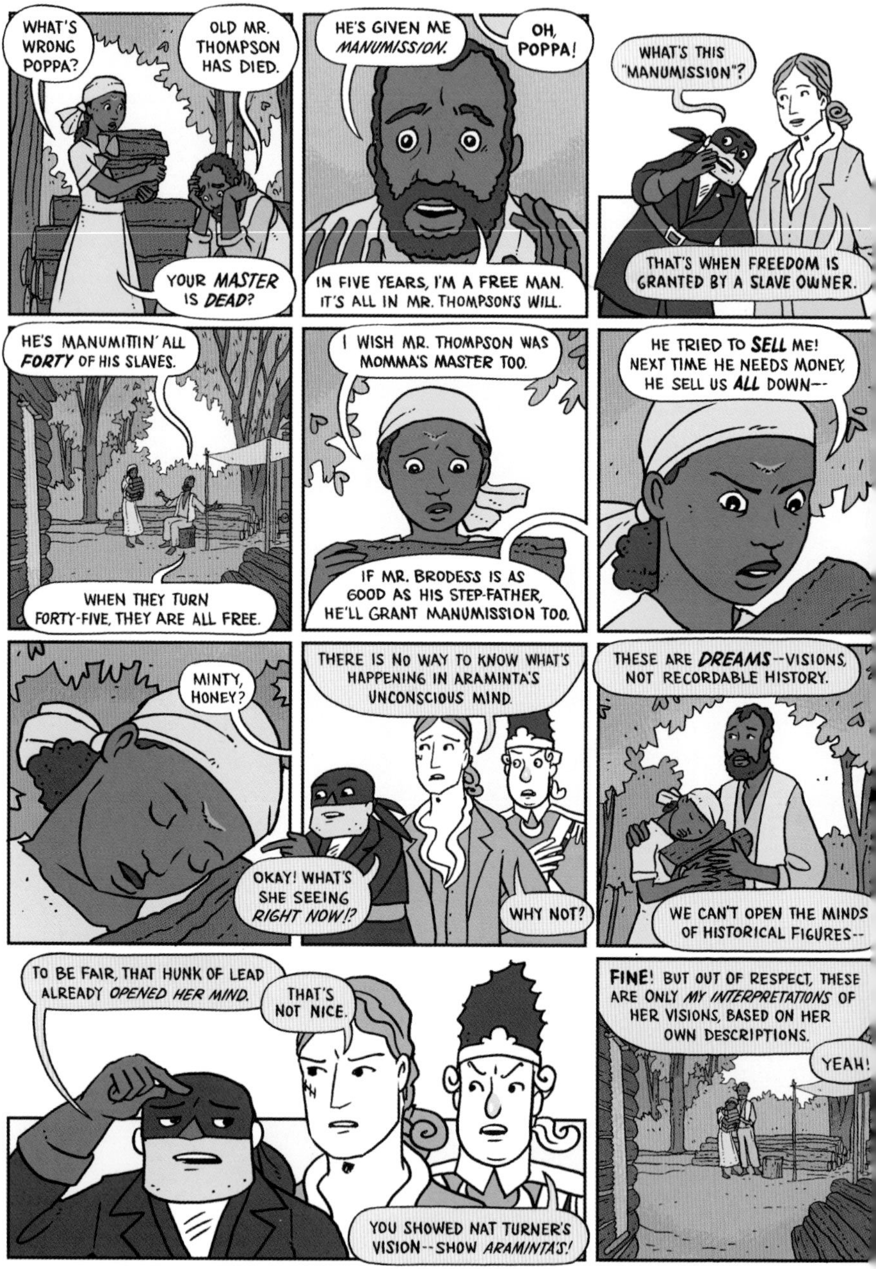
WHAT'S WRONG POPPA?
OLD MR. THOMPSON HAS DIED.
YOUR MASTER IS DEAD?
HE'S GIVEN ME MANUMISSION.
OH, POPPA!
IN FIVE YEARS, I'M A FREE MAN. IT'S ALL IN MR. THOMPSON'S WILL.
WHAT'S THIS "MANUMISSION"?
THAT'S WHEN FREEDOM IS GRANTED BY A SLAVE OWNER.
HE'S MANUMITTIN' ALL FORTY OF HIS SLAVES.
WHEN THEY TURN FORTY-FIVE, THEY ARE ALL FREE.
I WISH MR. THOMPSON WAS MOMMA'S MASTER TOO.
IF MR. BRODESS IS AS GOOD AS HIS STEP-FATHER, HE'LL GRANT MANUMISSION TOO.
HE TRIED TO SELL ME! NEXT TIME HE NEEDS MONEY, HE SELL US ALL DOWN--
MINTY, HONEY?
THERE IS NO WAY TO KNOW WHAT'S HAPPENING IN ARAMINTA'S UNCONSCIOUS MIND.
OKAY! WHAT'S SHE SEEING RIGHT NOW!?
WHY NOT?
THESE ARE DREAMS--VISIONS, NOT RECORDABLE HISTORY.
WE CAN'T OPEN THE MINDS OF HISTORICAL FIGURES--
TO BE FAIR, THAT HUNK OF LEAD ALREADY OPENED HER MIND.
THAT'S NOT NICE.
YOU SHOWED NAT TURNER'S VISION--SHOW ARAMINTA'S!
FINE! BUT OUT OF RESPECT, THESE ARE ONLY MY INTERPRETATIONS OF HER VISIONS, BASED ON HER OWN DESCRIPTIONS.
YEAH!

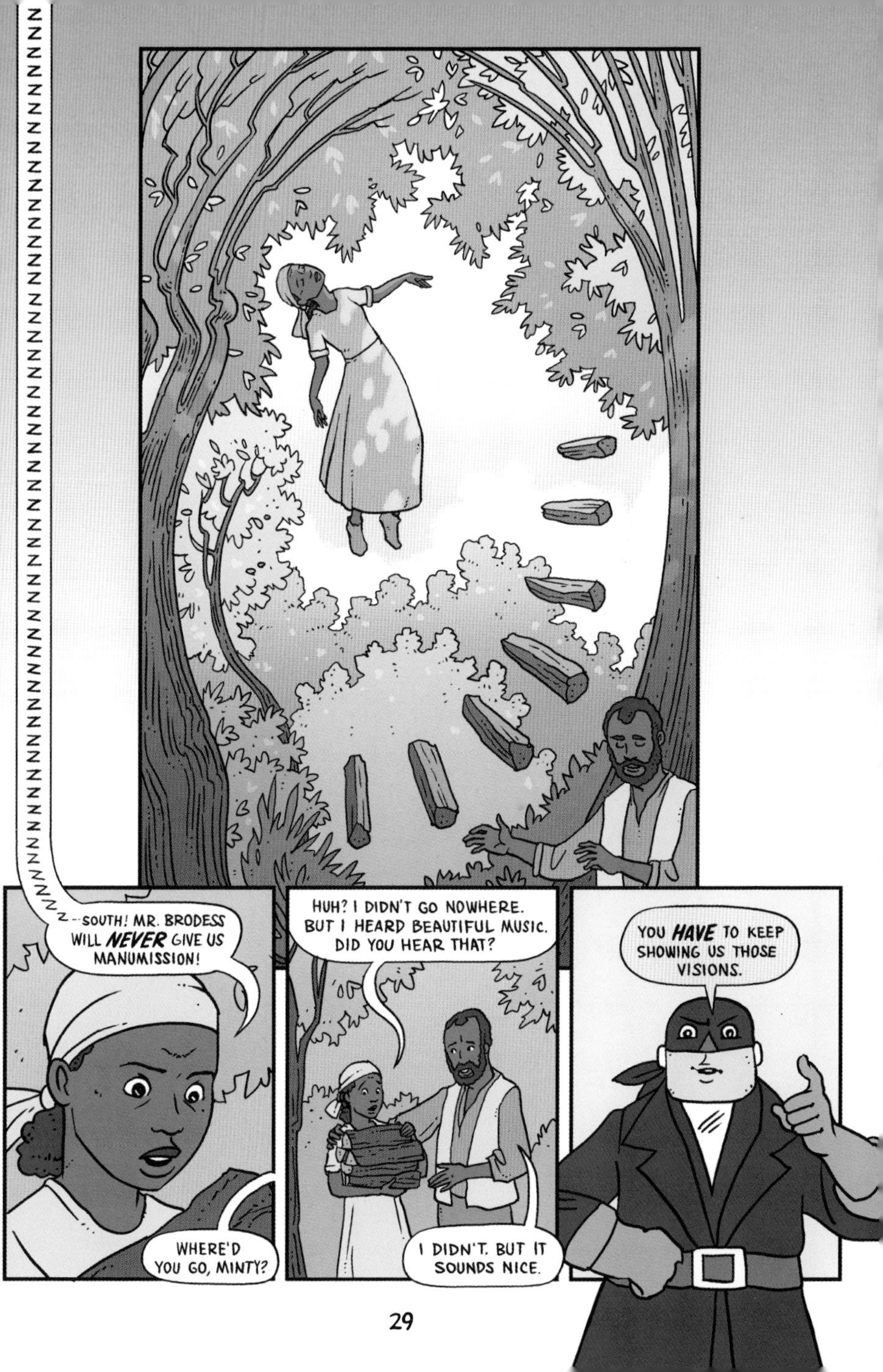
ZZZZZZZZZZZZZZZZZZZZZZZZZZZZZZZZZZZZZZZZZZZZZZZZZZZZZZZZZZZZZZ--SOUTH! MR. BRODESS WILL NEVER GIVE US MANUMISSION!
WHERE'D YOU GO, MINTY?
HUH? I DIDN'T GO NOWHERE. BUT I HEARD BEAUTIFUL MUSIC. DID YOU HEAR THAT?
I DIDN'T. BUT IT SOUNDS NICE.
YOU HAVE TO KEEP SHOWING US THOSE VISIONS.

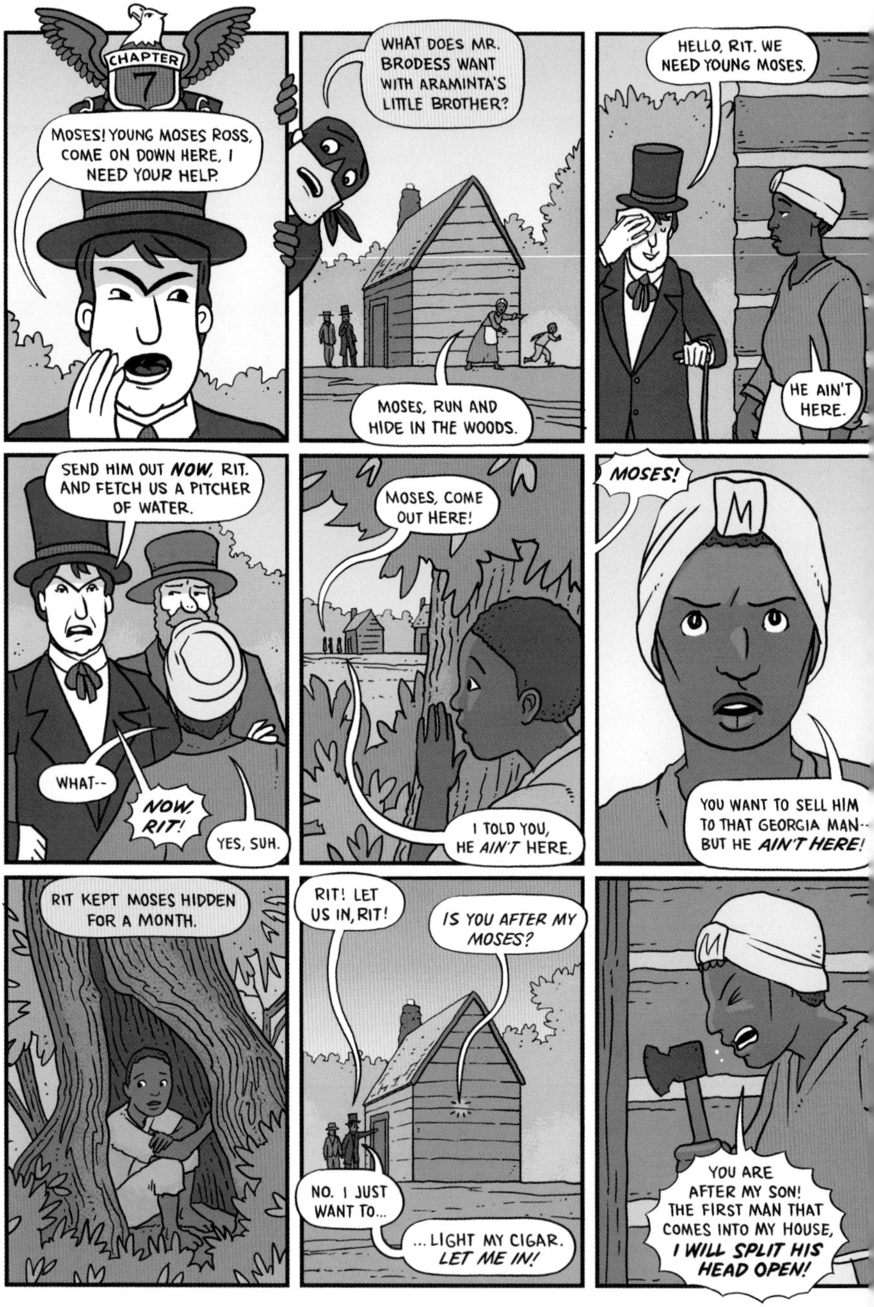
CHAPTER 7
MOSES! YOUNG MOSES ROSS, COME ON DOWN HERE, I NEED YOUR HELP.
WHAT DOES MR. BRODESS WANT WITH ARAMINTA'S LITTLE BROTHER?
MOSES, RUN AND HIDE IN THE WOODS.
HELLO, RIT. WE NEED YOUNG MOSES.
HE AIN'T HERE.
SEND HIM OUT NOW, RIT. AND FETCH US A PITCHER OF WATER.
WHAT--
NOW, RIT!
YES, SUH.
MOSES, COME OUT HERE!
I TOLD YOU, HE AIN'T HERE.
MOSES!
M
YOU WANT TO SELL HIM TO THAT GEORGIA MAN-- BUT HE AIN'T HERE!
RIT KEPT MOSES HIDDEN FOR A MONTH.
RIT! LET US IN, RIT!
IS YOU AFTER MY MOSES?
NO. I JUST WANT TO...
... LIGHT MY CIGAR. LET ME IN!
M
YOU ARE AFTER MY SON! THE FIRST MAN THAT COMES INTO MY HOUSE, I WILL SPLIT HIS HEAD OPEN!

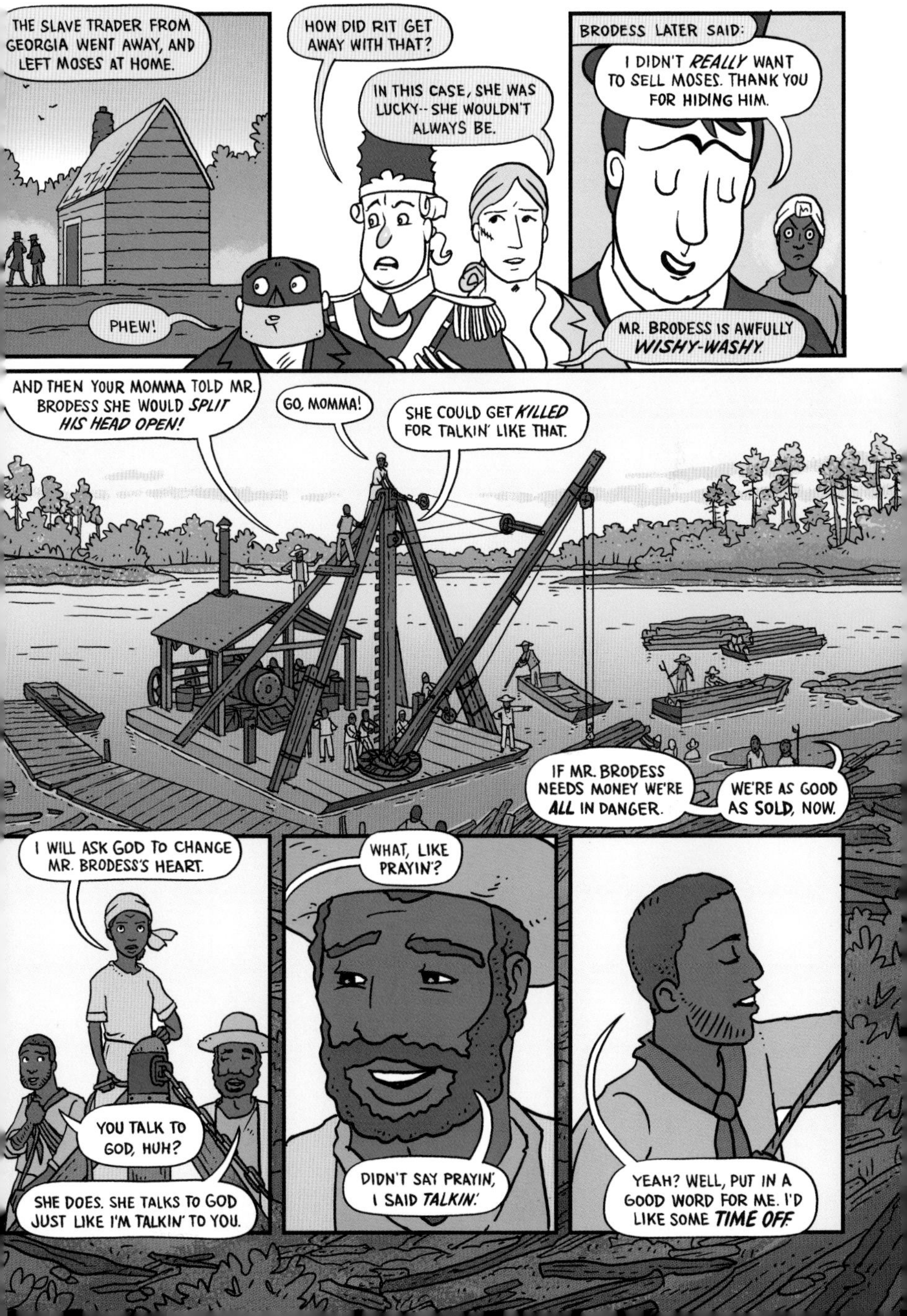
THE SLAVE TRADER FROM GEORGIA WENT AWAY, AND LEFT MOSES AT HOME.
HOW DID RIT GET AWAY WITH THAT?
IN THIS CASE, SHE WAS LUCKY-- SHE WOULDN'T ALWAYS BE.
PHEW!
BRODESS LATER SAID:
I DIDN'T *REALLY* WANT TO SELL MOSES. THANK YOU FOR HIDING HIM.
MR. BRODESS IS AWFULLY *WISHY-WASHY.*
AND THEN YOUR MOMMA TOLD MR. BRODESS SHE WOULD *SPLIT HIS HEAD OPEN!*
GO, MOMMA!
SHE COULD GET *KILLED* FOR TALKIN' LIKE THAT.
IF MR. BRODESS NEEDS MONEY WE'RE **ALL** IN DANGER.
WE'RE AS GOOD AS **SOLD**, NOW.
I WILL ASK GOD TO CHANGE MR. BRODESS'S HEART.
YOU TALK TO GOD, HUH?
SHE DOES. SHE TALKS TO GOD JUST LIKE I'M TALKIN' TO YOU.
WHAT, LIKE PRAYIN'?
DIDN'T SAY PRAYIN', I SAID *TALKIN'.*
YEAH? WELL, PUT IN A GOOD WORD FOR ME. I'D LIKE SOME ***TIME OFF.***

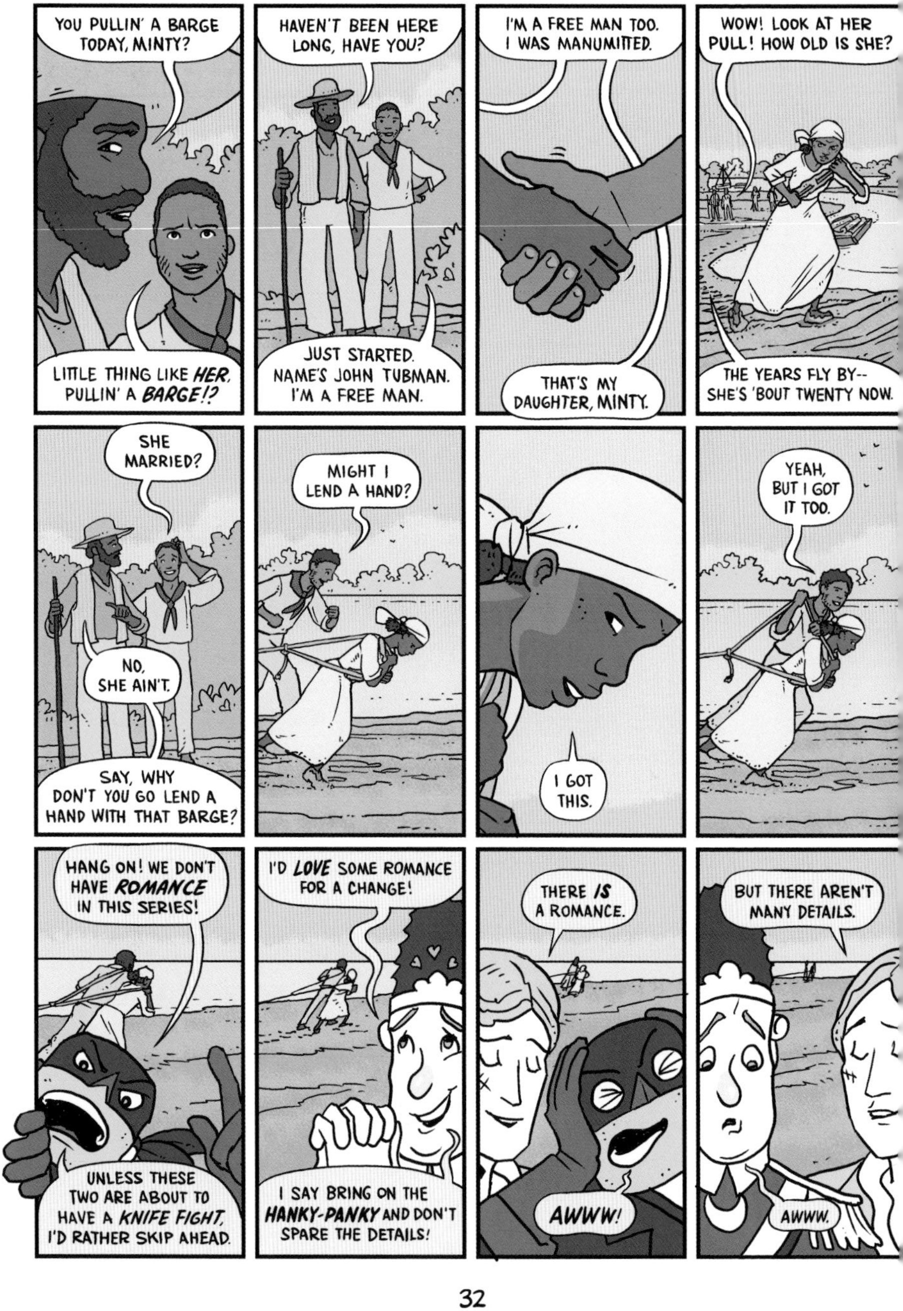
YOU PULLIN' A BARGE TODAY, MINTY?
LITTLE THING LIKE HER, PULLIN' A BARGE!?
HAVEN'T BEEN HERE LONG, HAVE YOU?
JUST STARTED. NAME'S JOHN TUBMAN. I'M A FREE MAN.
I'M A FREE MAN TOO. I WAS MANUMITTED.
THAT'S MY DAUGHTER, MINTY.
WOW! LOOK AT HER PULL! HOW OLD IS SHE?
THE YEARS FLY BY-- SHE'S 'BOUT TWENTY NOW.
SHE MARRIED?
NO, SHE AIN'T.
SAY, WHY DON'T YOU GO LEND A HAND WITH THAT BARGE?
MIGHT I LEND A HAND?
I GOT THIS.
YEAH, BUT I GOT IT TOO.
HANG ON! WE DON'T HAVE ROMANCE IN THIS SERIES!
UNLESS THESE TWO ARE ABOUT TO HAVE A KNIFE FIGHT, I'D RATHER SKIP AHEAD.
I'D LOVE SOME ROMANCE FOR A CHANGE!
I SAY BRING ON THE HANKY-PANKY AND DON'T SPARE THE DETAILS!
THERE IS A ROMANCE.
AWWW!
BUT THERE AREN'T MANY DETAILS.
AWWW.

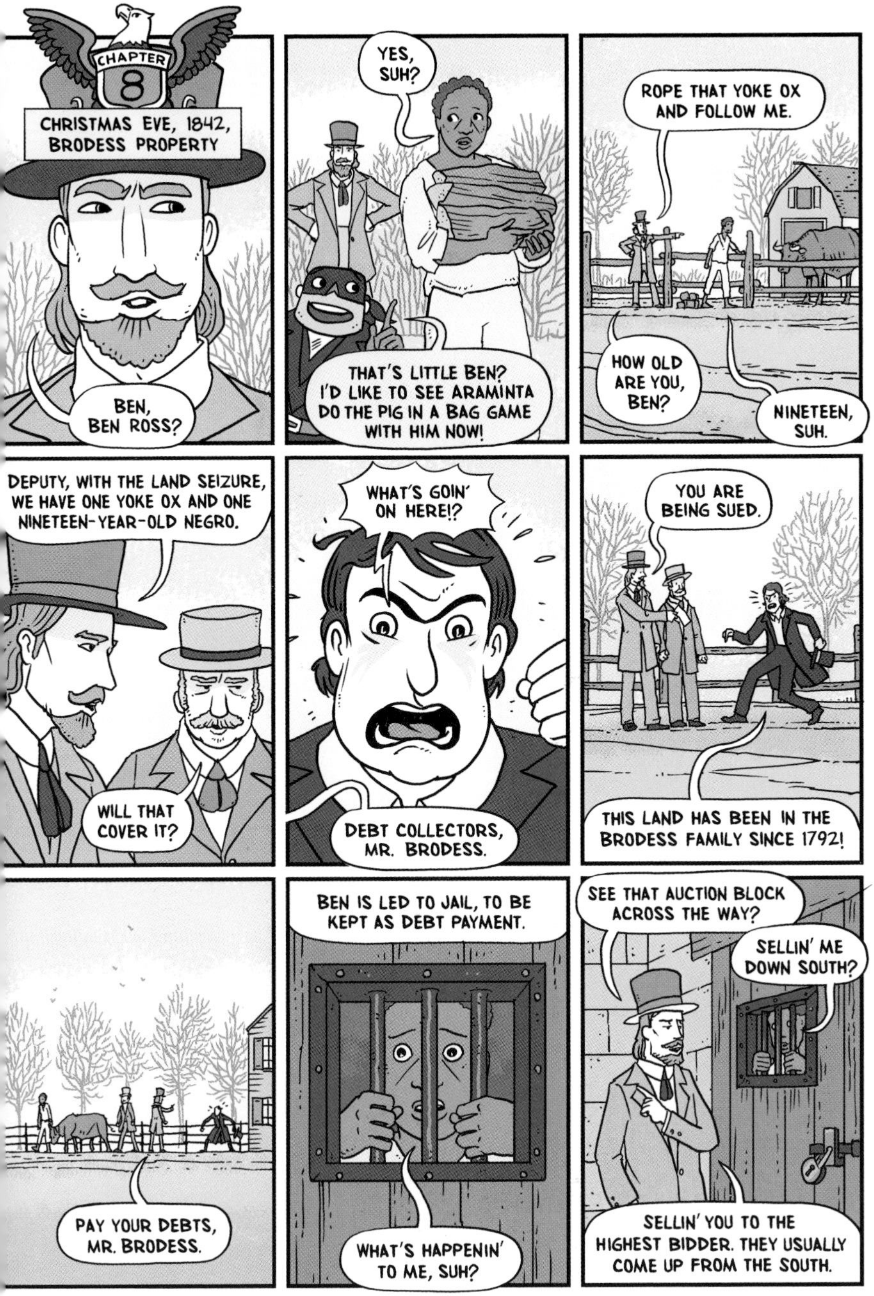
CHAPTER 8
CHRISTMAS EVE, 1842, BRODESS PROPERTY
BEN, BEN ROSS?
YES, SUH?
THAT'S LITTLE BEN? I'D LIKE TO SEE ARAMINTA DO THE PIG IN A BAG GAME WITH HIM NOW!
ROPE THAT YOKE OX AND FOLLOW ME.
HOW OLD ARE YOU, BEN?
NINETEEN, SUH.
DEPUTY, WITH THE LAND SEIZURE, WE HAVE ONE YOKE OX AND ONE NINETEEN-YEAR-OLD NEGRO.
WILL THAT COVER IT?
WHAT'S GOIN' ON HERE!?
DEBT COLLECTORS, MR. BRODESS.
YOU ARE BEING SUED.
THIS LAND HAS BEEN IN THE BRODESS FAMILY SINCE 1792!
PAY YOUR DEBTS, MR. BRODESS.
BEN IS LED TO JAIL, TO BE KEPT AS DEBT PAYMENT.
WHAT'S HAPPENIN' TO ME, SUH?
SEE THAT AUCTION BLOCK ACROSS THE WAY?
SELLIN' ME DOWN SOUTH?
SELLIN' YOU TO THE HIGHEST BIDDER. THEY USUALLY COME UP FROM THE SOUTH.

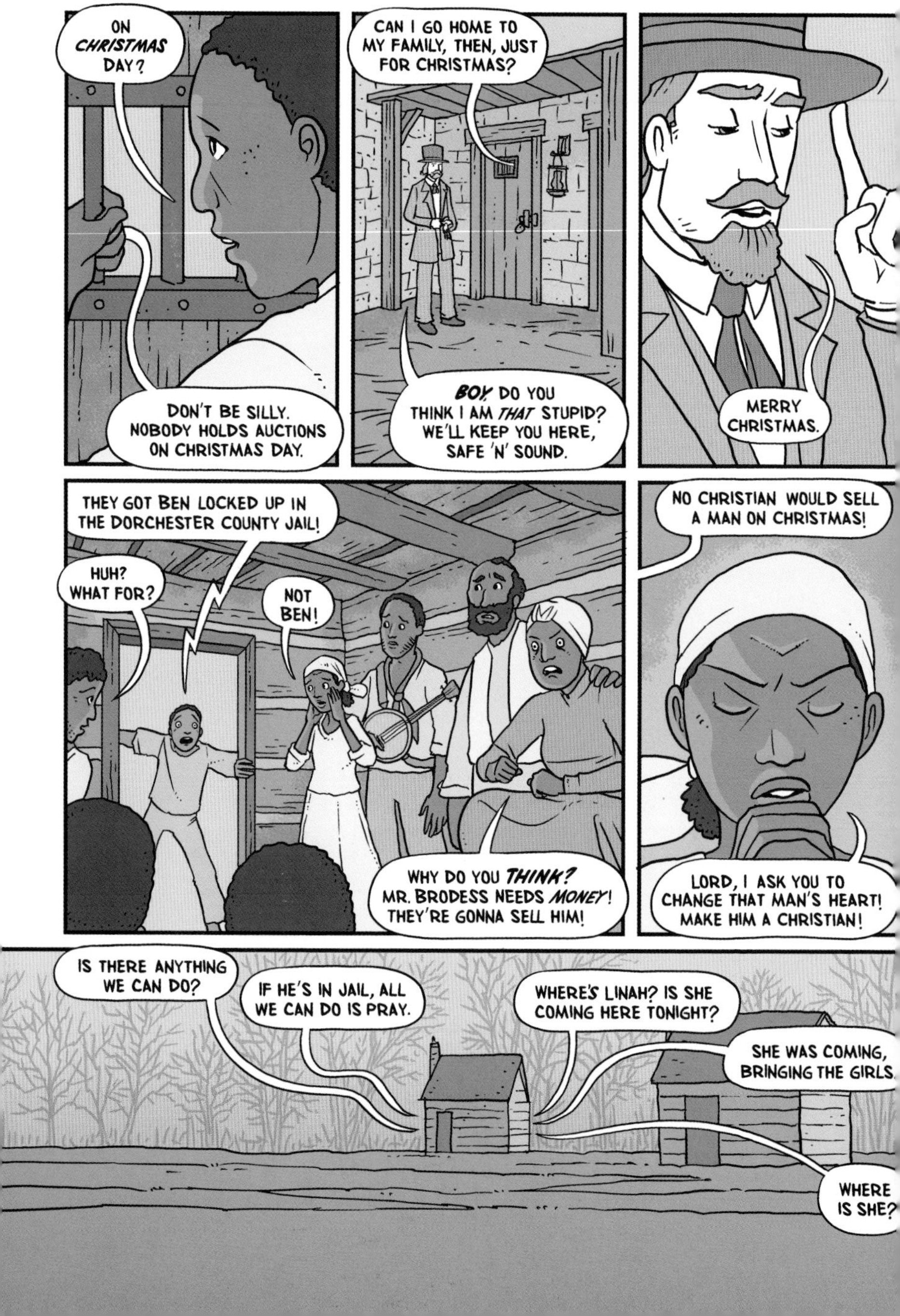
ON *CHRISTMAS* DAY?
DON'T BE SILLY. NOBODY HOLDS AUCTIONS ON CHRISTMAS DAY.
CAN I GO HOME TO MY FAMILY, THEN, JUST FOR CHRISTMAS?
BOY, DO YOU THINK I AM *THAT* STUPID? WE'LL KEEP YOU HERE, SAFE 'N' SOUND.
MERRY CHRISTMAS.
THEY GOT BEN LOCKED UP IN THE DORCHESTER COUNTY JAIL!
HUH? WHAT FOR?
NOT BEN!
WHY DO YOU *THINK?* MR. BRODESS NEEDS *MONEY*! THEY'RE GONNA SELL HIM!
NO CHRISTIAN WOULD SELL A MAN ON CHRISTMAS!
LORD, I ASK YOU TO CHANGE THAT MAN'S HEART! MAKE HIM A CHRISTIAN!
IS THERE ANYTHING WE CAN DO?
IF HE'S IN JAIL, ALL WE CAN DO IS PRAY.
WHERE'S LINAH? IS SHE COMING HERE TONIGHT?
SHE WAS COMING, BRINGING THE GIRLS.
WHERE IS SHE?

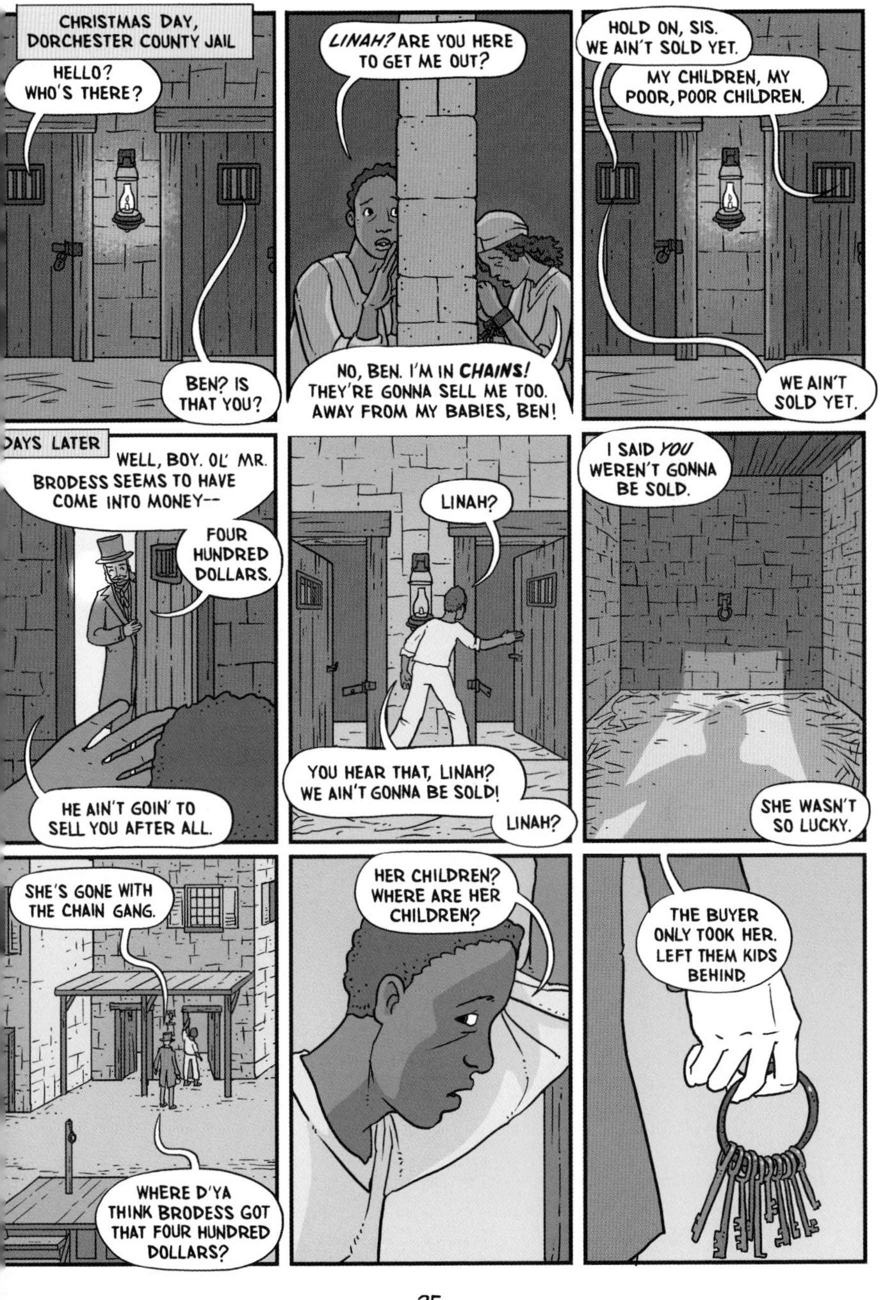
CHRISTMAS DAY, DORCHESTER COUNTY JAIL
HELLO? WHO'S THERE?
BEN? IS THAT YOU?
LINAH? ARE YOU HERE TO GET ME OUT?
NO, BEN. I'M IN CHAINS! THEY'RE GONNA SELL ME TOO. AWAY FROM MY BABIES, BEN!
HOLD ON, SIS. WE AIN'T SOLD YET.
MY CHILDREN, MY POOR, POOR CHILDREN.
WE AIN'T SOLD YET.
DAYS LATER
WELL, BOY. OL' MR. BRODESS SEEMS TO HAVE COME INTO MONEY--
FOUR HUNDRED DOLLARS.
HE AIN'T GOIN' TO SELL YOU AFTER ALL.
LINAH?
YOU HEAR THAT, LINAH? WE AIN'T GONNA BE SOLD!
LINAH?
I SAID YOU WEREN'T GONNA BE SOLD.
SHE WASN'T SO LUCKY.
SHE'S GONE WITH THE CHAIN GANG.
WHERE D'YA THINK BRODESS GOT THAT FOUR HUNDRED DOLLARS?
HER CHILDREN? WHERE ARE HER CHILDREN?
THE BUYER ONLY TOOK HER. LEFT THEM KIDS BEHIND.

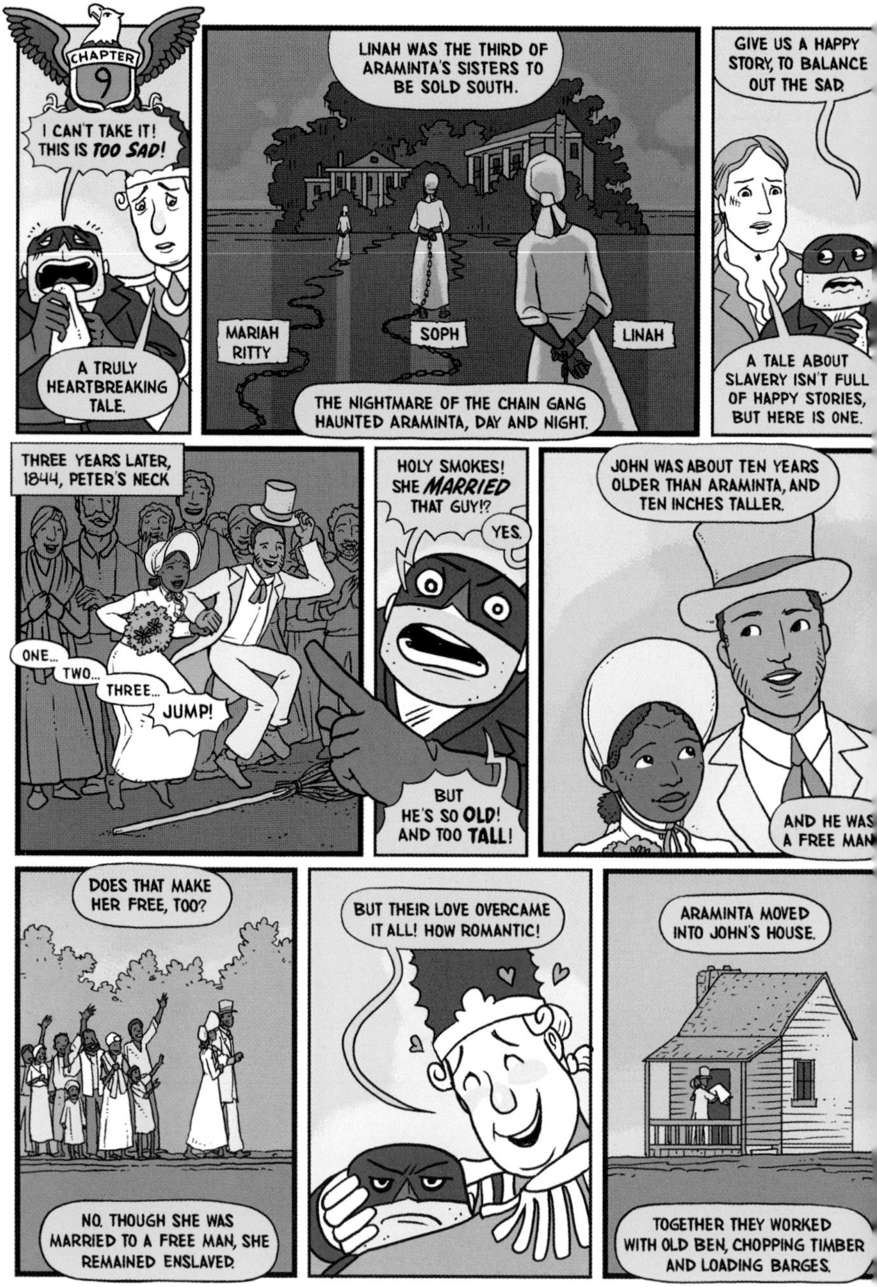
CHAPTER 9
I CAN'T TAKE IT! THIS IS *TOO SAD*!
A TRULY HEARTBREAKING TALE.
LINAH WAS THE THIRD OF ARAMINTA'S SISTERS TO BE SOLD SOUTH.
MARIAH RITTY
SOPH
LINAH
THE NIGHTMARE OF THE CHAIN GANG HAUNTED ARAMINTA, DAY AND NIGHT.
GIVE US A HAPPY STORY, TO BALANCE OUT THE SAD.
A TALE ABOUT SLAVERY ISN'T FULL OF HAPPY STORIES, BUT HERE IS ONE.
THREE YEARS LATER, 1844, PETER'S NECK
ONE...
TWO...
THREE...
JUMP!
HOLY SMOKES! SHE *MARRIED* THAT GUY!?
YES.
BUT HE'S SO **OLD**! AND TOO **TALL**!
JOHN WAS ABOUT TEN YEARS OLDER THAN ARAMINTA, AND TEN INCHES TALLER.
AND HE WAS A FREE MAN
DOES THAT MAKE HER FREE, TOO?
NO. THOUGH SHE WAS MARRIED TO A FREE MAN, SHE REMAINED ENSLAVED.
BUT THEIR LOVE OVERCAME IT ALL! HOW ROMANTIC!
ARAMINTA MOVED INTO JOHN'S HOUSE.
TOGETHER THEY WORKED WITH OLD BEN, CHOPPING TIMBER AND LOADING BARGES.

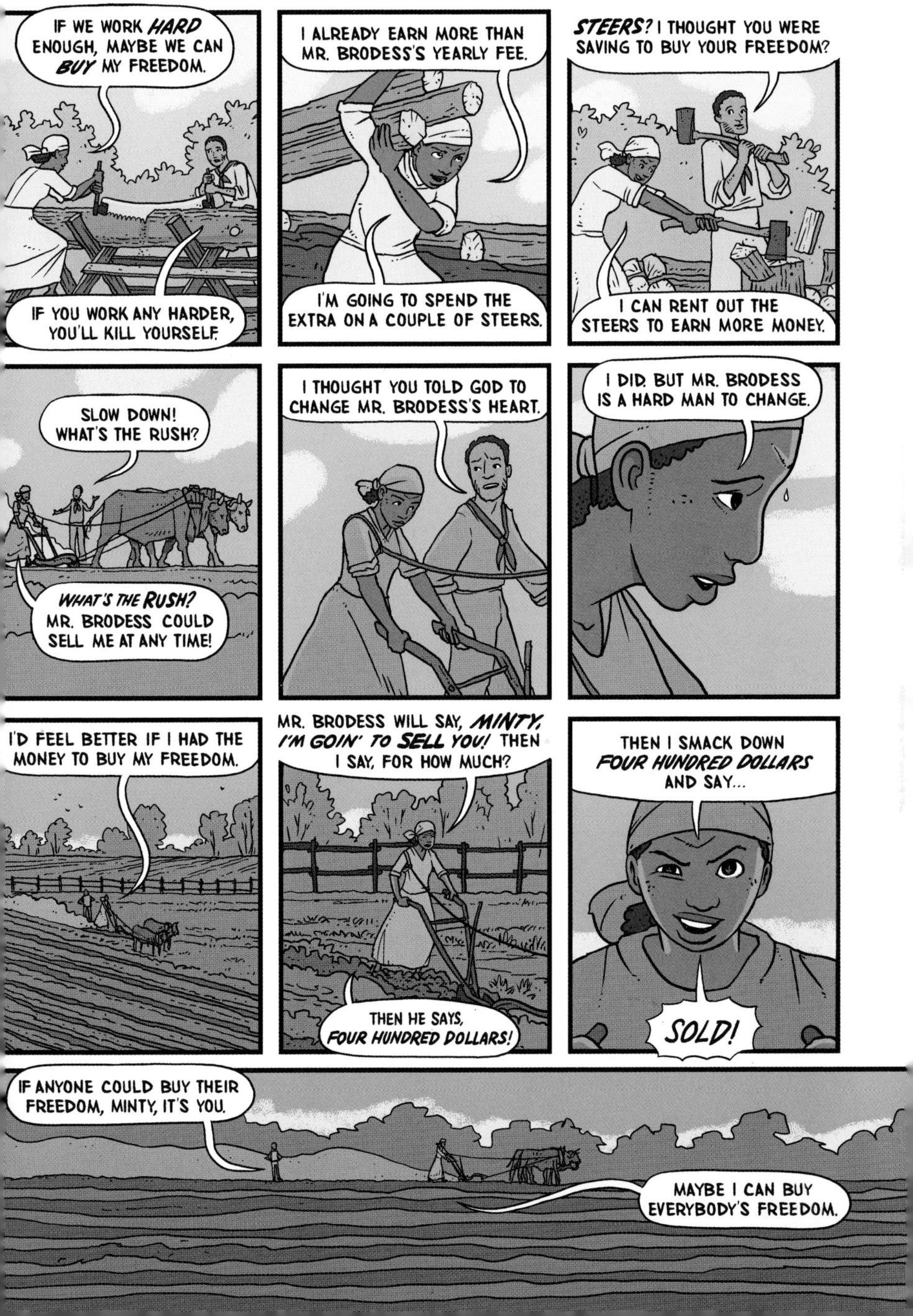
IF WE WORK HARD ENOUGH, MAYBE WE CAN BUY MY FREEDOM.
IF YOU WORK ANY HARDER, YOU'LL KILL YOURSELF.
I ALREADY EARN MORE THAN MR. BRODESS'S YEARLY FEE.
I'M GOING TO SPEND THE EXTRA ON A COUPLE OF STEERS.
STEERS? I THOUGHT YOU WERE SAVING TO BUY YOUR FREEDOM?
I CAN RENT OUT THE STEERS TO EARN MORE MONEY.
SLOW DOWN! WHAT'S THE RUSH?
WHAT'S THE RUSH? MR. BRODESS COULD SELL ME AT ANY TIME!
I THOUGHT YOU TOLD GOD TO CHANGE MR. BRODESS'S HEART.
I DID. BUT MR. BRODESS IS A HARD MAN TO CHANGE.
I'D FEEL BETTER IF I HAD THE MONEY TO BUY MY FREEDOM.
MR. BRODESS WILL SAY, MINTY, I'M GOIN' TO SELL YOU! THEN I SAY, FOR HOW MUCH?
THEN HE SAYS, FOUR HUNDRED DOLLARS!
THEN I SMACK DOWN FOUR HUNDRED DOLLARS AND SAY...
SOLD!
IF ANYONE COULD BUY THEIR FREEDOM, MINTY, IT'S YOU.
MAYBE I CAN BUY EVERYBODY'S FREEDOM.

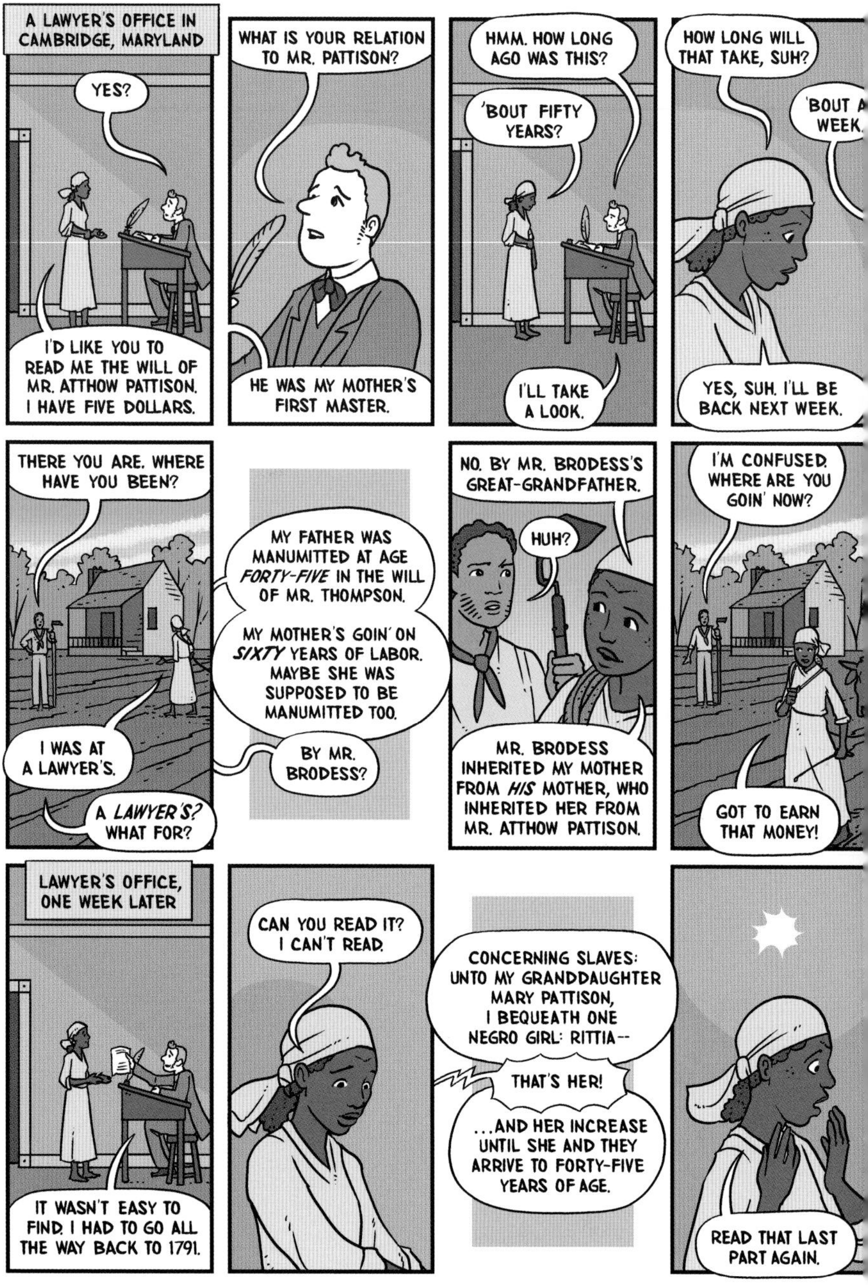
A LAWYER'S OFFICE IN CAMBRIDGE, MARYLAND
YES?
I'D LIKE YOU TO READ ME THE WILL OF MR. ATTHOW PATTISON. I HAVE FIVE DOLLARS.
WHAT IS YOUR RELATION TO MR. PATTISON?
HE WAS MY MOTHER'S FIRST MASTER.
HMM. HOW LONG AGO WAS THIS?
'BOUT FIFTY YEARS?
I'LL TAKE A LOOK.
HOW LONG WILL THAT TAKE, SUH?
'BOUT A WEEK.
YES, SUH. I'LL BE BACK NEXT WEEK.
THERE YOU ARE. WHERE HAVE YOU BEEN?
I WAS AT A LAWYER'S.
A *LAWYER'S?* WHAT FOR?
MY FATHER WAS MANUMITTED AT AGE *FORTY-FIVE* IN THE WILL OF MR. THOMPSON.
MY MOTHER'S GOIN' ON *SIXTY* YEARS OF LABOR. MAYBE SHE WAS SUPPOSED TO BE MANUMITTED TOO.
BY MR. BRODESS?
NO. BY MR. BRODESS'S GREAT-GRANDFATHER.
HUH?
MR. BRODESS INHERITED MY MOTHER FROM *HIS* MOTHER, WHO INHERITED HER FROM MR. ATTHOW PATTISON.
I'M CONFUSED. WHERE ARE YOU GOIN' NOW?
GOT TO EARN THAT MONEY!
LAWYER'S OFFICE, ONE WEEK LATER
IT WASN'T EASY TO FIND. I HAD TO GO ALL THE WAY BACK TO 1791.
CAN YOU READ IT? I CAN'T READ.
CONCERNING SLAVES: UNTO MY GRANDDAUGHTER MARY PATTISON, I BEQUEATH ONE NEGRO GIRL: RITTIA--
THAT'S HER!
...AND HER INCREASE UNTIL SHE AND THEY ARRIVE TO FORTY-FIVE YEARS OF AGE.
READ THAT LAST PART AGAIN.

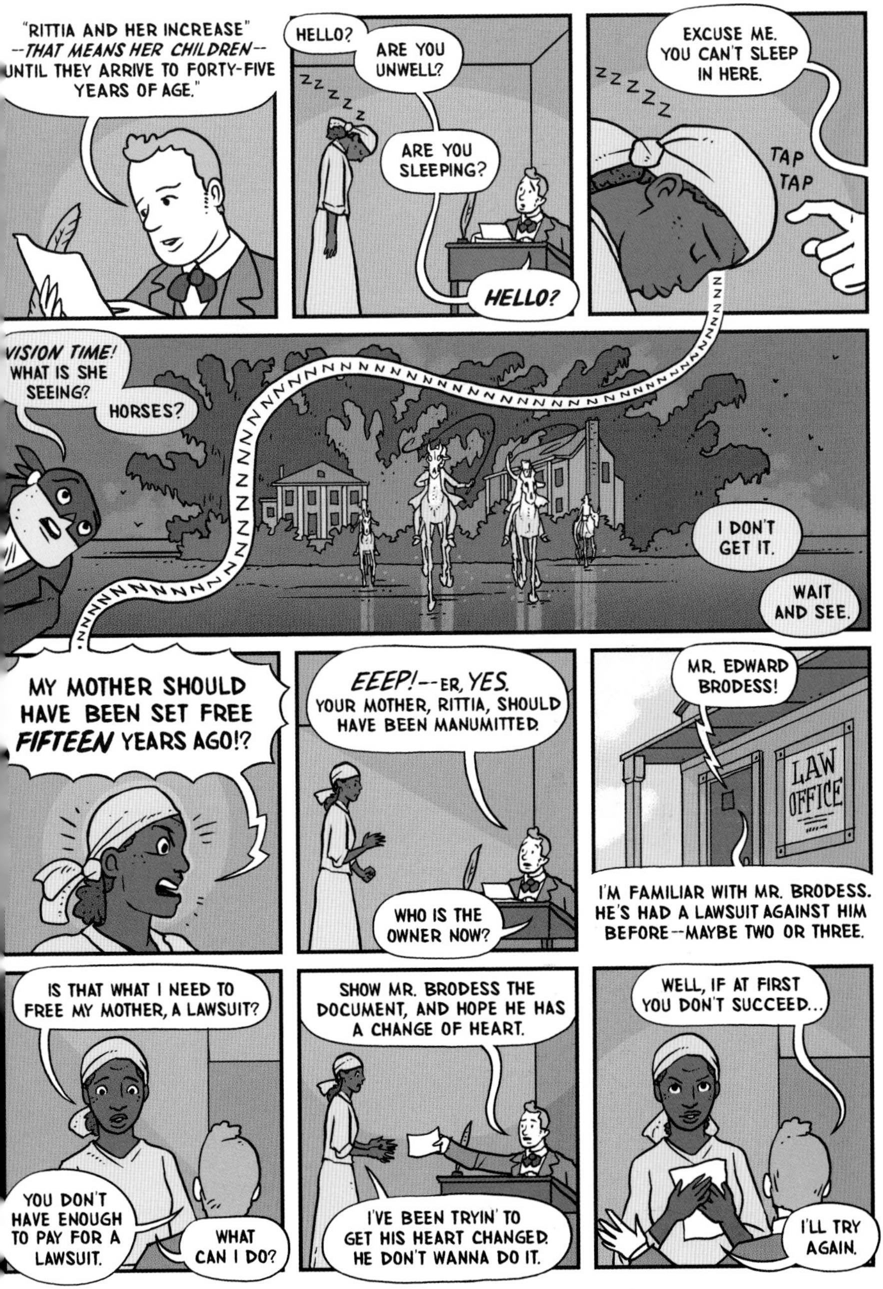
"RITTIA AND HER INCREASE" --*THAT MEANS HER CHILDREN*-- UNTIL THEY ARRIVE TO FORTY-FIVE YEARS OF AGE."
HELLO?
ARE YOU UNWELL?
Z Z Z Z Z
ARE YOU SLEEPING?
HELLO?
EXCUSE ME. YOU CAN'T SLEEP IN HERE.
Z Z Z Z Z
TAP TAP
VISION TIME! WHAT IS SHE SEEING?
HORSES?
I DON'T GET IT.
WAIT AND SEE.
MY MOTHER SHOULD HAVE BEEN SET FREE ***FIFTEEN*** YEARS AGO!?
EEEP!--ER, *YES.* YOUR MOTHER, RITTIA, SHOULD HAVE BEEN MANUMITTED.
WHO IS THE OWNER NOW?
MR. EDWARD BRODESS!
LAW OFFICE
I'M FAMILIAR WITH MR. BRODESS. HE'S HAD A LAWSUIT AGAINST HIM BEFORE--MAYBE TWO OR THREE.
IS THAT WHAT I NEED TO FREE MY MOTHER, A LAWSUIT?
YOU DON'T HAVE ENOUGH TO PAY FOR A LAWSUIT.
WHAT CAN I DO?
SHOW MR. BRODESS THE DOCUMENT, AND HOPE HE HAS A CHANGE OF HEART.
I'VE BEEN TRYIN' TO GET HIS HEART CHANGED. HE DON'T WANNA DO IT.
WELL, IF AT FIRST YOU DON'T SUCCEED...
I'LL TRY AGAIN.

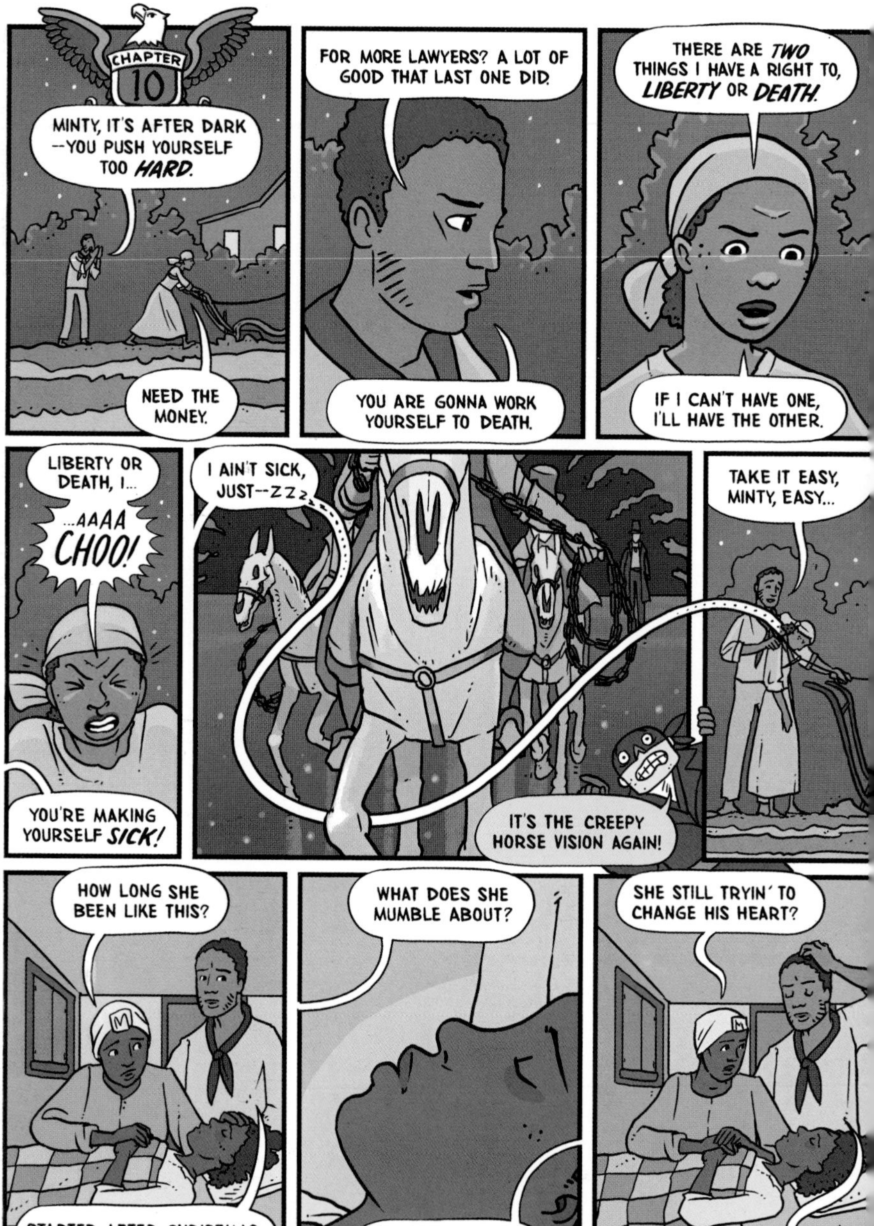
CHAPTER 10
MINTY, IT'S AFTER DARK --YOU PUSH YOURSELF TOO HARD.
NEED THE MONEY.
FOR MORE LAWYERS? A LOT OF GOOD THAT LAST ONE DID.
YOU ARE GONNA WORK YOURSELF TO DEATH.
THERE ARE TWO THINGS I HAVE A RIGHT TO, LIBERTY OR DEATH.
IF I CAN'T HAVE ONE, I'LL HAVE THE OTHER.
LIBERTY OR DEATH, I...
...AAAA CHOO!
YOU'RE MAKING YOURSELF SICK!
I AIN'T SICK, JUST--ZZZ
IT'S THE CREEPY HORSE VISION AGAIN!
TAKE IT EASY, MINTY, EASY...
HOW LONG SHE BEEN LIKE THIS?
STARTED AFTER CHRISTMAS. SHE'S IN AND OUT OF FEVER, MUMBLIN' ALL THE TIME.
WHAT DOES SHE MUMBLE ABOUT?
FREEDOM. LIBERTY. MR. BRODESS.
SHE STILL TRYIN' TO CHANGE HIS HEART?
EVERY DAY.

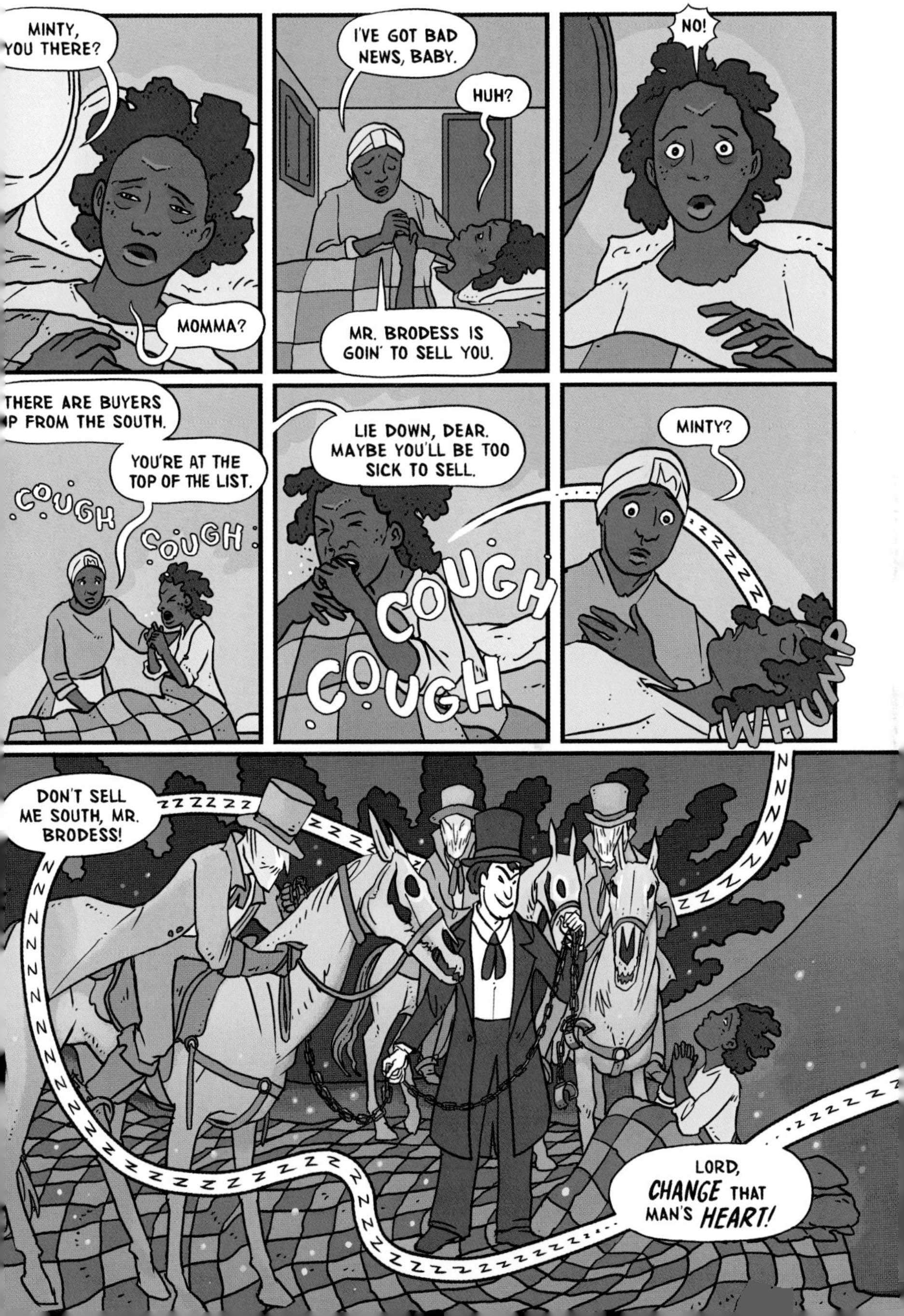
MINTY, YOU THERE?
MOMMA?
I'VE GOT BAD NEWS, BABY.
HUH?
MR. BRODESS IS GOIN' TO SELL YOU.
NO!
THERE ARE BUYERS UP FROM THE SOUTH.
YOU'RE AT THE TOP OF THE LIST.
COUGH
COUGH
LIE DOWN, DEAR. MAYBE YOU'LL BE TOO SICK TO SELL.
COUGH
COUGH
MINTY?
WHUMP
DON'T SELL ME SOUTH, MR. BRODESS!
LORD, CHANGE THAT MAN'S HEART!

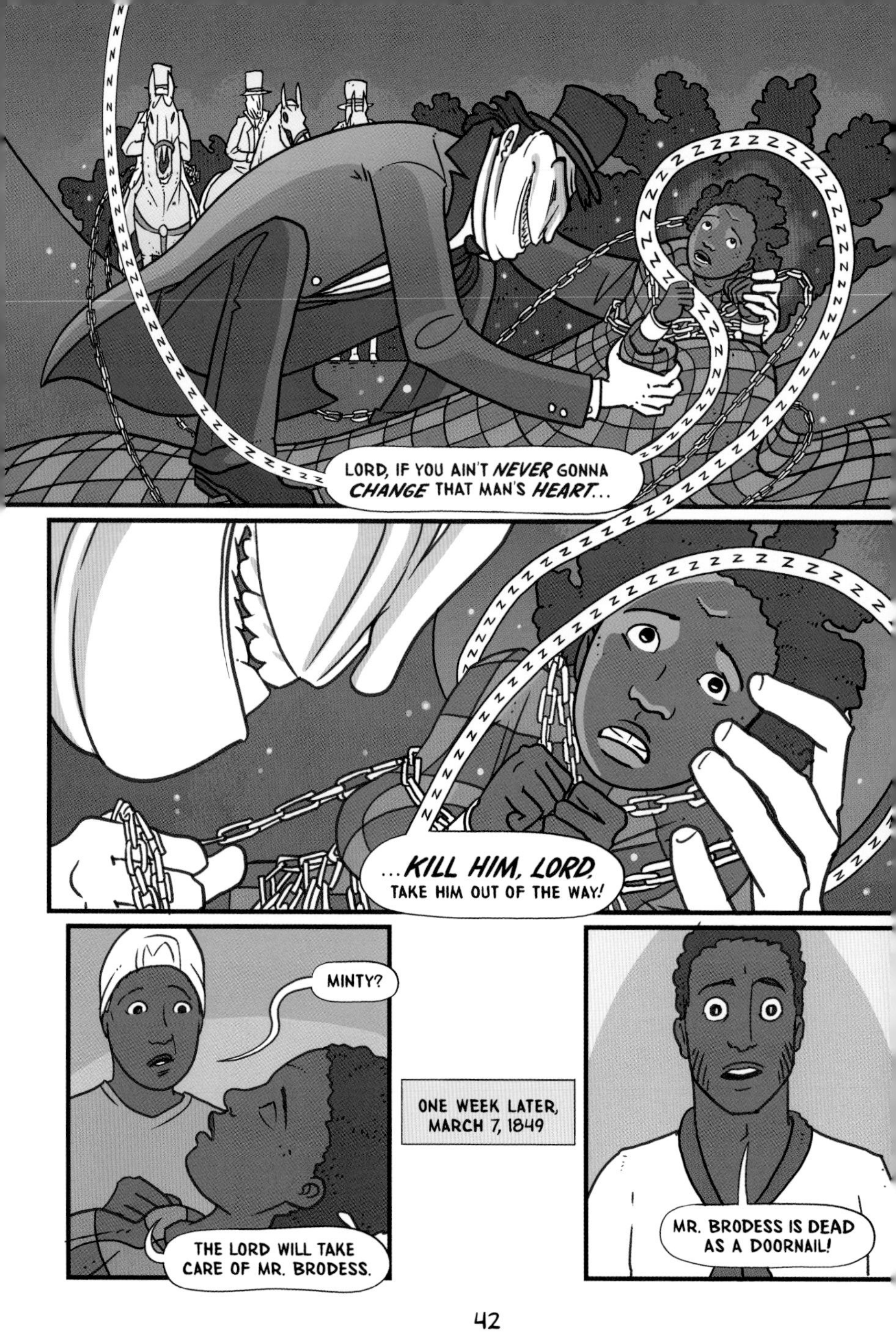
LORD, IF YOU AIN'T NEVER GONNA CHANGE THAT MAN'S HEART...
...KILL HIM, LORD. TAKE HIM OUT OF THE WAY!
MINTY?
THE LORD WILL TAKE CARE OF MR. BRODESS.
ONE WEEK LATER, MARCH 7, 1849
MR. BRODESS IS DEAD AS A DOORNAIL!

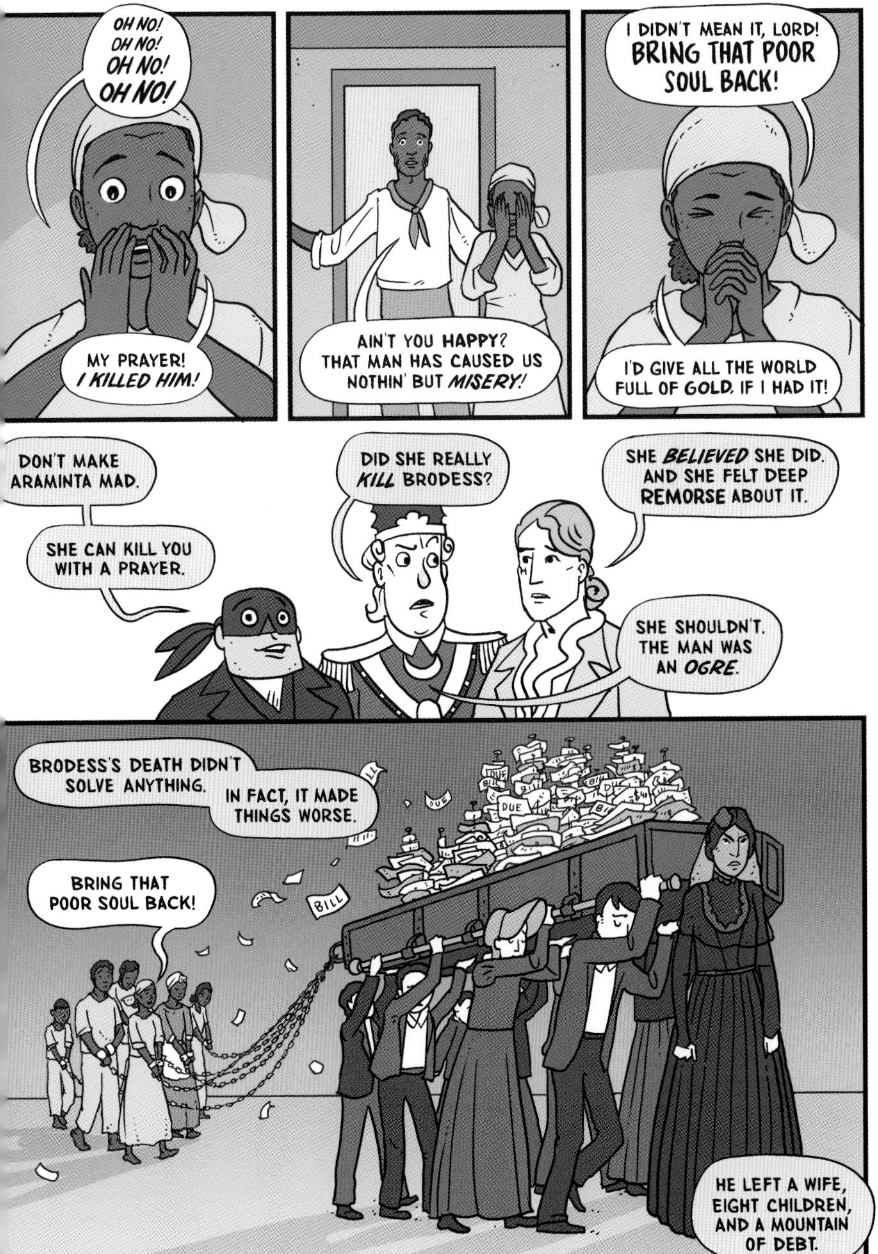
OH NO! OH NO! OH NO! OH NO!
MY PRAYER! I KILLED HIM!
AIN'T YOU HAPPY? THAT MAN HAS CAUSED US NOTHIN' BUT MISERY!
I DIDN'T MEAN IT, LORD! BRING THAT POOR SOUL BACK!
I'D GIVE ALL THE WORLD FULL OF GOLD, IF I HAD IT!
DON'T MAKE ARAMINTA MAD.
SHE CAN KILL YOU WITH A PRAYER.
DID SHE REALLY KILL BRODESS?
SHE BELIEVED SHE DID. AND SHE FELT DEEP REMORSE ABOUT IT.
SHE SHOULDN'T. THE MAN WAS AN OGRE.
BRODESS'S DEATH DIDN'T SOLVE ANYTHING.
IN FACT, IT MADE THINGS WORSE.
BRING THAT POOR SOUL BACK!
DUE
BILL
HE LEFT A WIFE, EIGHT CHILDREN, AND A MOUNTAIN OF DEBT.

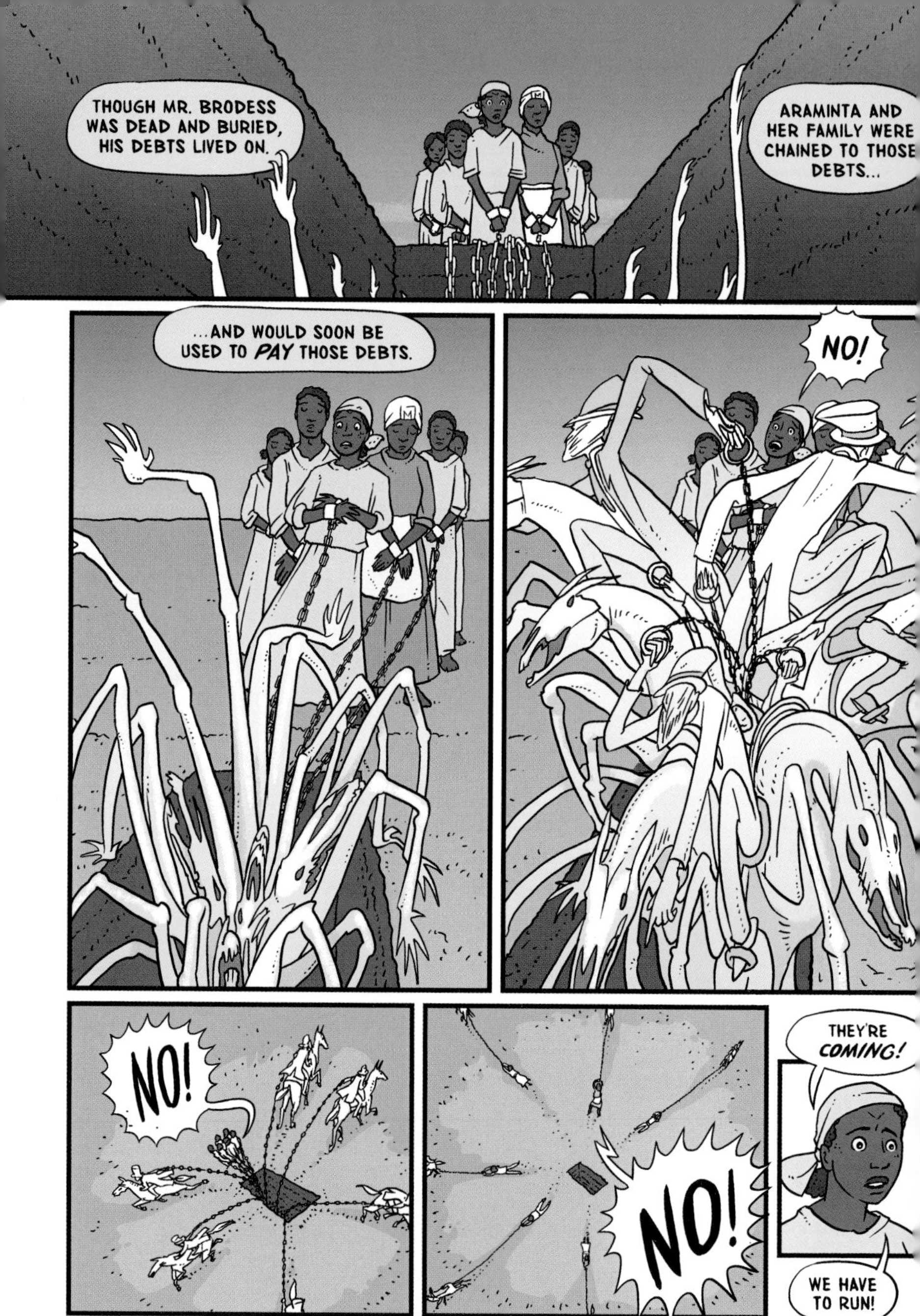
THOUGH MR. BRODESS WAS DEAD AND BURIED, HIS DEBTS LIVED ON.
ARAMINTA AND HER FAMILY WERE CHAINED TO THOSE DEBTS...
...AND WOULD SOON BE USED TO *PAY* THOSE DEBTS.
NO!
NO!
NO!
THEY'RE *COMING!*
WE HAVE TO RUN!

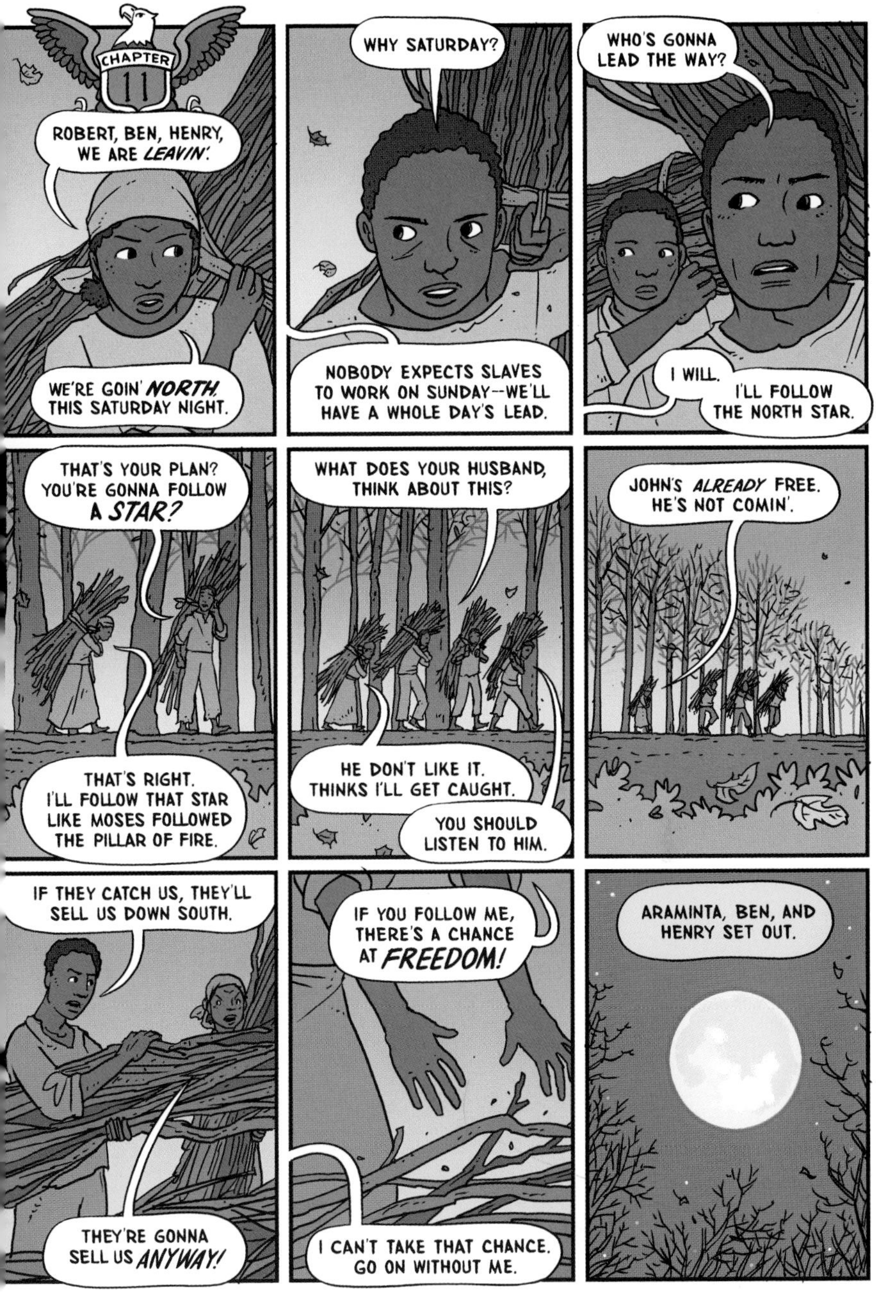
CHAPTER 11
ROBERT, BEN, HENRY, WE ARE LEAVIN'.
WE'RE GOIN' NORTH, THIS SATURDAY NIGHT.
WHY SATURDAY?
NOBODY EXPECTS SLAVES TO WORK ON SUNDAY--WE'LL HAVE A WHOLE DAY'S LEAD.
WHO'S GONNA LEAD THE WAY?
I WILL.
I'LL FOLLOW THE NORTH STAR.
THAT'S YOUR PLAN? YOU'RE GONNA FOLLOW A STAR?
THAT'S RIGHT. I'LL FOLLOW THAT STAR LIKE MOSES FOLLOWED THE PILLAR OF FIRE.
WHAT DOES YOUR HUSBAND, THINK ABOUT THIS?
HE DON'T LIKE IT. THINKS I'LL GET CAUGHT.
YOU SHOULD LISTEN TO HIM.
JOHN'S ALREADY FREE. HE'S NOT COMIN'.
IF THEY CATCH US, THEY'LL SELL US DOWN SOUTH.
THEY'RE GONNA SELL US ANYWAY!
IF YOU FOLLOW ME, THERE'S A CHANCE AT FREEDOM!
I CAN'T TAKE THAT CHANCE. GO ON WITHOUT ME.
ARAMINTA, BEN, AND HENRY SET OUT.

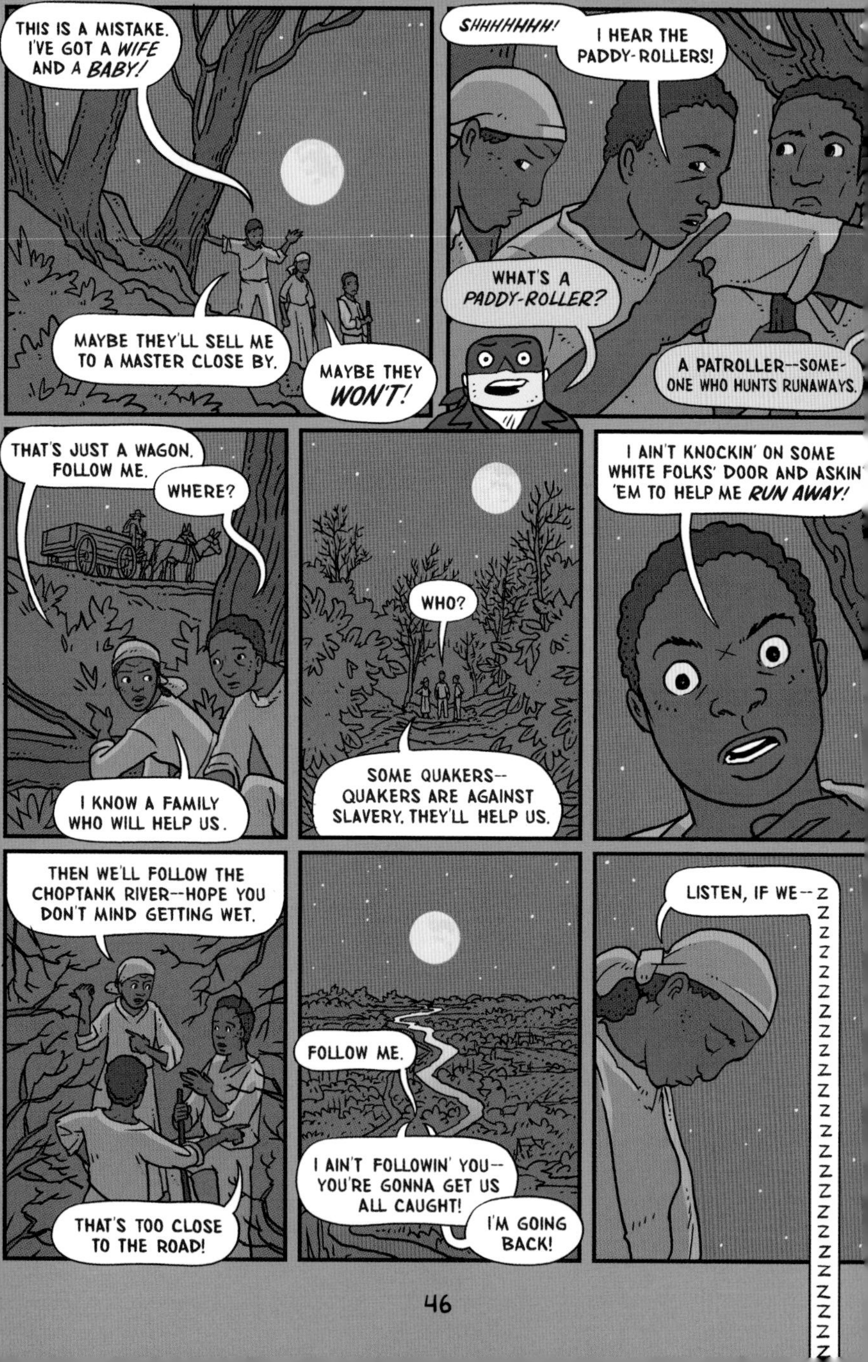
THIS IS A MISTAKE. I'VE GOT A *WIFE* AND A *BABY!*
MAYBE THEY'LL SELL ME TO A MASTER CLOSE BY.
MAYBE THEY *WON'T!*
SHHHHHHH!
I HEAR THE PADDY-ROLLERS!
WHAT'S A *PADDY-ROLLER?*
A PATROLLER--SOMEONE WHO HUNTS RUNAWAYS.
THAT'S JUST A WAGON. FOLLOW ME.
WHERE?
I KNOW A FAMILY WHO WILL HELP US.
WHO?
SOME QUAKERS-- QUAKERS ARE AGAINST SLAVERY. THEY'LL HELP US.
I AIN'T KNOCKIN' ON SOME WHITE FOLKS' DOOR AND ASKIN' 'EM TO HELP ME *RUN AWAY!*
THEN WE'LL FOLLOW THE CHOPTANK RIVER--HOPE YOU DON'T MIND GETTING WET.
THAT'S TOO CLOSE TO THE ROAD!
FOLLOW ME.
I AIN'T FOLLOWIN' YOU-- YOU'RE GONNA GET US ALL CAUGHT!
I'M GOING BACK!
LISTEN, IF WE-- ZZZZZZZZZZZZZZZZZZZZZZZZZZZZ

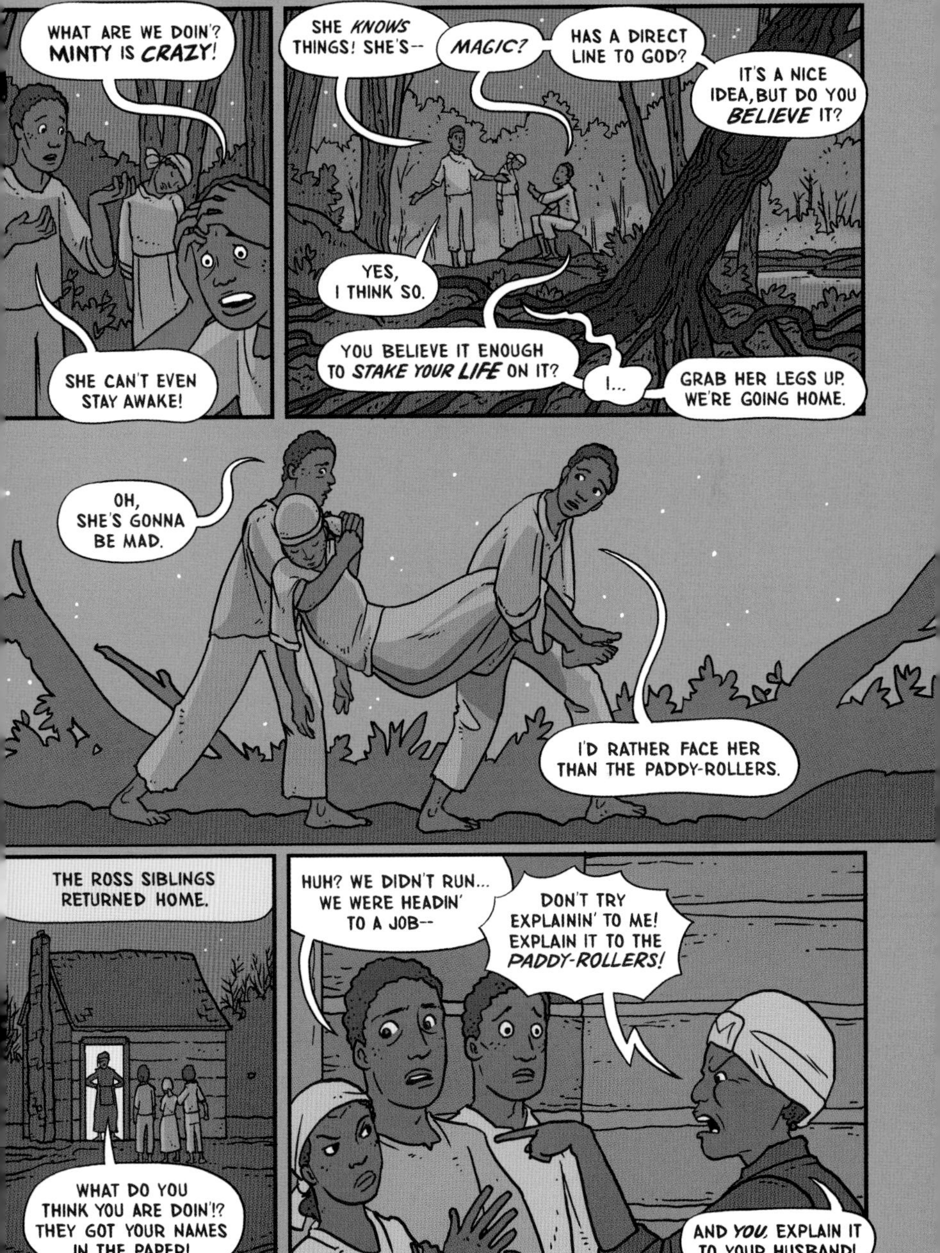
WHAT ARE WE DOIN'? MINTY IS *CRAZY*!
SHE CAN'T EVEN STAY AWAKE!
SHE *KNOWS* THINGS! SHE'S--
MAGIC?
HAS A DIRECT LINE TO GOD?
IT'S A NICE IDEA, BUT DO YOU *BELIEVE* IT?
YES, I THINK SO.
YOU BELIEVE IT ENOUGH TO *STAKE YOUR LIFE* ON IT?
I...
GRAB HER LEGS UP. WE'RE GOING HOME.
OH, SHE'S GONNA BE MAD.
I'D RATHER FACE HER THAN THE PADDY-ROLLERS.
THE ROSS SIBLINGS RETURNED HOME.
WHAT DO YOU THINK YOU ARE DOIN'!? THEY GOT YOUR NAMES IN THE PAPER!
HUH? WE DIDN'T RUN... WE WERE HEADIN' TO A JOB--
DON'T TRY EXPLAININ' TO ME! EXPLAIN IT TO THE *PADDY-ROLLERS!*
AND *YOU*, EXPLAIN IT TO YOUR HUSBAND!

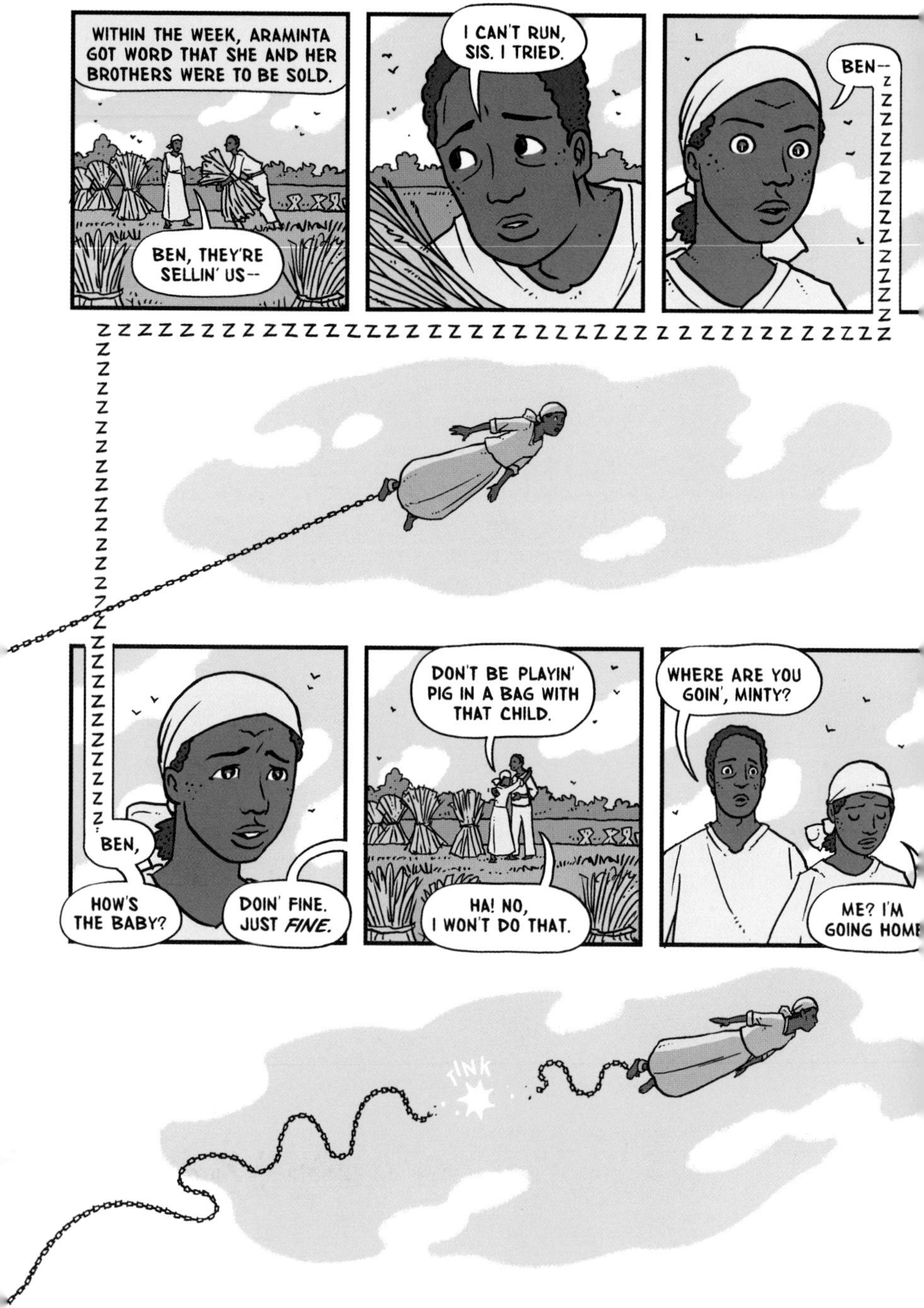

WITHIN THE WEEK, ARAMINTA GOT WORD THAT SHE AND HER BROTHERS WERE TO BE SOLD.
BEN, THEY'RE SELLIN' US--
I CAN'T RUN, SIS. I TRIED.
BEN--
ZZZZZZZZZZZZZZZZZZZZZZZZZZZZZZZ
BEN,
HOW'S THE BABY?
DOIN' FINE. JUST *FINE.*
DON'T BE PLAYIN' PIG IN A BAG WITH THAT CHILD.
HA! NO, I WON'T DO THAT.
WHERE ARE YOU GOIN', MINTY?
ME? I'M GOING HOME
TINK

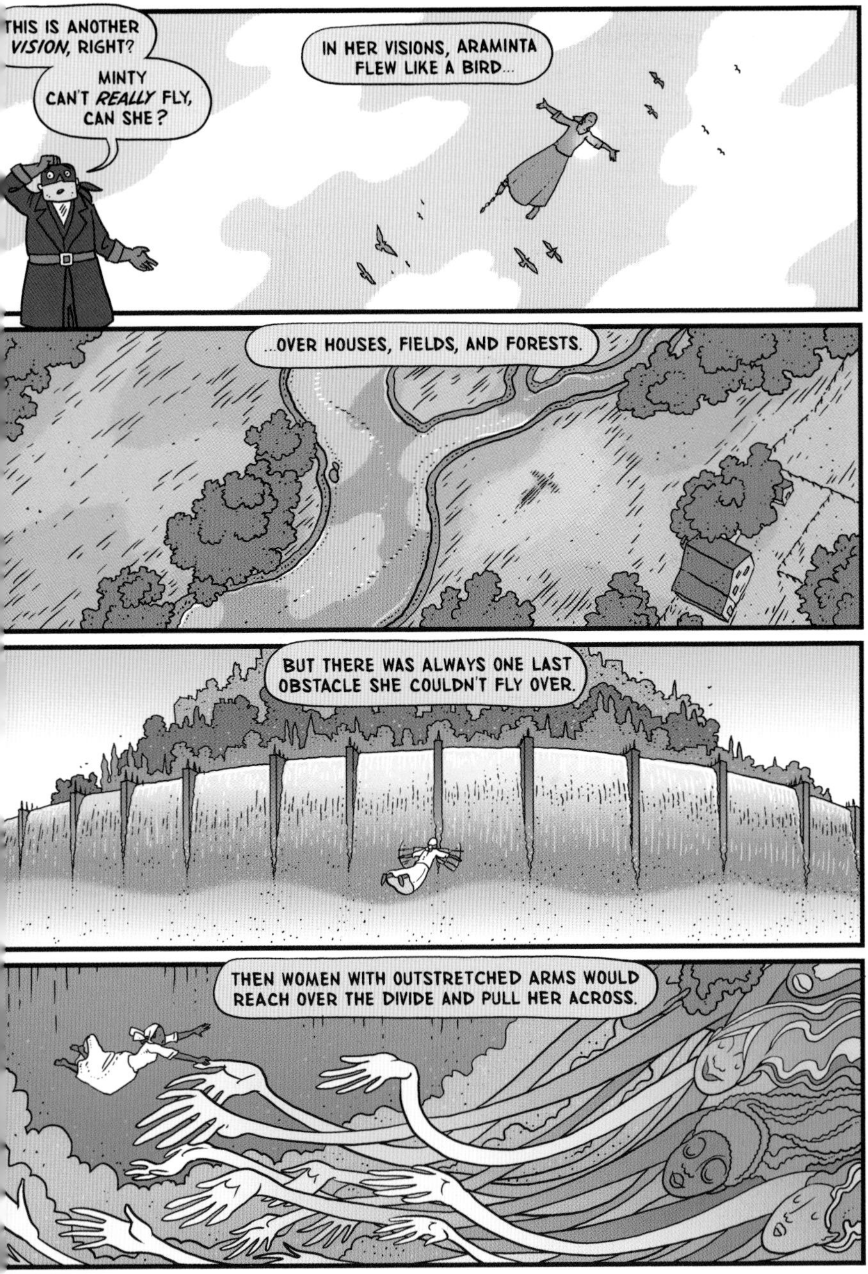
THIS IS ANOTHER VISION, RIGHT?
MINTY CAN'T REALLY FLY, CAN SHE?
IN HER VISIONS, ARAMINTA FLEW LIKE A BIRD...
...OVER HOUSES, FIELDS, AND FORESTS.
BUT THERE WAS ALWAYS ONE LAST OBSTACLE SHE COULDN'T FLY OVER.
THEN WOMEN WITH OUTSTRETCHED ARMS WOULD REACH OVER THE DIVIDE AND PULL HER ACROSS.

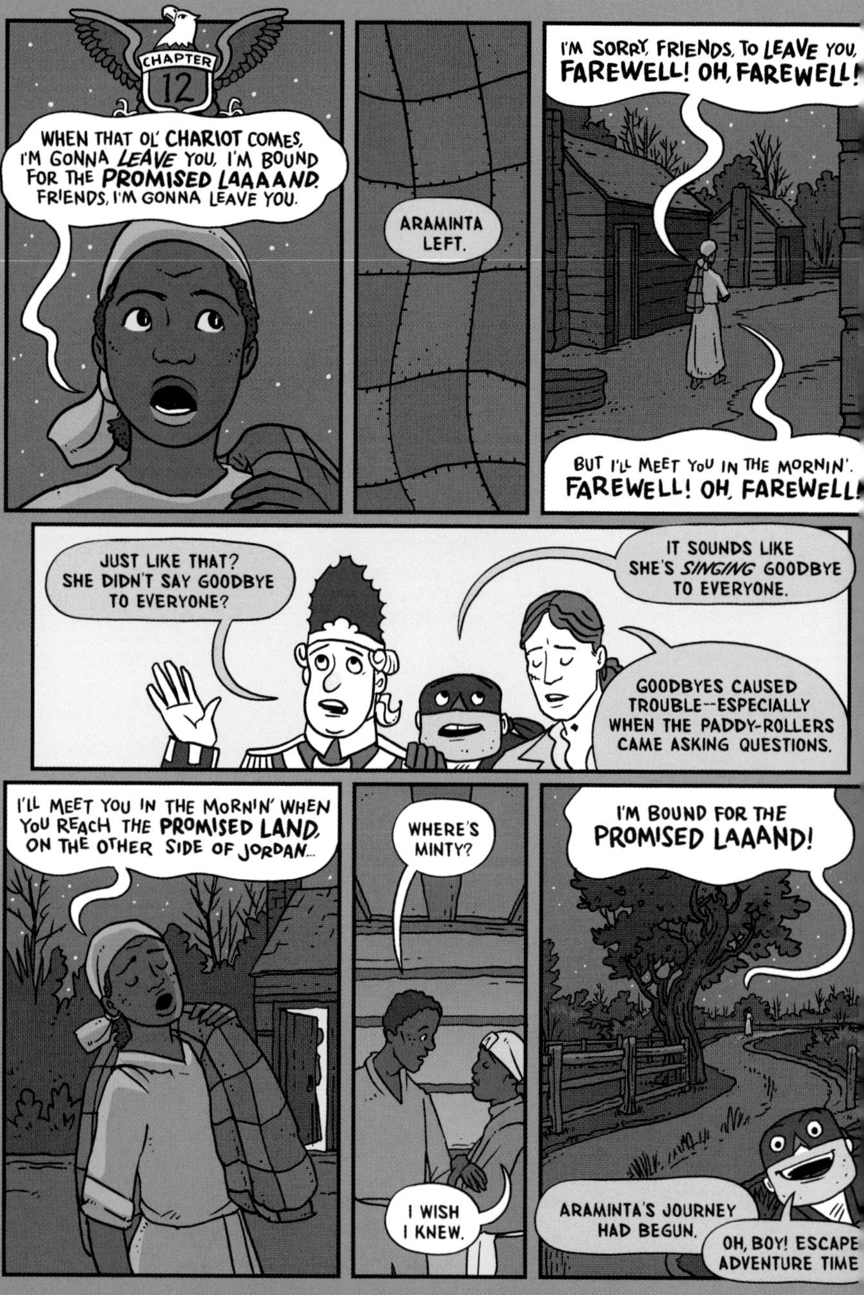
CHAPTER 12
WHEN THAT OL' CHARIOT COMES, I'M GONNA LEAVE YOU, I'M BOUND FOR THE PROMISED LAAAAND. FRIENDS, I'M GONNA LEAVE YOU.
ARAMINTA LEFT.
I'M SORRY, FRIENDS, TO LEAVE YOU, FAREWELL! OH, FAREWELL!
BUT I'LL MEET YOU IN THE MORNIN'. FAREWELL! OH, FAREWELL!
JUST LIKE THAT? SHE DIDN'T SAY GOODBYE TO EVERYONE?
IT SOUNDS LIKE SHE'S SINGING GOODBYE TO EVERYONE.
GOODBYES CAUSED TROUBLE--ESPECIALLY WHEN THE PADDY-ROLLERS CAME ASKING QUESTIONS.
I'LL MEET YOU IN THE MORNIN' WHEN YOU REACH THE PROMISED LAND, ON THE OTHER SIDE OF JORDAN...
WHERE'S MINTY?
I WISH I KNEW.
I'M BOUND FOR THE PROMISED LAAAND!
ARAMINTA'S JOURNEY HAD BEGUN.
OH, BOY! ESCAPE ADVENTURE TIME

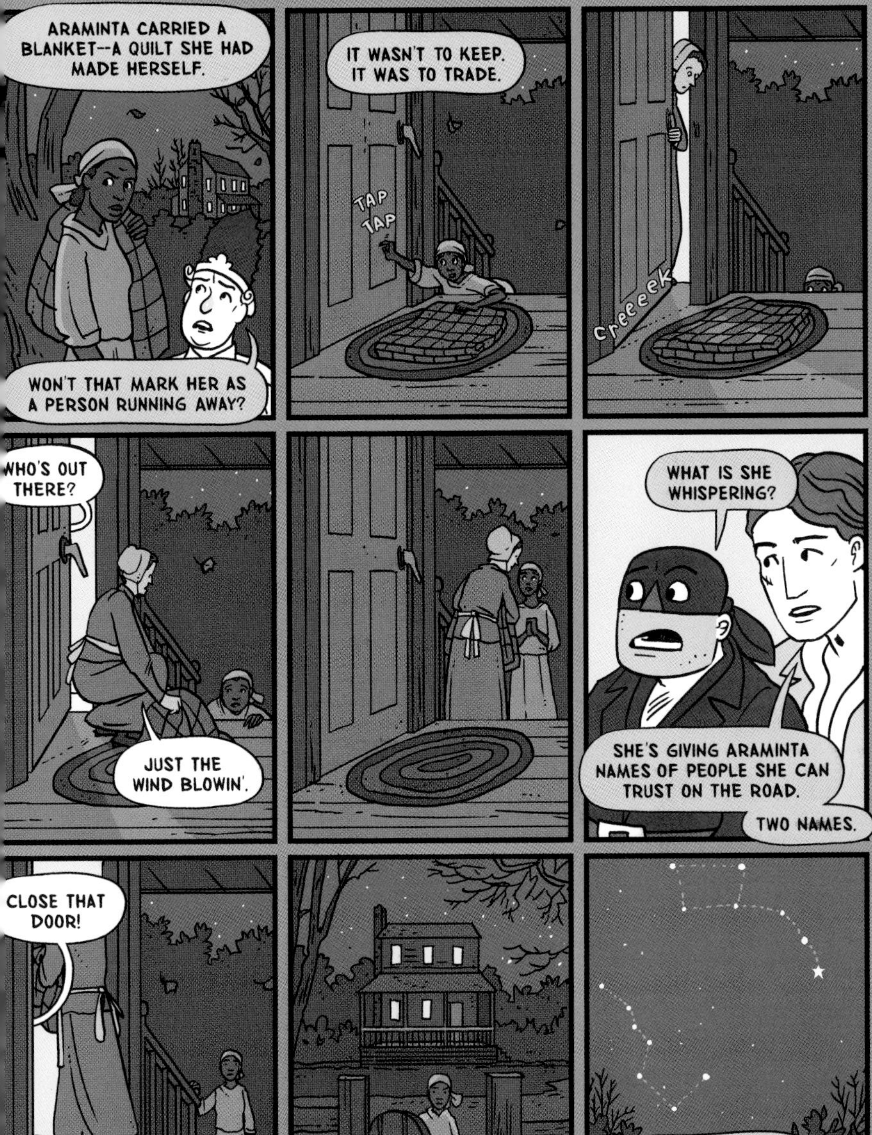
ARAMINTA CARRIED A BLANKET--A QUILT SHE HAD MADE HERSELF.
WON'T THAT MARK HER AS A PERSON RUNNING AWAY?
IT WASN'T TO KEEP. IT WAS TO TRADE.
TAP
TAP
creeeek
WHO'S OUT THERE?
JUST THE WIND BLOWIN'.
WHAT IS SHE WHISPERING?
SHE'S GIVING ARAMINTA NAMES OF PEOPLE SHE CAN TRUST ON THE ROAD.
TWO NAMES.
CLOSE THAT DOOR!
YES, YES, HERE I COME.
WITH TWO NAMES AND A STAR TO FOLLOW, ARAMINTA SET OUT.

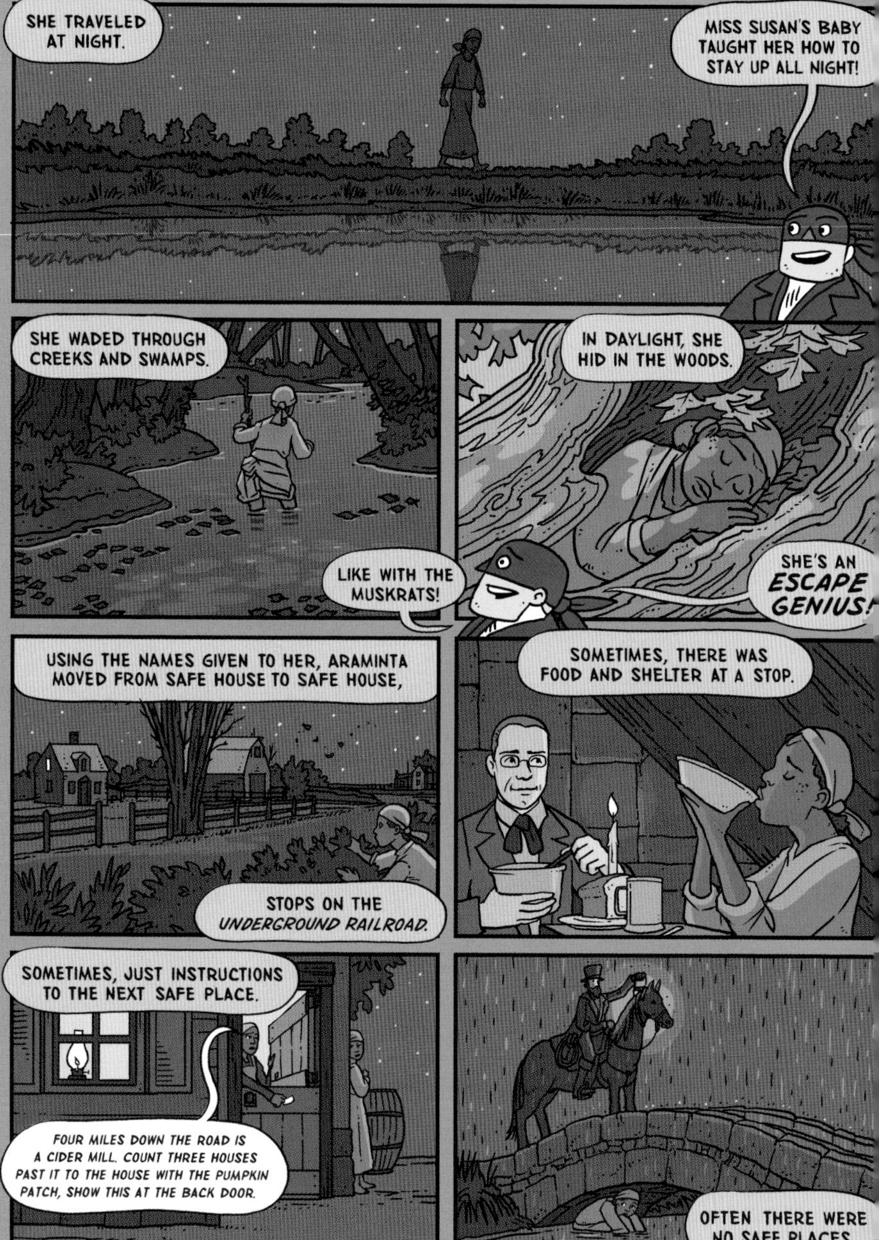
SHE TRAVELED AT NIGHT.
MISS SUSAN'S BABY TAUGHT HER HOW TO STAY UP ALL NIGHT!
SHE WADED THROUGH CREEKS AND SWAMPS.
LIKE WITH THE MUSKRATS!
IN DAYLIGHT, SHE HID IN THE WOODS.
SHE'S AN *ESCAPE GENIUS!*
USING THE NAMES GIVEN TO HER, ARAMINTA MOVED FROM SAFE HOUSE TO SAFE HOUSE,
STOPS ON THE *UNDERGROUND RAILROAD.*
SOMETIMES, THERE WAS FOOD AND SHELTER AT A STOP.
SOMETIMES, JUST INSTRUCTIONS TO THE NEXT SAFE PLACE.
FOUR MILES DOWN THE ROAD IS A CIDER MILL. COUNT THREE HOUSES PAST IT TO THE HOUSE WITH THE PUMPKIN PATCH, SHOW THIS AT THE BACK DOOR.
OFTEN THERE WERE NO SAFE PLACES.

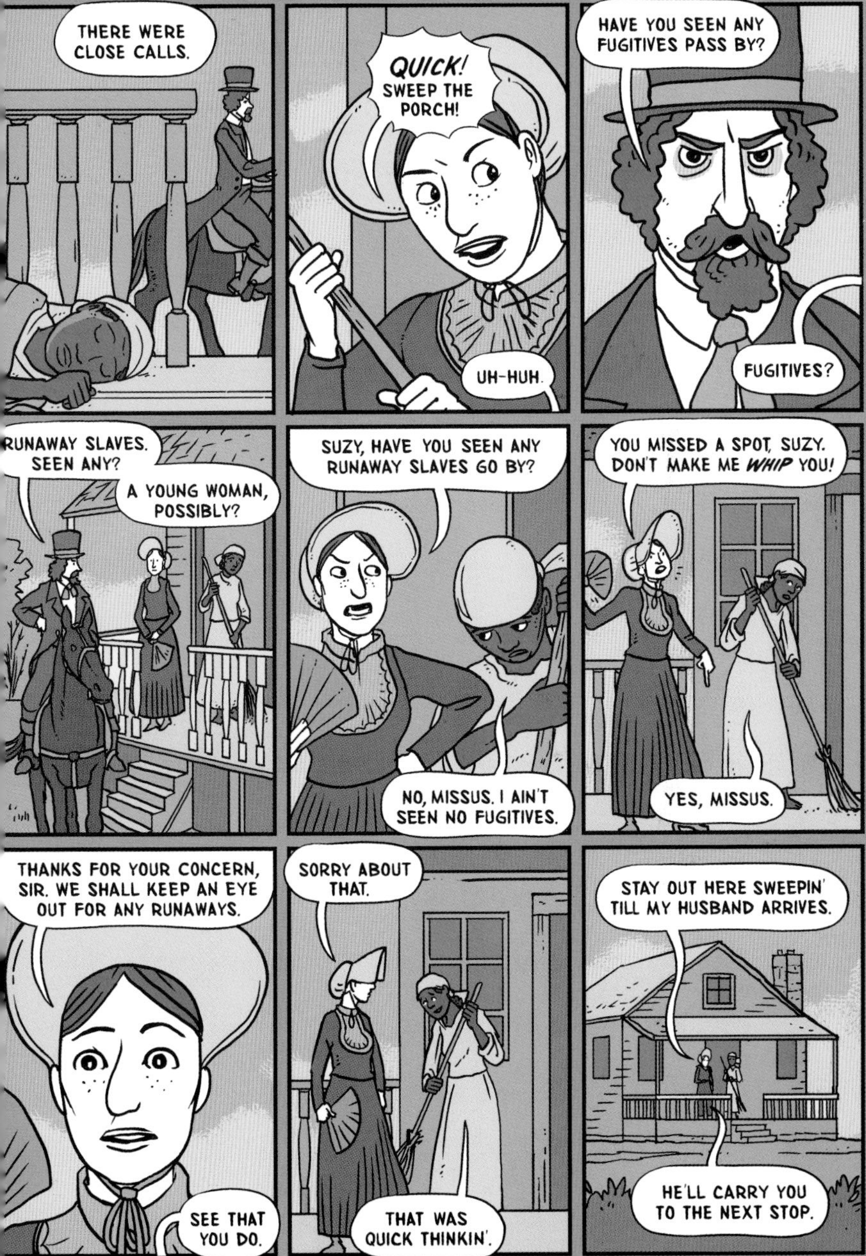
THERE WERE CLOSE CALLS.
QUICK! SWEEP THE PORCH!
UH-HUH.
HAVE YOU SEEN ANY FUGITIVES PASS BY?
FUGITIVES?
RUNAWAY SLAVES. SEEN ANY?
A YOUNG WOMAN, POSSIBLY?
SUZY, HAVE YOU SEEN ANY RUNAWAY SLAVES GO BY?
NO, MISSUS. I AIN'T SEEN NO FUGITIVES.
YOU MISSED A SPOT, SUZY. DON'T MAKE ME *WHIP* YOU!
YES, MISSUS.
THANKS FOR YOUR CONCERN, SIR. WE SHALL KEEP AN EYE OUT FOR ANY RUNAWAYS.
SEE THAT YOU DO.
SORRY ABOUT THAT.
THAT WAS QUICK THINKIN'.
STAY OUT HERE SWEEPIN' TILL MY HUSBAND ARRIVES.
HE'LL CARRY YOU TO THE NEXT STOP.

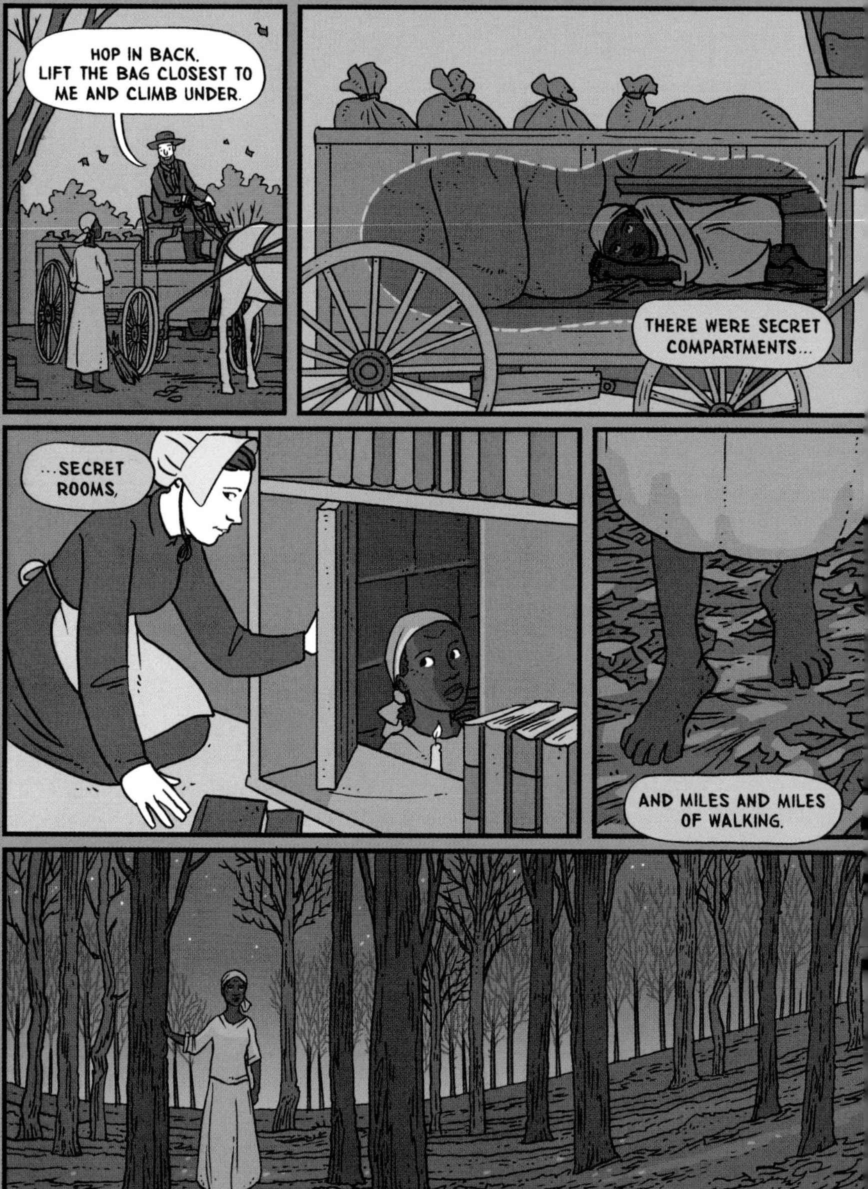
HOP IN BACK. LIFT THE BAG CLOSEST TO ME AND CLIMB UNDER.
THERE WERE SECRET COMPARTMENTS...
...SECRET ROOMS,
AND MILES AND MILES OF WALKING.
ARAMINTA MADE HER WAY NEARLY ONE HUNDRED MILES NORTH

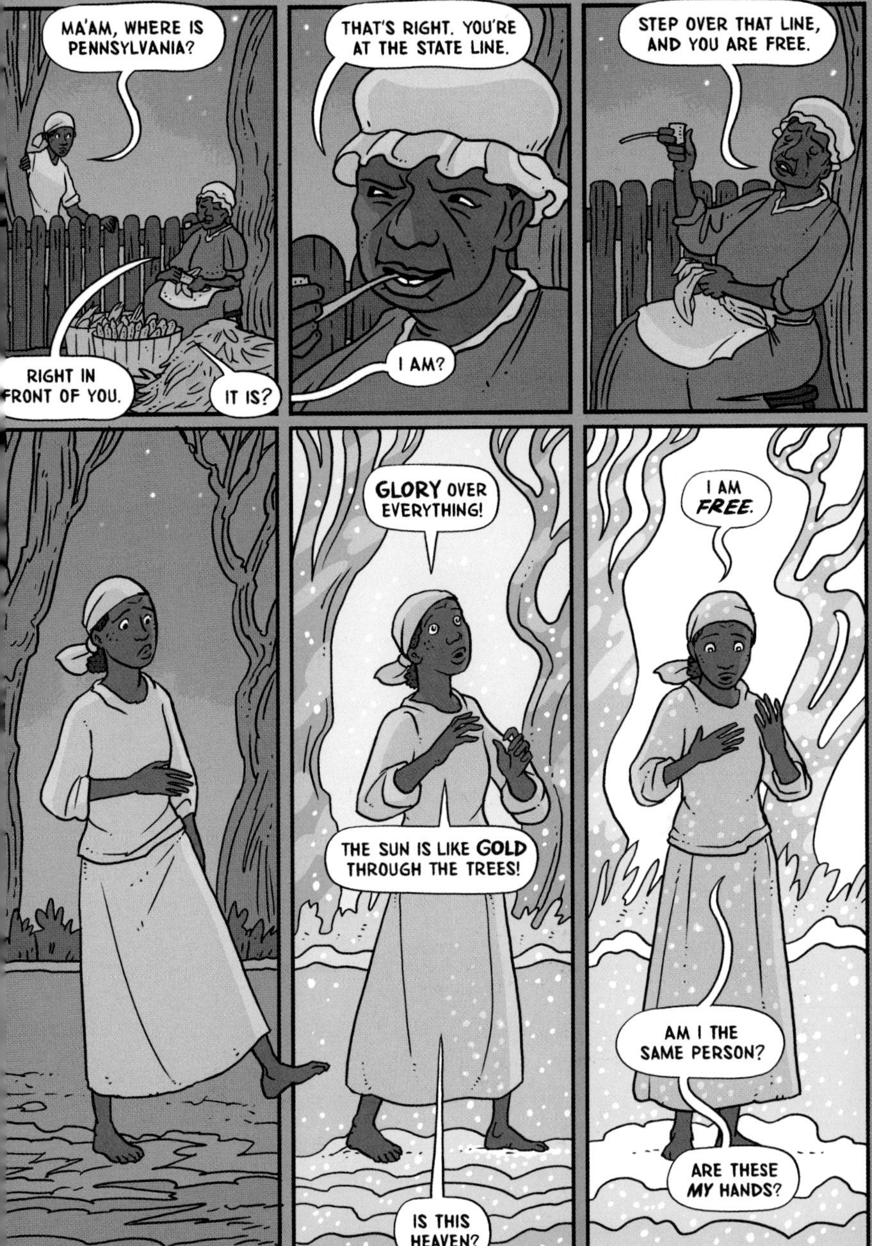
MA'AM, WHERE IS PENNSYLVANIA?
RIGHT IN FRONT OF YOU.
IT IS?
THAT'S RIGHT. YOU'RE AT THE STATE LINE.
I AM?
STEP OVER THAT LINE, AND YOU ARE FREE.
GLORY OVER EVERYTHING!
THE SUN IS LIKE GOLD THROUGH THE TREES!
IS THIS HEAVEN?
I AM *FREE*.
AM I THE SAME PERSON?
ARE THESE *MY* HANDS?

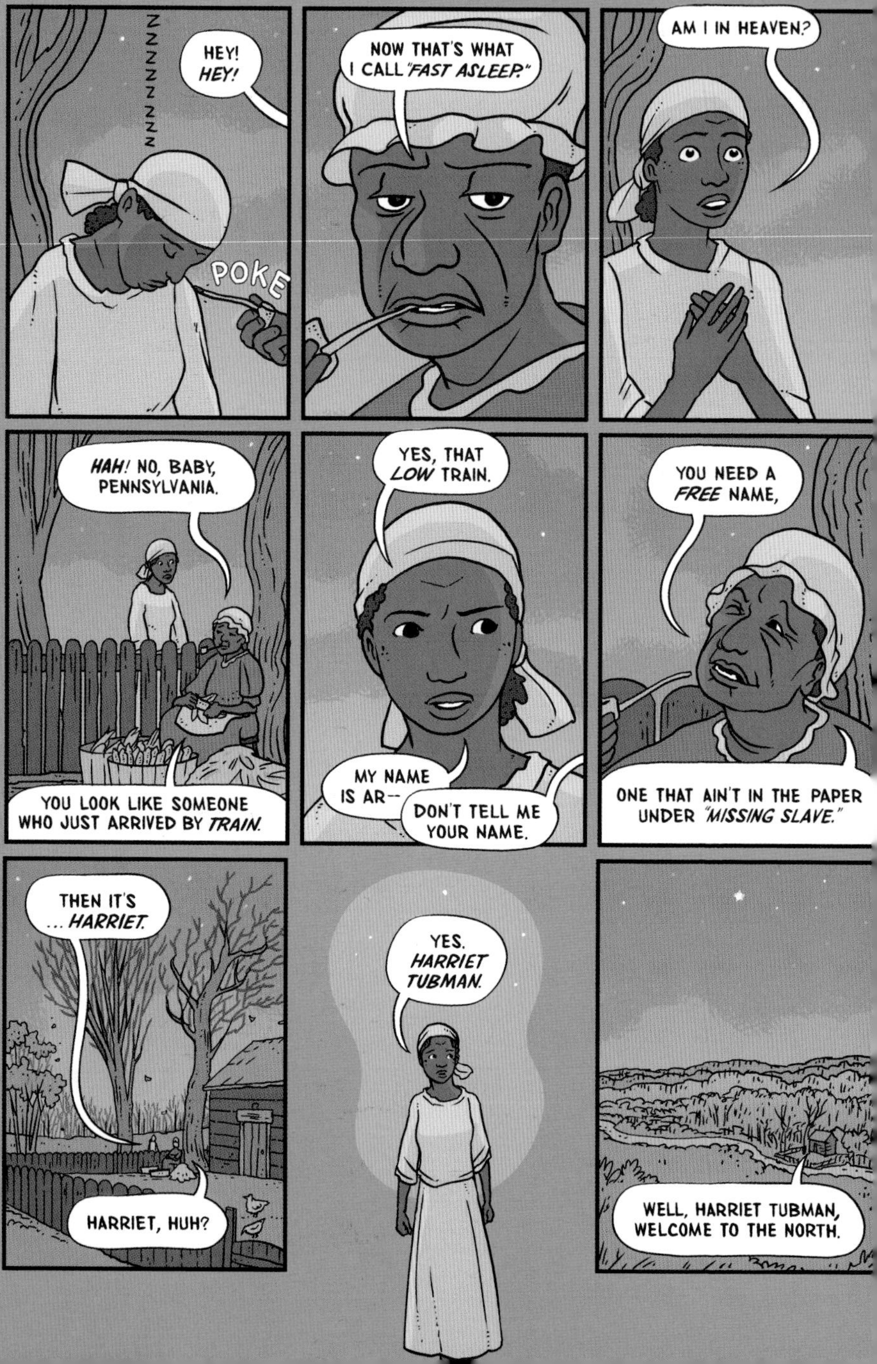
ZZZZZZZZ
HEY! *HEY!*
POKE
NOW THAT'S WHAT I CALL *"FAST ASLEEP."*
AM I IN HEAVEN?
HAH! NO, BABY, PENNSYLVANIA.
YOU LOOK LIKE SOMEONE WHO JUST ARRIVED BY *TRAIN.*
YES, THAT *LOW* TRAIN.
MY NAME IS AR--
DON'T TELL ME YOUR NAME.
YOU NEED A *FREE* NAME,
ONE THAT AIN'T IN THE PAPER UNDER *"MISSING SLAVE."*
THEN IT'S ...*HARRIET.*
HARRIET, HUH?
YES. *HARRIET TUBMAN.*
WELL, HARRIET TUBMAN, WELCOME TO THE NORTH.

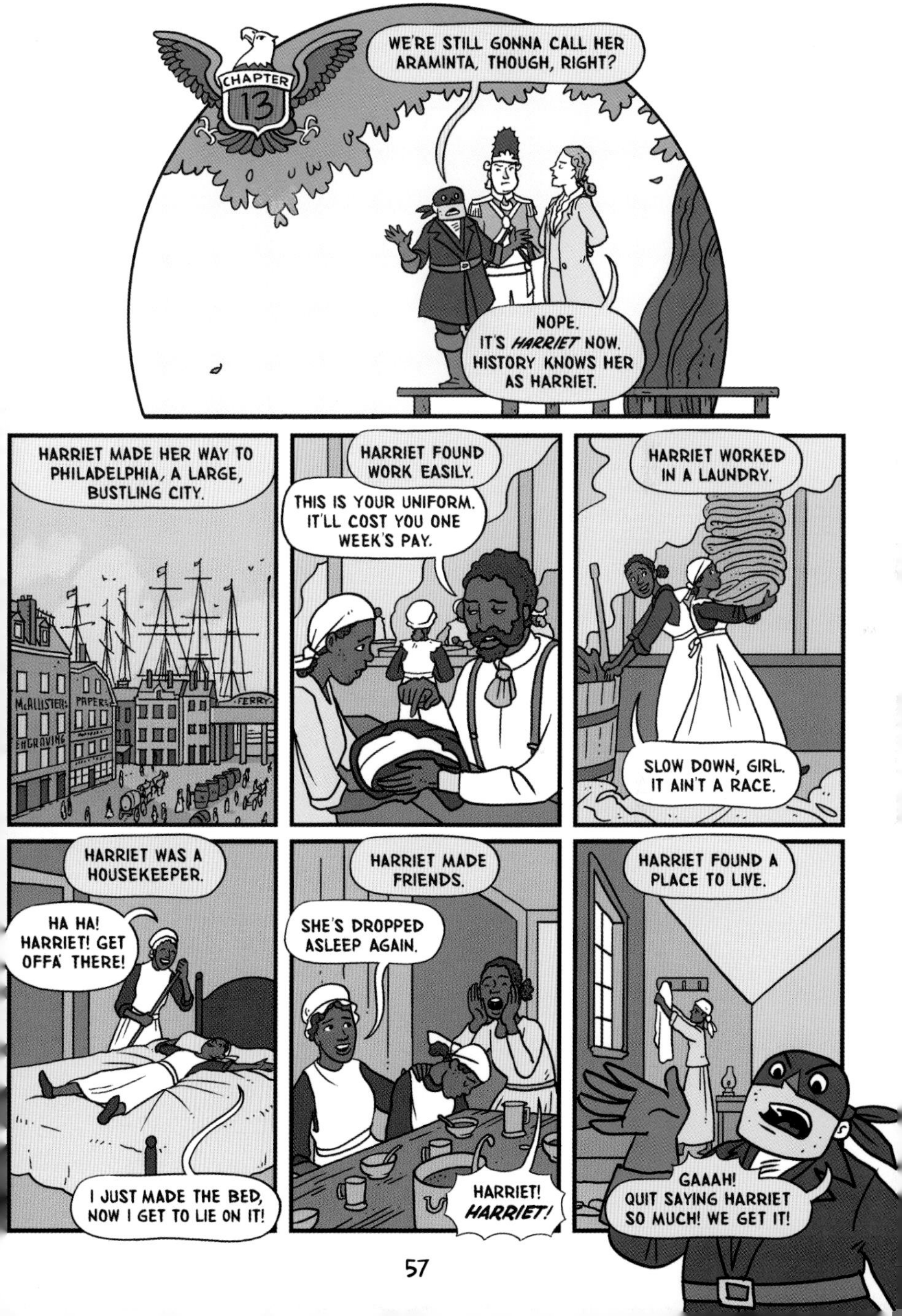
CHAPTER 13
WE'RE STILL GONNA CALL HER ARAMINTA, THOUGH, RIGHT?
NOPE. IT'S *HARRIET* NOW. HISTORY KNOWS HER AS HARRIET.
HARRIET MADE HER WAY TO PHILADELPHIA, A LARGE, BUSTLING CITY.
McALLISTER ENGRAVING
PAPER
FERRY
HARRIET FOUND WORK EASILY.
THIS IS YOUR UNIFORM. IT'LL COST YOU ONE WEEK'S PAY.
HARRIET WORKED IN A LAUNDRY.
SLOW DOWN, GIRL. IT AIN'T A RACE.
HARRIET WAS A HOUSEKEEPER.
HA HA! HARRIET! GET OFFA' THERE!
I JUST MADE THE BED, NOW I GET TO LIE ON IT!
HARRIET MADE FRIENDS.
SHE'S DROPPED ASLEEP AGAIN.
HARRIET! *HARRIET!*
HARRIET FOUND A PLACE TO LIVE.
GAAAH! QUIT SAYING HARRIET SO MUCH! WE GET IT!

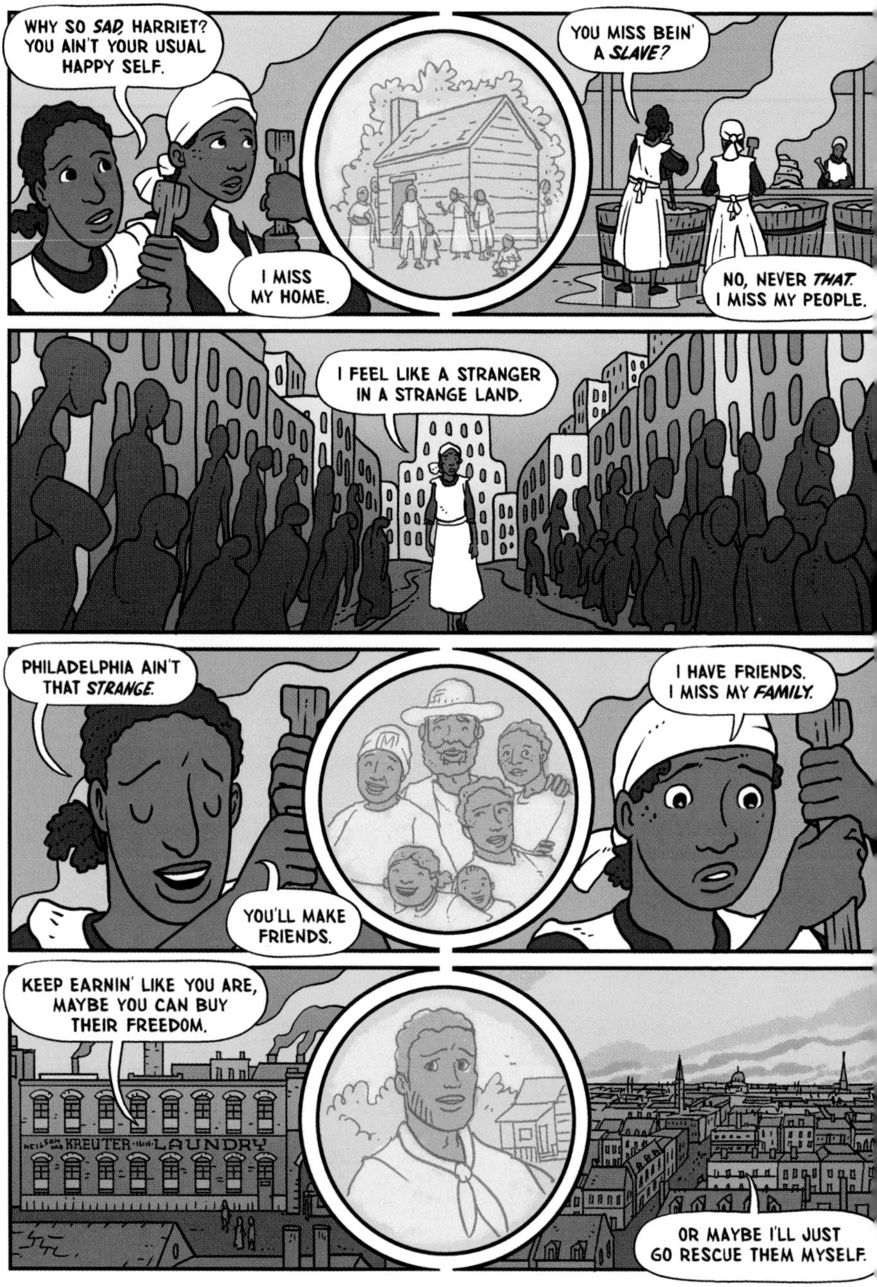
WHY SO SAD, HARRIET? YOU AIN'T YOUR USUAL HAPPY SELF.
I MISS MY HOME.
YOU MISS BEIN' A SLAVE?
NO, NEVER THAT. I MISS MY PEOPLE.
I FEEL LIKE A STRANGER IN A STRANGE LAND.
PHILADELPHIA AIN'T THAT STRANGE.
YOU'LL MAKE FRIENDS.
I HAVE FRIENDS. I MISS MY FAMILY.
KEEP EARNIN' LIKE YOU ARE, MAYBE YOU CAN BUY THEIR FREEDOM.
NEILSON AND KREUTER LAUNDRY
OR MAYBE I'LL JUST GO RESCUE THEM MYSELF.

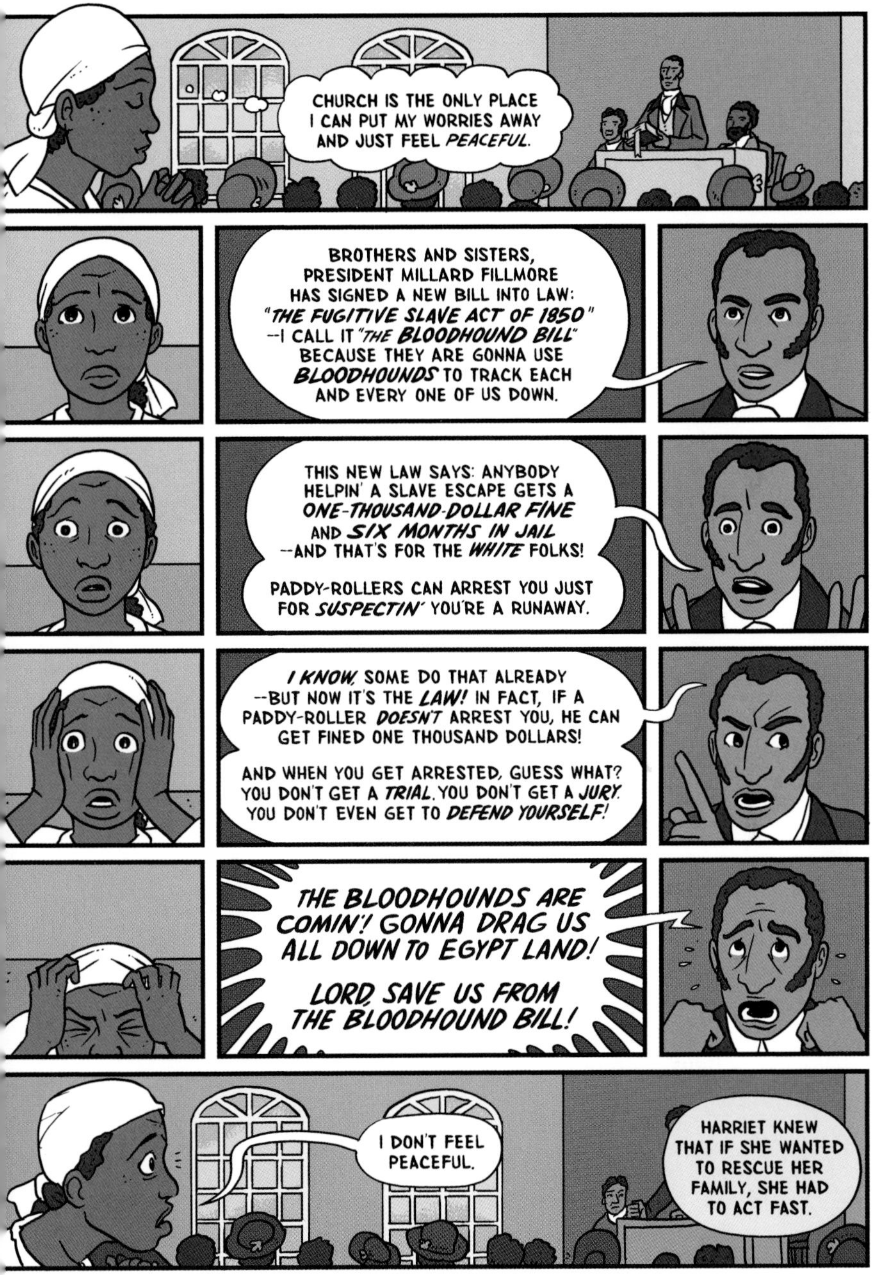

CHURCH IS THE ONLY PLACE I CAN PUT MY WORRIES AWAY AND JUST FEEL *PEACEFUL.*
BROTHERS AND SISTERS, PRESIDENT MILLARD FILLMORE HAS SIGNED A NEW BILL INTO LAW: "*THE FUGITIVE SLAVE ACT OF 1850*" --I CALL IT "*THE BLOODHOUND BILL*" BECAUSE THEY ARE GONNA USE *BLOODHOUNDS* TO TRACK EACH AND EVERY ONE OF US DOWN.
THIS NEW LAW SAYS: ANYBODY HELPIN' A SLAVE ESCAPE GETS A *ONE-THOUSAND-DOLLAR FINE* AND *SIX MONTHS IN JAIL* --AND THAT'S FOR THE *WHITE* FOLKS!
PADDY-ROLLERS CAN ARREST YOU JUST FOR *SUSPECTIN'* YOU'RE A RUNAWAY.
I KNOW, SOME DO THAT ALREADY --BUT NOW IT'S THE *LAW!* IN FACT, IF A PADDY-ROLLER *DOESN'T* ARREST YOU, HE CAN GET FINED ONE THOUSAND DOLLARS!
AND WHEN YOU GET ARRESTED, GUESS WHAT? YOU DON'T GET A *TRIAL*. YOU DON'T GET A *JURY*. YOU DON'T EVEN GET TO *DEFEND YOURSELF!*
THE BLOODHOUNDS ARE COMIN'! GONNA DRAG US ALL DOWN TO EGYPT LAND!
LORD, SAVE US FROM THE BLOODHOUND BILL!
I DON'T FEEL PEACEFUL.
HARRIET KNEW THAT IF SHE WANTED TO RESCUE HER FAMILY, SHE HAD TO ACT FAST.

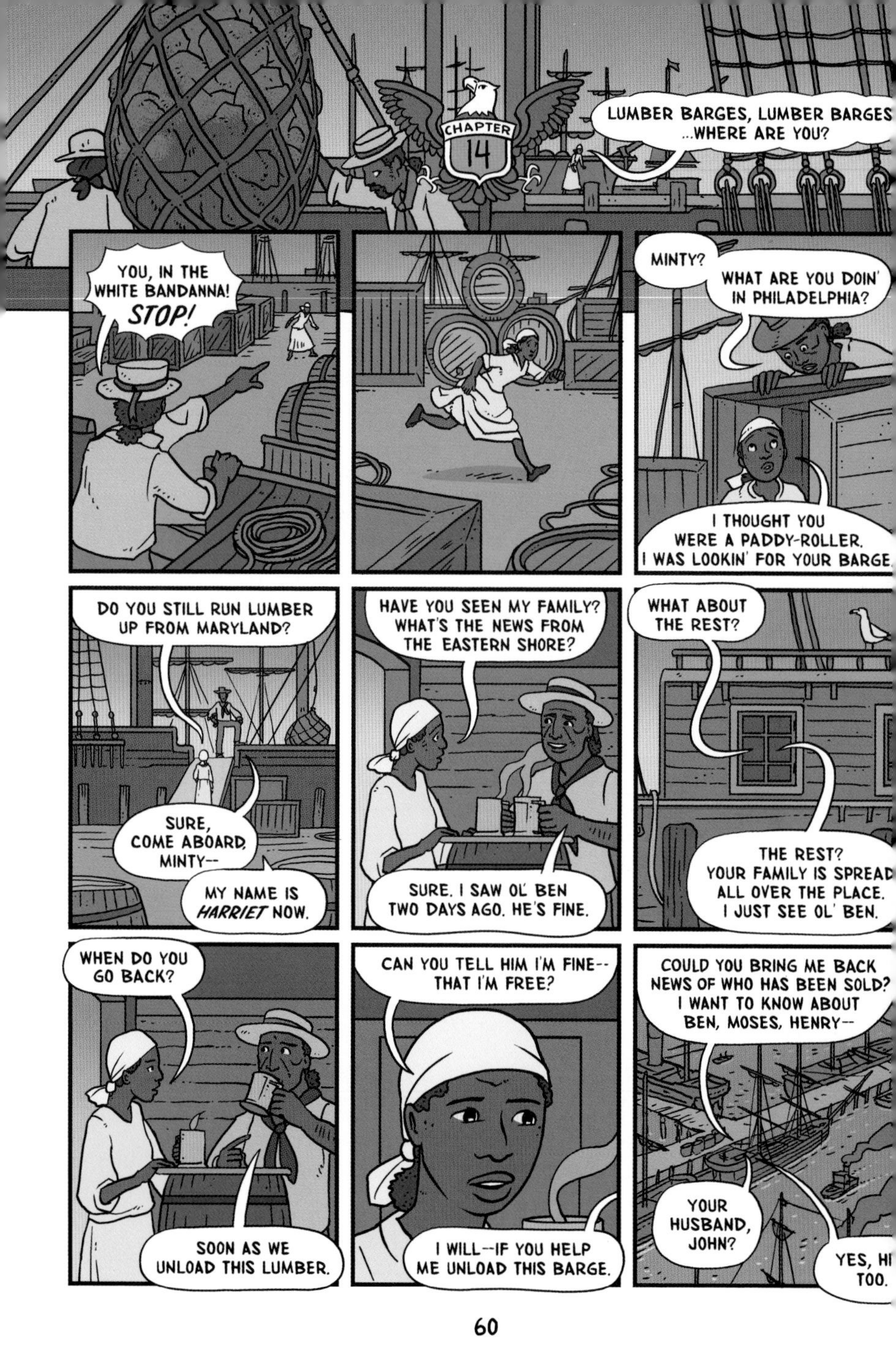
CHAPTER 14
LUMBER BARGES, LUMBER BARGES ...WHERE ARE YOU?
YOU, IN THE WHITE BANDANNA! *STOP!*
MINTY?
WHAT ARE YOU DOIN' IN PHILADELPHIA?
I THOUGHT YOU WERE A PADDY-ROLLER. I WAS LOOKIN' FOR YOUR BARGE.
DO YOU STILL RUN LUMBER UP FROM MARYLAND?
SURE, COME ABOARD, MINTY--
MY NAME IS *HARRIET* NOW.
HAVE YOU SEEN MY FAMILY? WHAT'S THE NEWS FROM THE EASTERN SHORE?
SURE. I SAW OL' BEN TWO DAYS AGO. HE'S FINE.
WHAT ABOUT THE REST?
THE REST? YOUR FAMILY IS SPREAD ALL OVER THE PLACE. I JUST SEE OL' BEN.
WHEN DO YOU GO BACK?
SOON AS WE UNLOAD THIS LUMBER.
CAN YOU TELL HIM I'M FINE-- THAT I'M FREE?
I WILL--IF YOU HELP ME UNLOAD THIS BARGE.
COULD YOU BRING ME BACK NEWS OF WHO HAS BEEN SOLD? I WANT TO KNOW ABOUT BEN, MOSES, HENRY--
YOUR HUSBAND, JOHN?
YES, HI TOO.

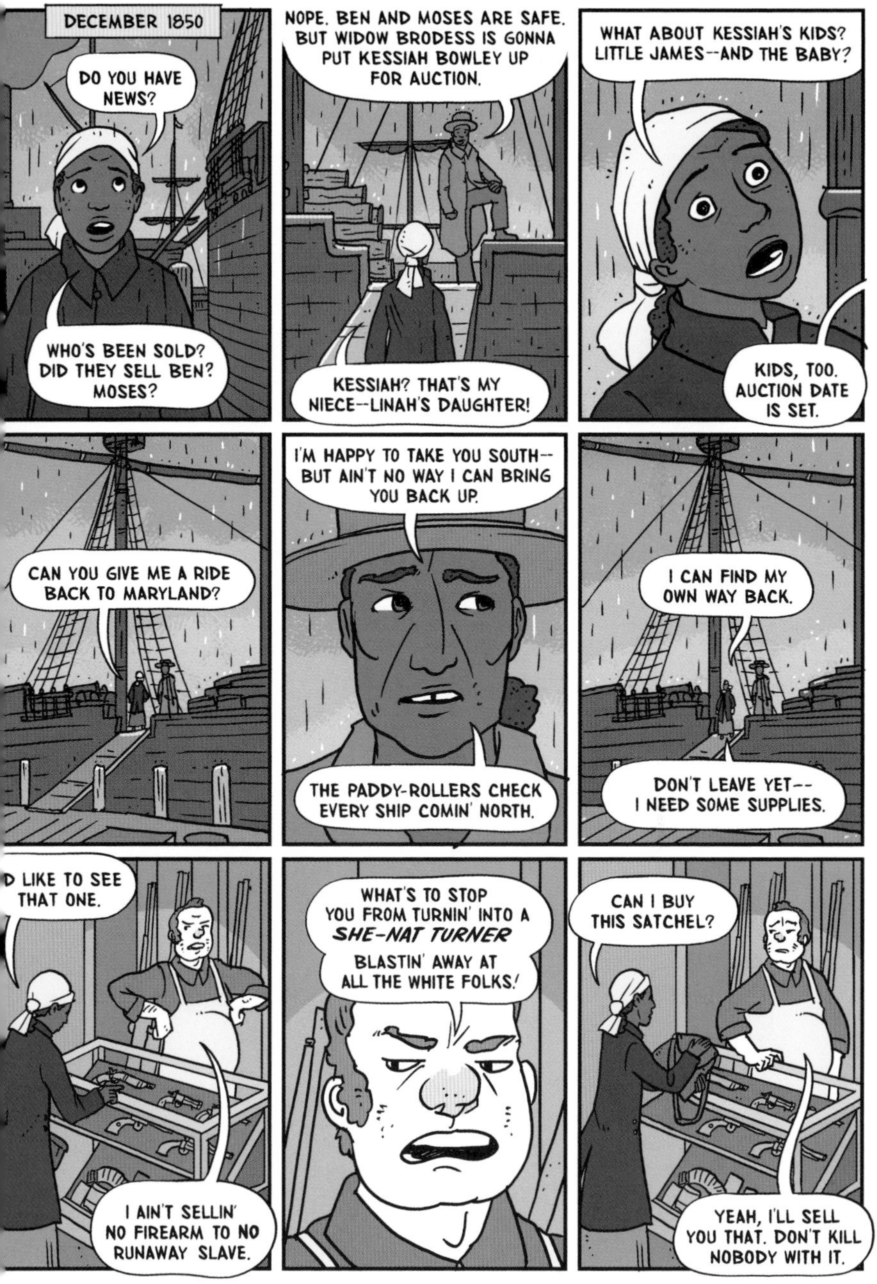
DECEMBER 1850
DO YOU HAVE NEWS?
WHO'S BEEN SOLD? DID THEY SELL BEN? MOSES?
NOPE. BEN AND MOSES ARE SAFE. BUT WIDOW BRODESS IS GONNA PUT KESSIAH BOWLEY UP FOR AUCTION.
KESSIAH? THAT'S MY NIECE--LINAH'S DAUGHTER!
WHAT ABOUT KESSIAH'S KIDS? LITTLE JAMES--AND THE BABY?
KIDS, TOO. AUCTION DATE IS SET.
CAN YOU GIVE ME A RIDE BACK TO MARYLAND?
I'M HAPPY TO TAKE YOU SOUTH-- BUT AIN'T NO WAY I CAN BRING YOU BACK UP.
THE PADDY-ROLLERS CHECK EVERY SHIP COMIN' NORTH.
I CAN FIND MY OWN WAY BACK.
DON'T LEAVE YET-- I NEED SOME SUPPLIES.
D LIKE TO SEE THAT ONE.
I AIN'T SELLIN' NO FIREARM TO NO RUNAWAY SLAVE.
WHAT'S TO STOP YOU FROM TURNIN' INTO A *SHE-NAT TURNER*
BLASTIN' AWAY AT ALL THE WHITE FOLKS!
CAN I BUY THIS SATCHEL?
YEAH, I'LL SELL YOU THAT. DON'T KILL NOBODY WITH IT.

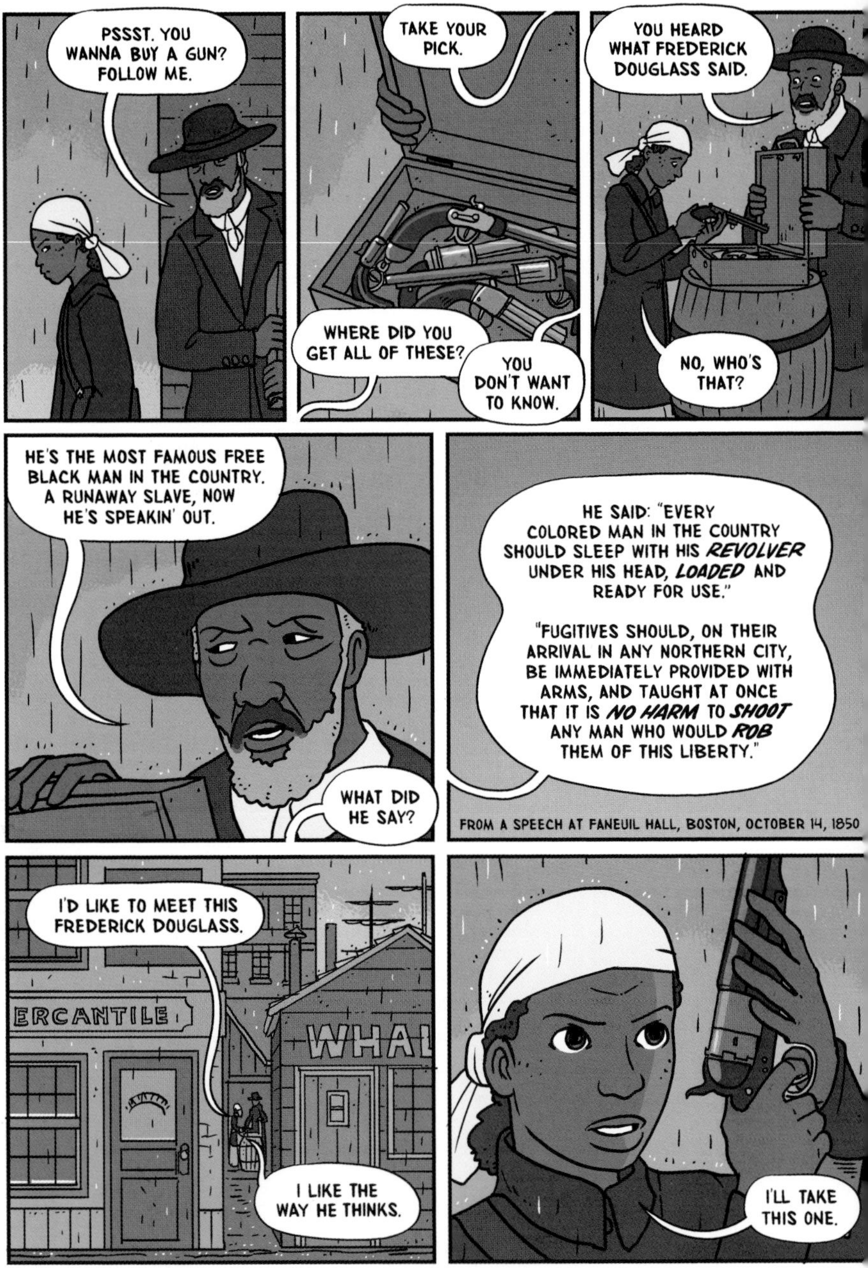
PSSST. YOU WANNA BUY A GUN? FOLLOW ME.
TAKE YOUR PICK.
WHERE DID YOU GET ALL OF THESE?
YOU DON'T WANT TO KNOW.
YOU HEARD WHAT FREDERICK DOUGLASS SAID.
NO, WHO'S THAT?
HE'S THE MOST FAMOUS FREE BLACK MAN IN THE COUNTRY. A RUNAWAY SLAVE, NOW HE'S SPEAKIN' OUT.
WHAT DID HE SAY?
HE SAID: "EVERY COLORED MAN IN THE COUNTRY SHOULD SLEEP WITH HIS *REVOLVER* UNDER HIS HEAD, *LOADED* AND READY FOR USE."
"FUGITIVES SHOULD, ON THEIR ARRIVAL IN ANY NORTHERN CITY, BE IMMEDIATELY PROVIDED WITH ARMS, AND TAUGHT AT ONCE THAT IT IS *NO HARM* TO *SHOOT* ANY MAN WHO WOULD *ROB* THEM OF THIS LIBERTY."
FROM A SPEECH AT FANEUIL HALL, BOSTON, OCTOBER 14, 1850
ERCANTILE
WHAL
I'D LIKE TO MEET THIS FREDERICK DOUGLASS.
I LIKE THE WAY HE THINKS.
I'LL TAKE THIS ONE.

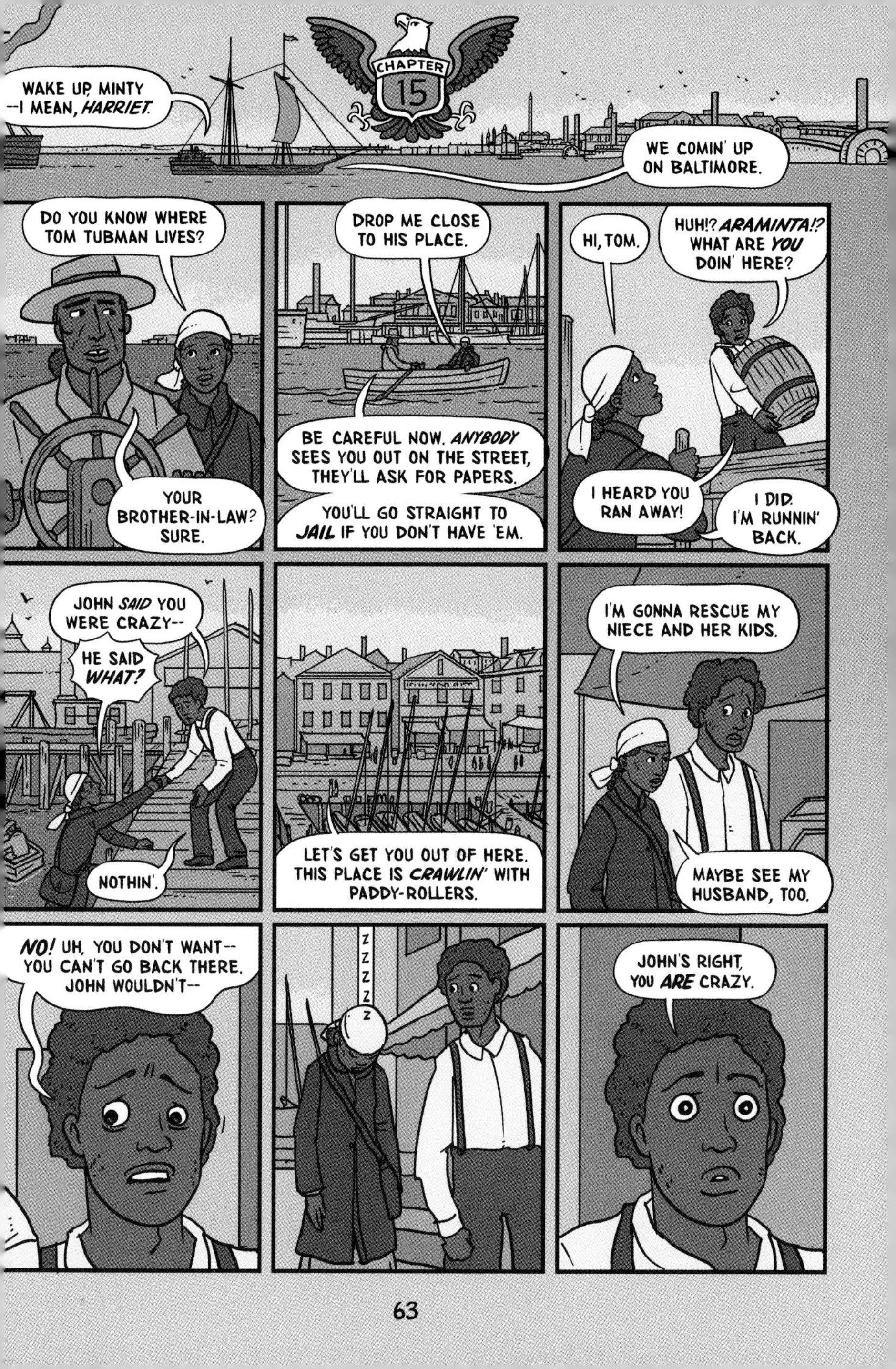
CHAPTER 15
WAKE UP, MINTY --I MEAN, HARRIET.
WE COMIN' UP ON BALTIMORE.
DO YOU KNOW WHERE TOM TUBMAN LIVES?
YOUR BROTHER-IN-LAW? SURE.
DROP ME CLOSE TO HIS PLACE.
BE CAREFUL NOW. ANYBODY SEES YOU OUT ON THE STREET, THEY'LL ASK FOR PAPERS.
YOU'LL GO STRAIGHT TO JAIL IF YOU DON'T HAVE 'EM.
HI, TOM.
HUH!? ARAMINTA!? WHAT ARE YOU DOIN' HERE?
I HEARD YOU RAN AWAY!
I DID. I'M RUNNIN' BACK.
JOHN SAID YOU WERE CRAZY--
HE SAID WHAT?
NOTHIN'.
LET'S GET YOU OUT OF HERE. THIS PLACE IS CRAWLIN' WITH PADDY-ROLLERS.
I'M GONNA RESCUE MY NIECE AND HER KIDS.
MAYBE SEE MY HUSBAND, TOO.
NO! UH, YOU DON'T WANT-- YOU CAN'T GO BACK THERE. JOHN WOULDN'T--
Z Z Z Z Z
JOHN'S RIGHT, YOU ARE CRAZY.

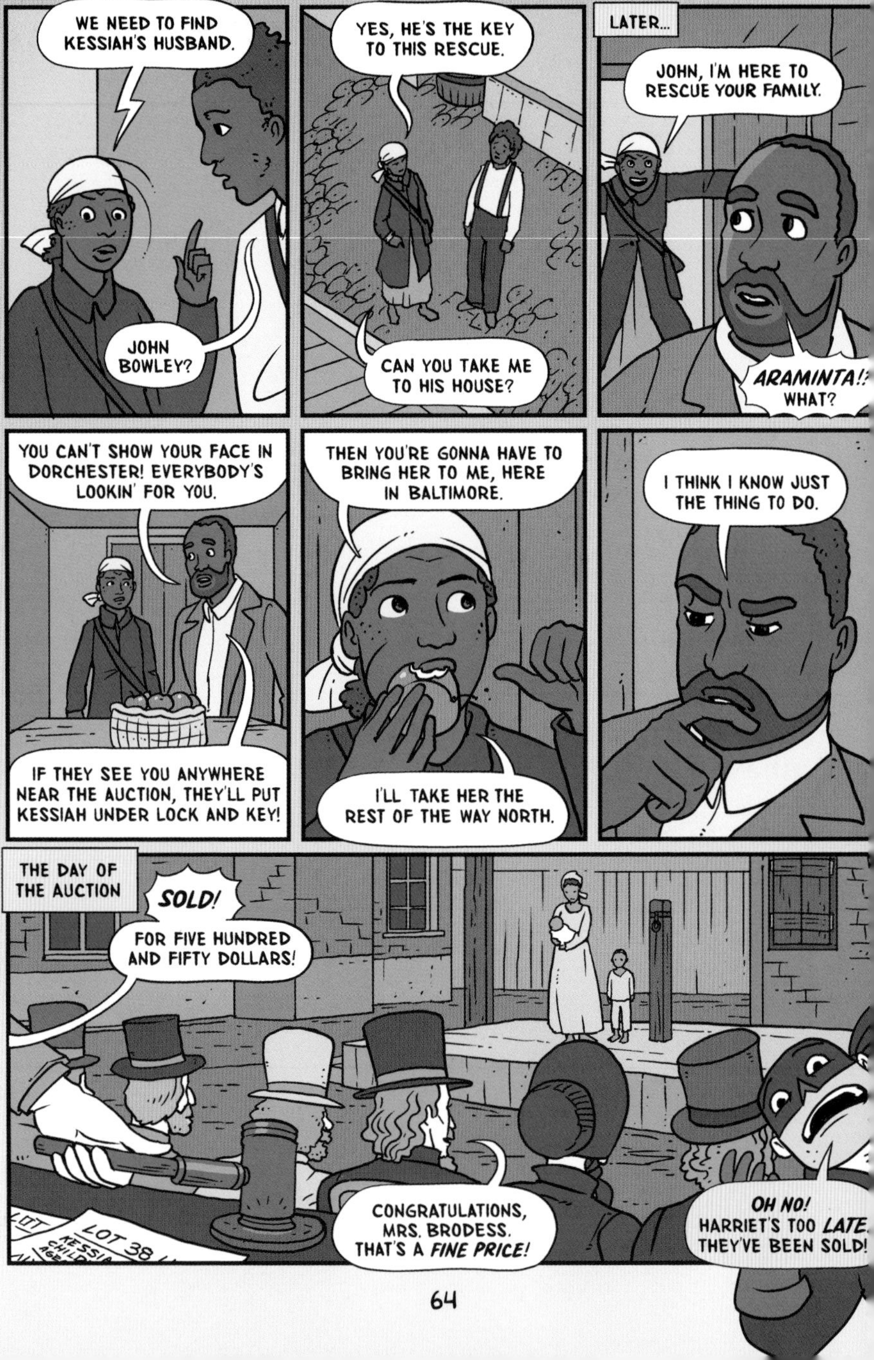
WE NEED TO FIND KESSIAH'S HUSBAND.
JOHN BOWLEY?
YES, HE'S THE KEY TO THIS RESCUE.
CAN YOU TAKE ME TO HIS HOUSE?
LATER...
JOHN, I'M HERE TO RESCUE YOUR FAMILY.
ARAMINTA!? WHAT?
YOU CAN'T SHOW YOUR FACE IN DORCHESTER! EVERYBODY'S LOOKIN' FOR YOU.
IF THEY SEE YOU ANYWHERE NEAR THE AUCTION, THEY'LL PUT KESSIAH UNDER LOCK AND KEY!
THEN YOU'RE GONNA HAVE TO BRING HER TO ME, HERE IN BALTIMORE.
I'LL TAKE HER THE REST OF THE WAY NORTH.
I THINK I KNOW JUST THE THING TO DO.
THE DAY OF THE AUCTION
SOLD!
FOR FIVE HUNDRED AND FIFTY DOLLARS!
LOT 38
CONGRATULATIONS, MRS. BRODESS. THAT'S A FINE PRICE!
OH NO! HARRIET'S TOO LATE. THEY'VE BEEN SOLD!

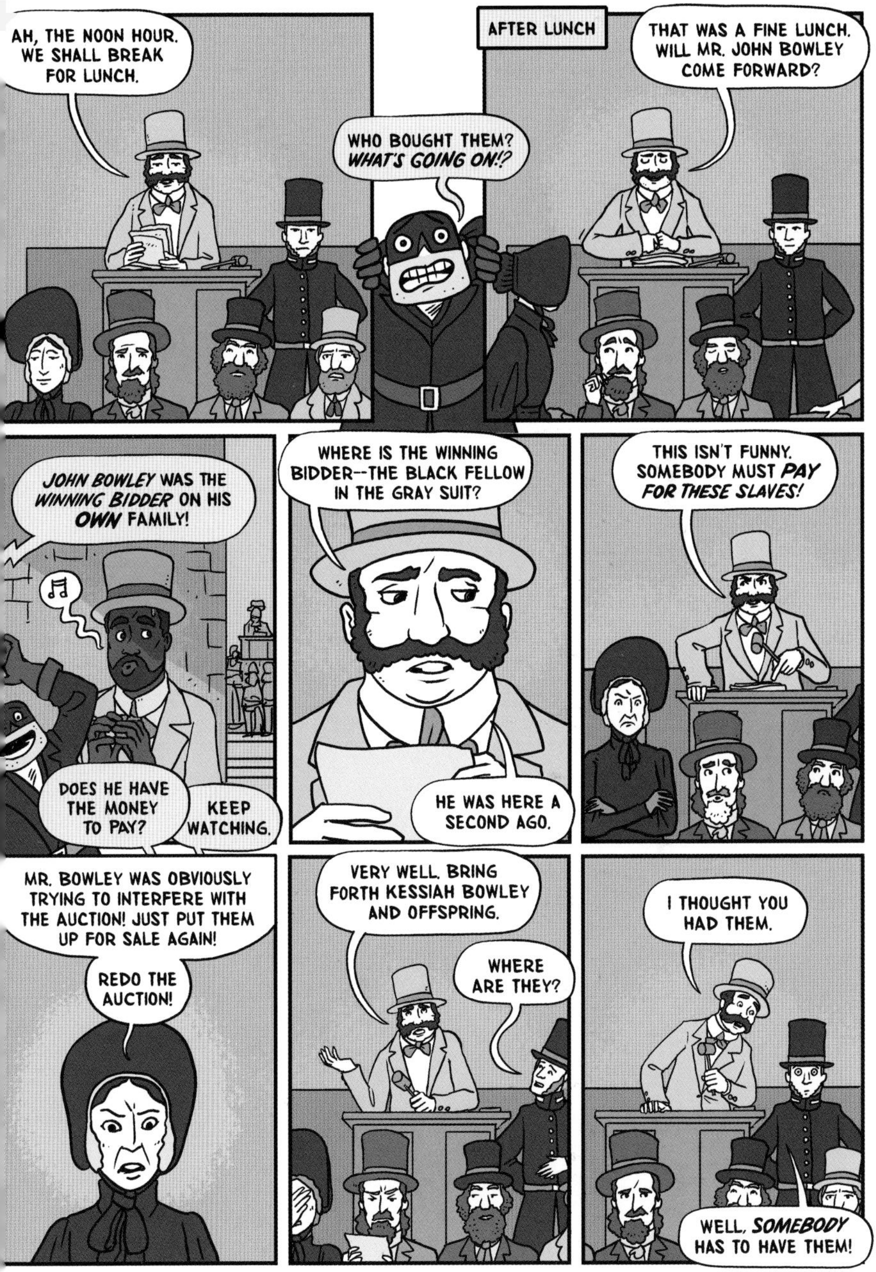
AH, THE NOON HOUR. WE SHALL BREAK FOR LUNCH.
WHO BOUGHT THEM? WHAT'S GOING ON!?
AFTER LUNCH
THAT WAS A FINE LUNCH. WILL MR. JOHN BOWLEY COME FORWARD?
JOHN BOWLEY WAS THE WINNING BIDDER ON HIS OWN FAMILY!
DOES HE HAVE THE MONEY TO PAY?
KEEP WATCHING.
WHERE IS THE WINNING BIDDER--THE BLACK FELLOW IN THE GRAY SUIT?
HE WAS HERE A SECOND AGO.
THIS ISN'T FUNNY. SOMEBODY MUST PAY FOR THESE SLAVES!
MR. BOWLEY WAS OBVIOUSLY TRYING TO INTERFERE WITH THE AUCTION! JUST PUT THEM UP FOR SALE AGAIN!
REDO THE AUCTION!
VERY WELL. BRING FORTH KESSIAH BOWLEY AND OFFSPRING.
WHERE ARE THEY?
I THOUGHT YOU HAD THEM.
WELL, SOMEBODY HAS TO HAVE THEM!

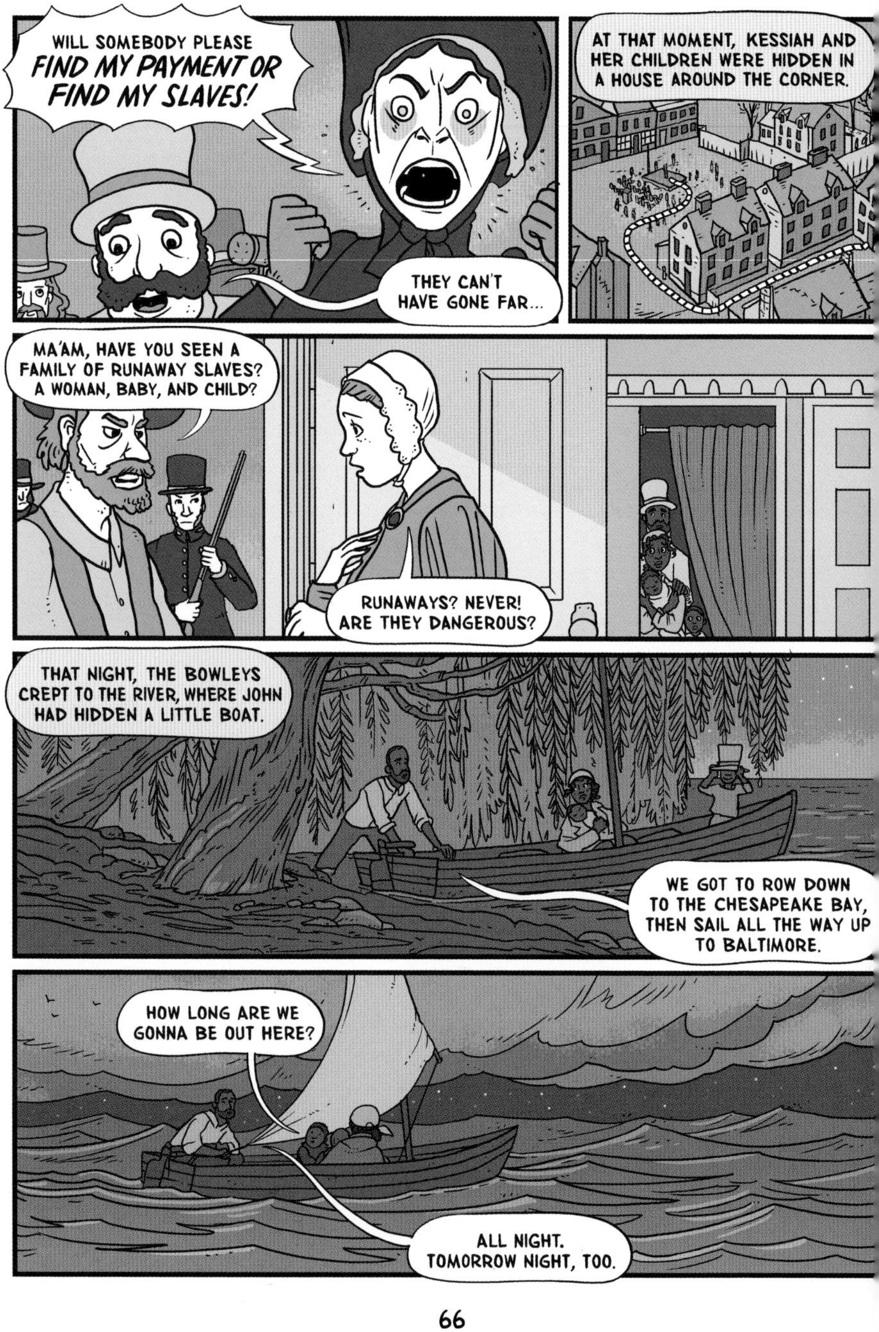
WILL SOMEBODY PLEASE FIND MY PAYMENT OR FIND MY SLAVES!
THEY CAN'T HAVE GONE FAR...
AT THAT MOMENT, KESSIAH AND HER CHILDREN WERE HIDDEN IN A HOUSE AROUND THE CORNER.
MA'AM, HAVE YOU SEEN A FAMILY OF RUNAWAY SLAVES? A WOMAN, BABY, AND CHILD?
RUNAWAYS? NEVER! ARE THEY DANGEROUS?
THAT NIGHT, THE BOWLEYS CREPT TO THE RIVER, WHERE JOHN HAD HIDDEN A LITTLE BOAT.
WE GOT TO ROW DOWN TO THE CHESAPEAKE BAY, THEN SAIL ALL THE WAY UP TO BALTIMORE.
HOW LONG ARE WE GONNA BE OUT HERE?
ALL NIGHT. TOMORROW NIGHT, TOO.

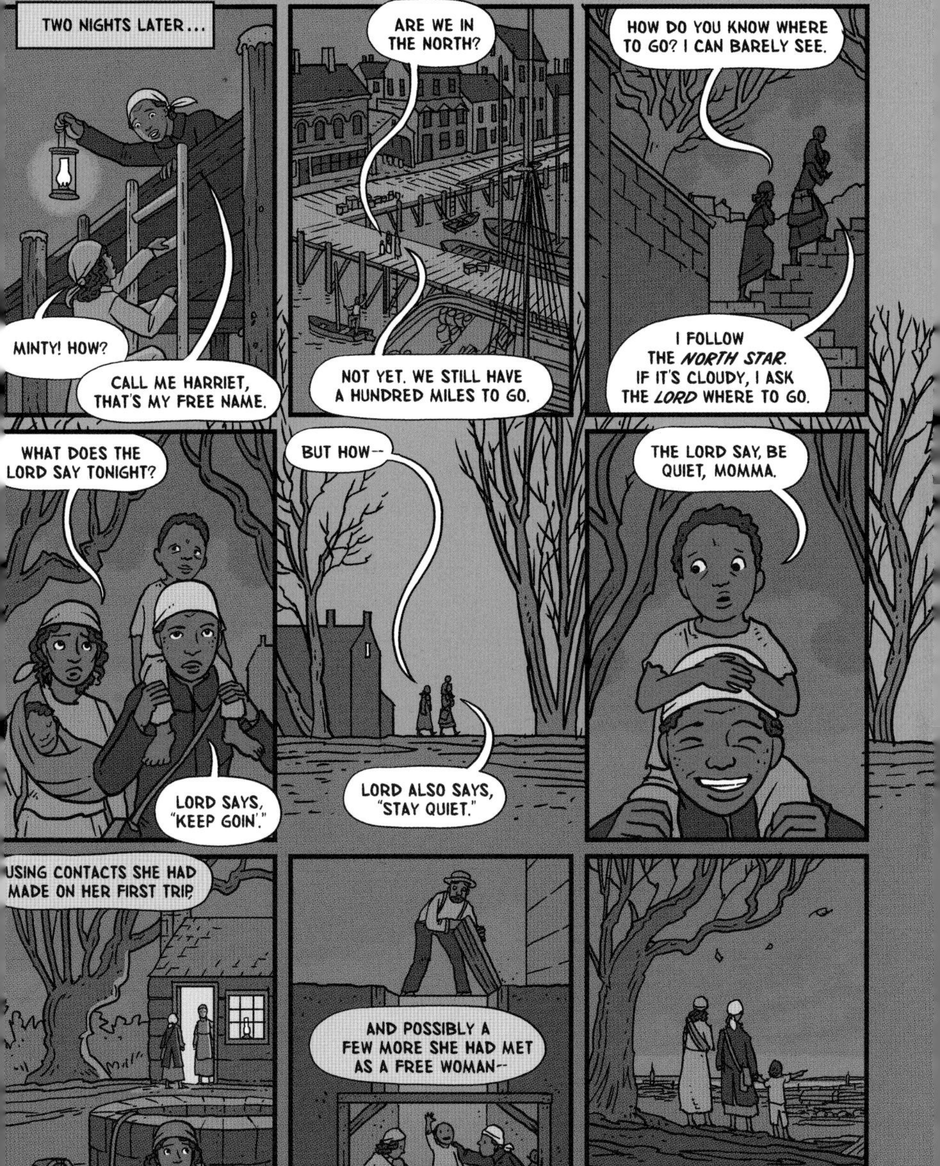

TWO NIGHTS LATER...
MINTY! HOW?
CALL ME HARRIET, THAT'S MY FREE NAME.
ARE WE IN THE NORTH?
NOT YET. WE STILL HAVE A HUNDRED MILES TO GO.
HOW DO YOU KNOW WHERE TO GO? I CAN BARELY SEE.
I FOLLOW THE *NORTH STAR*. IF IT'S CLOUDY, I ASK THE *LORD* WHERE TO GO.
WHAT DOES THE LORD SAY TONIGHT?
LORD SAYS, "KEEP GOIN'."
BUT HOW--
LORD ALSO SAYS, "STAY QUIET."
THE LORD SAY, BE QUIET, MOMMA.
USING CONTACTS SHE HAD MADE ON HER FIRST TRIP,
AND POSSIBLY A FEW MORE SHE HAD MET AS A FREE WOMAN--
HARRIET BROUGHT KESSIAH AND HER CHILDREN TO PHILADELPHIA.

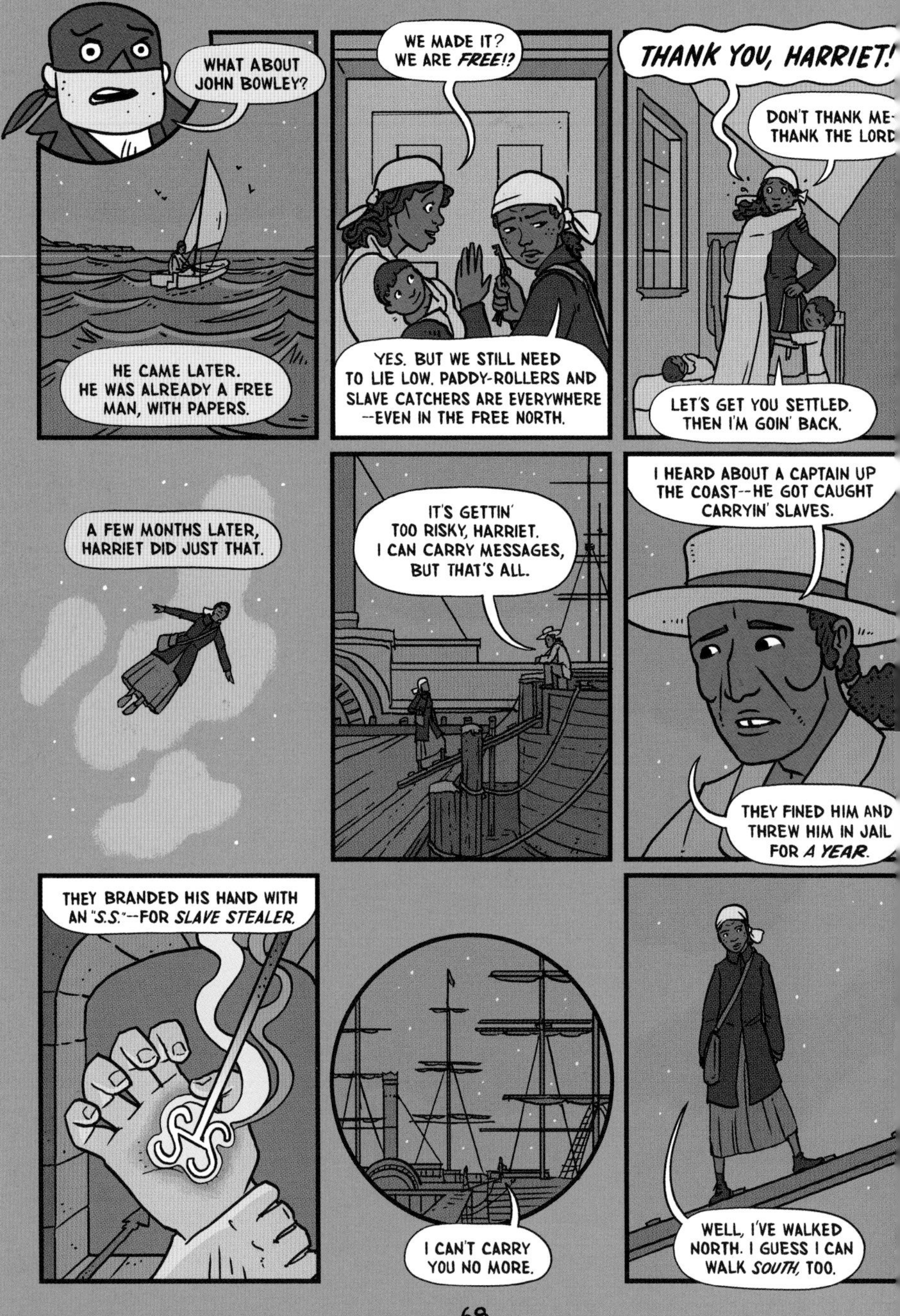
WHAT ABOUT JOHN BOWLEY?
HE CAME LATER. HE WAS ALREADY A FREE MAN, WITH PAPERS.
WE MADE IT? WE ARE *FREE*!?
YES. BUT WE STILL NEED TO LIE LOW. PADDY-ROLLERS AND SLAVE CATCHERS ARE EVERYWHERE --EVEN IN THE FREE NORTH.
THANK YOU, HARRIET!
DON'T THANK ME-THANK THE LORD
LET'S GET YOU SETTLED. THEN I'M GOIN' BACK.
A FEW MONTHS LATER, HARRIET DID JUST THAT.
IT'S GETTIN' TOO RISKY, HARRIET. I CAN CARRY MESSAGES, BUT THAT'S ALL.
I HEARD ABOUT A CAPTAIN UP THE COAST--HE GOT CAUGHT CARRYIN' SLAVES.
THEY FINED HIM AND THREW HIM IN JAIL FOR *A YEAR*.
THEY BRANDED HIS HAND WITH AN "*S.S.*"--FOR *SLAVE STEALER*.
I CAN'T CARRY YOU NO MORE.
WELL, I'VE WALKED NORTH. I GUESS I CAN WALK *SOUTH*, TOO.

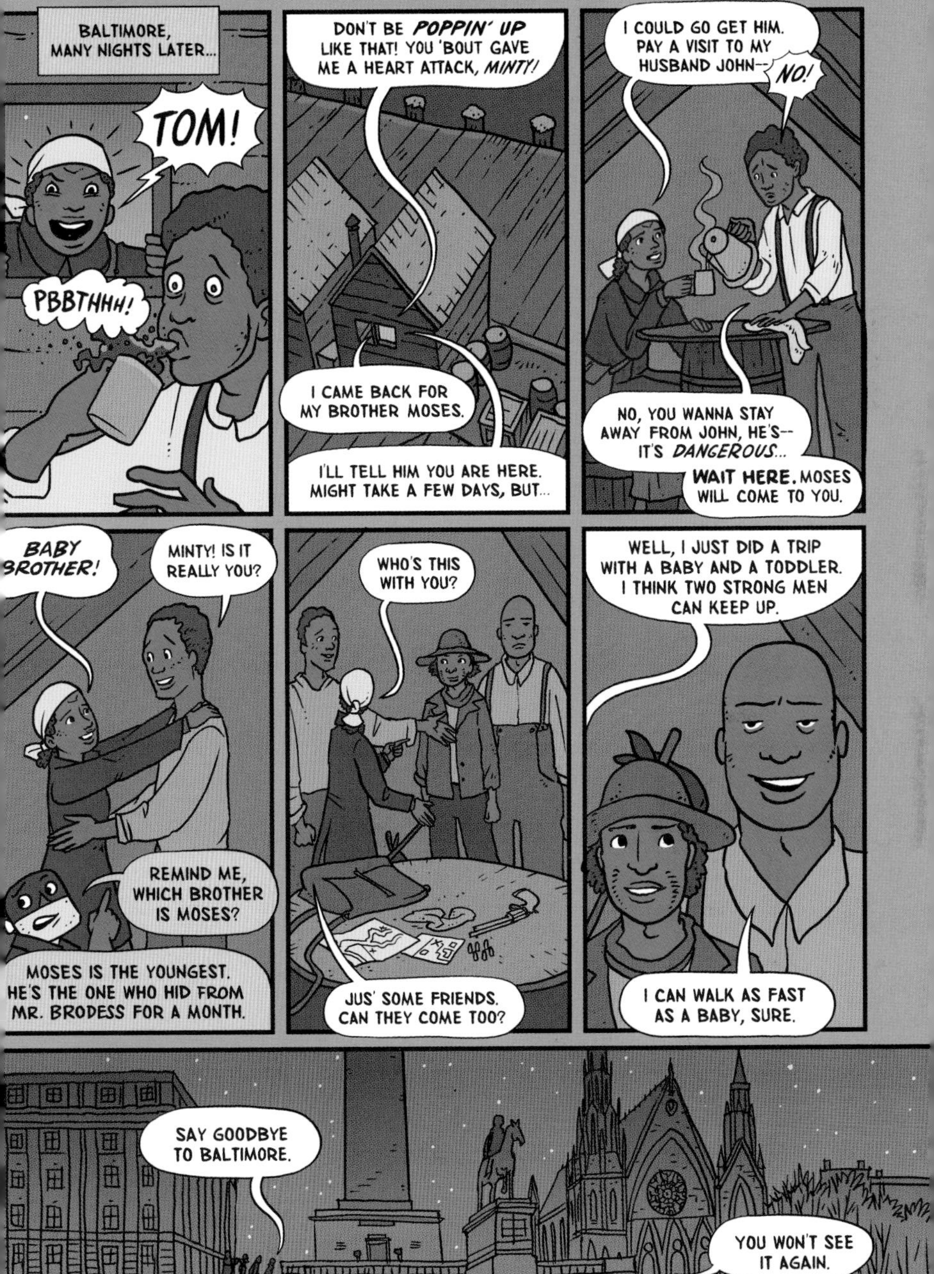
BALTIMORE, MANY NIGHTS LATER...
TOM!
PBBTHHH!
DON'T BE POPPIN' UP LIKE THAT! YOU 'BOUT GAVE ME A HEART ATTACK, MINTY!
I CAME BACK FOR MY BROTHER MOSES.
I'LL TELL HIM YOU ARE HERE. MIGHT TAKE A FEW DAYS, BUT...
I COULD GO GET HIM. PAY A VISIT TO MY HUSBAND JOHN--
NO!
NO, YOU WANNA STAY AWAY FROM JOHN, HE'S-- IT'S DANGEROUS...
WAIT HERE. MOSES WILL COME TO YOU.
BABY BROTHER!
MINTY! IS IT REALLY YOU?
REMIND ME, WHICH BROTHER IS MOSES?
MOSES IS THE YOUNGEST. HE'S THE ONE WHO HID FROM MR. BRODESS FOR A MONTH.
WHO'S THIS WITH YOU?
JUS' SOME FRIENDS. CAN THEY COME TOO?
WELL, I JUST DID A TRIP WITH A BABY AND A TODDLER. I THINK TWO STRONG MEN CAN KEEP UP.
I CAN WALK AS FAST AS A BABY, SURE.
SAY GOODBYE TO BALTIMORE.
YOU WON'T SEE IT AGAIN.

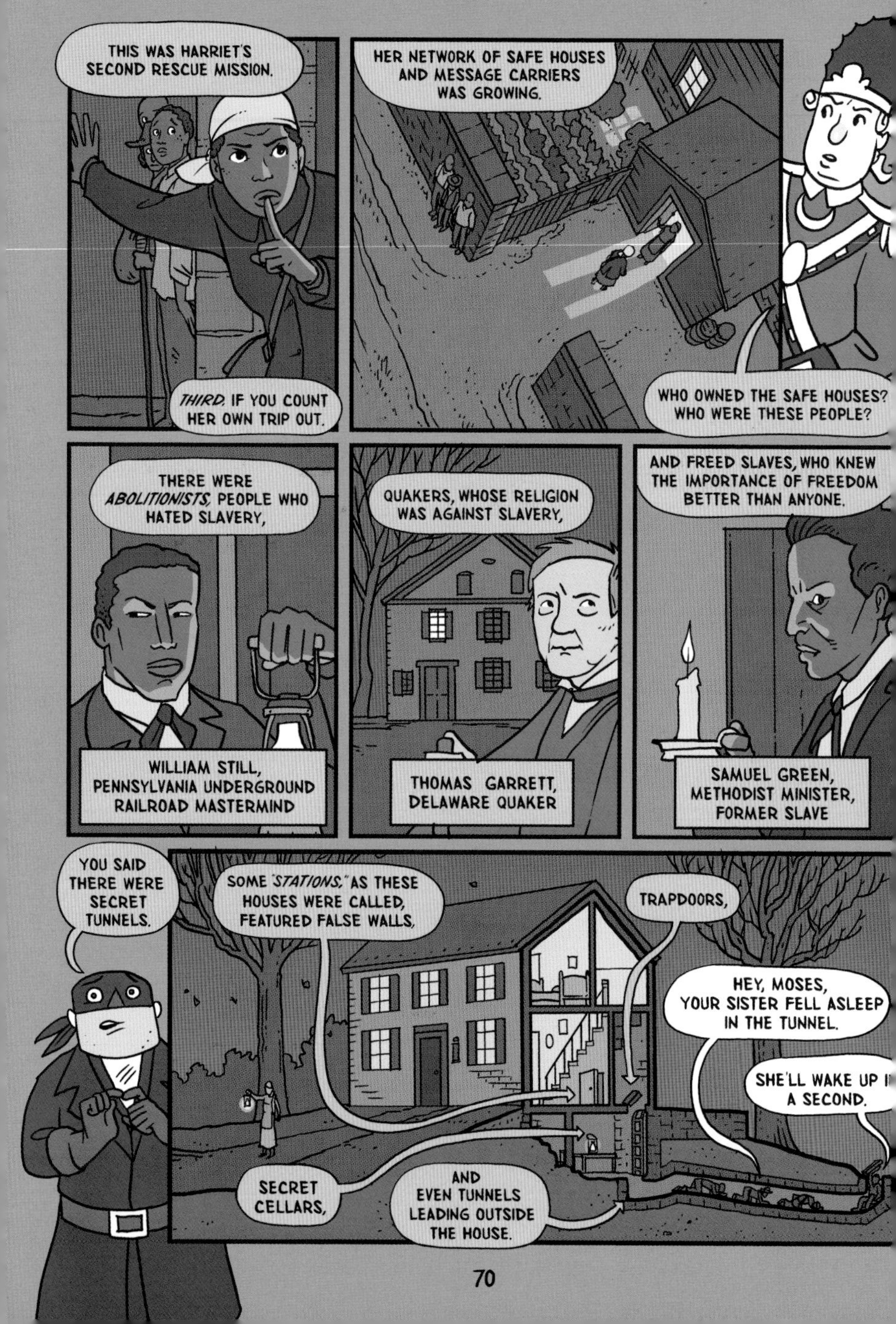
THIS WAS HARRIET'S SECOND RESCUE MISSION.
THIRD, IF YOU COUNT HER OWN TRIP OUT.
HER NETWORK OF SAFE HOUSES AND MESSAGE CARRIERS WAS GROWING.
WHO OWNED THE SAFE HOUSES? WHO WERE THESE PEOPLE?
THERE WERE ABOLITIONISTS, PEOPLE WHO HATED SLAVERY,
WILLIAM STILL, PENNSYLVANIA UNDERGROUND RAILROAD MASTERMIND
QUAKERS, WHOSE RELIGION WAS AGAINST SLAVERY,
THOMAS GARRETT, DELAWARE QUAKER
AND FREED SLAVES, WHO KNEW THE IMPORTANCE OF FREEDOM BETTER THAN ANYONE.
SAMUEL GREEN, METHODIST MINISTER, FORMER SLAVE
YOU SAID THERE WERE SECRET TUNNELS.
SOME "STATIONS," AS THESE HOUSES WERE CALLED, FEATURED FALSE WALLS,
TRAPDOORS,
SECRET CELLARS,
AND EVEN TUNNELS LEADING OUTSIDE THE HOUSE.
HEY, MOSES, YOUR SISTER FELL ASLEEP IN THE TUNNEL.
SHE'LL WAKE UP I A SECOND.

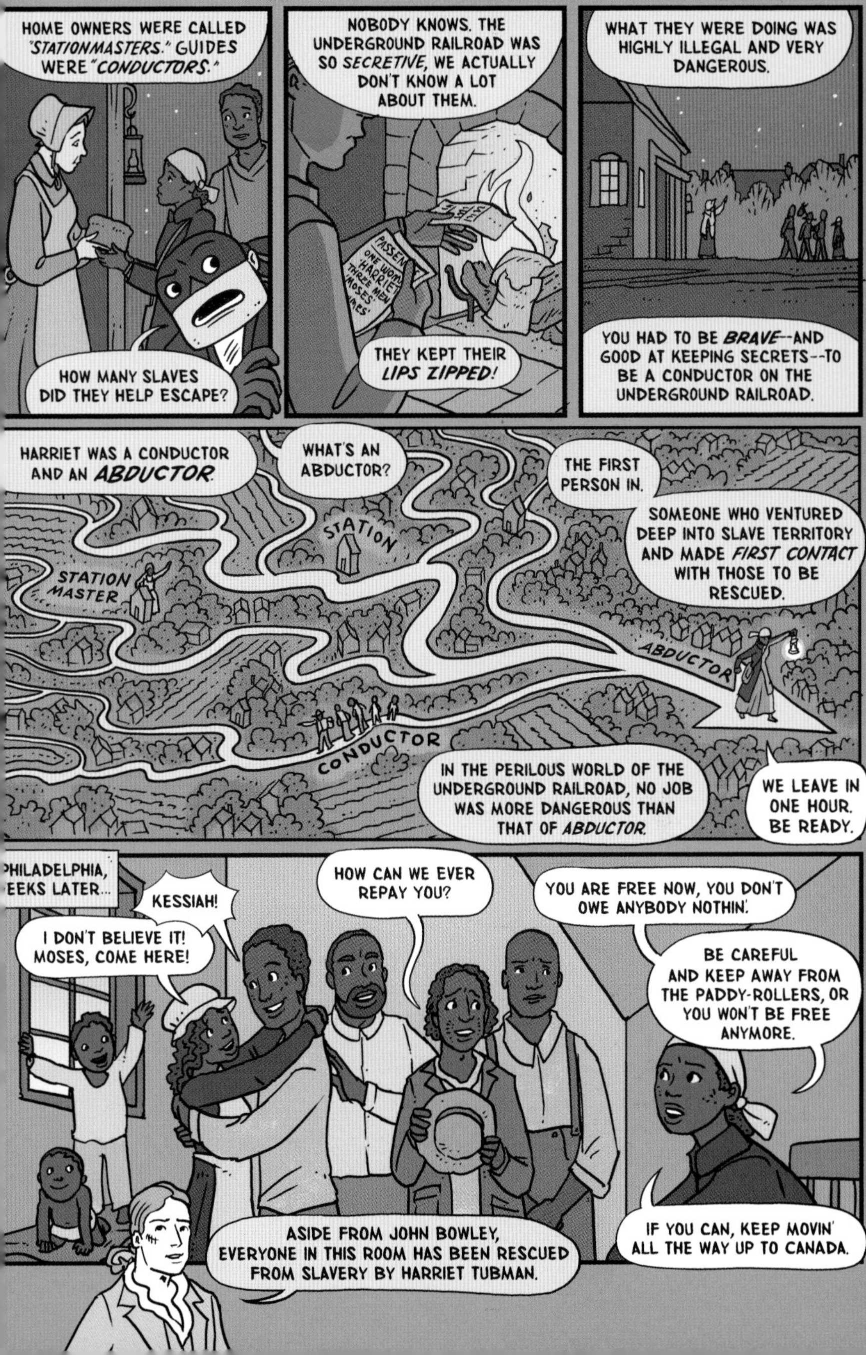

HOME OWNERS WERE CALLED "STATIONMASTERS." GUIDES WERE "CONDUCTORS."
HOW MANY SLAVES DID THEY HELP ESCAPE?
NOBODY KNOWS. THE UNDERGROUND RAILROAD WAS SO SECRETIVE, WE ACTUALLY DON'T KNOW A LOT ABOUT THEM.
THEY KEPT THEIR LIPS ZIPPED!
WHAT THEY WERE DOING WAS HIGHLY ILLEGAL AND VERY DANGEROUS.
YOU HAD TO BE BRAVE--AND GOOD AT KEEPING SECRETS--TO BE A CONDUCTOR ON THE UNDERGROUND RAILROAD.
HARRIET WAS A CONDUCTOR AND AN ABDUCTOR.
WHAT'S AN ABDUCTOR?
THE FIRST PERSON IN.
SOMEONE WHO VENTURED DEEP INTO SLAVE TERRITORY AND MADE FIRST CONTACT WITH THOSE TO BE RESCUED.
STATION
STATION MASTER
ABDUCTOR
CONDUCTOR
IN THE PERILOUS WORLD OF THE UNDERGROUND RAILROAD, NO JOB WAS MORE DANGEROUS THAN THAT OF ABDUCTOR.
WE LEAVE IN ONE HOUR. BE READY.
PHILADELPHIA, EEKS LATER...
KESSIAH!
I DON'T BELIEVE IT! MOSES, COME HERE!
HOW CAN WE EVER REPAY YOU?
YOU ARE FREE NOW, YOU DON'T OWE ANYBODY NOTHIN'.
BE CAREFUL AND KEEP AWAY FROM THE PADDY-ROLLERS, OR YOU WON'T BE FREE ANYMORE.
ASIDE FROM JOHN BOWLEY, EVERYONE IN THIS ROOM HAS BEEN RESCUED FROM SLAVERY BY HARRIET TUBMAN.
IF YOU CAN, KEEP MOVIN' ALL THE WAY UP TO CANADA.

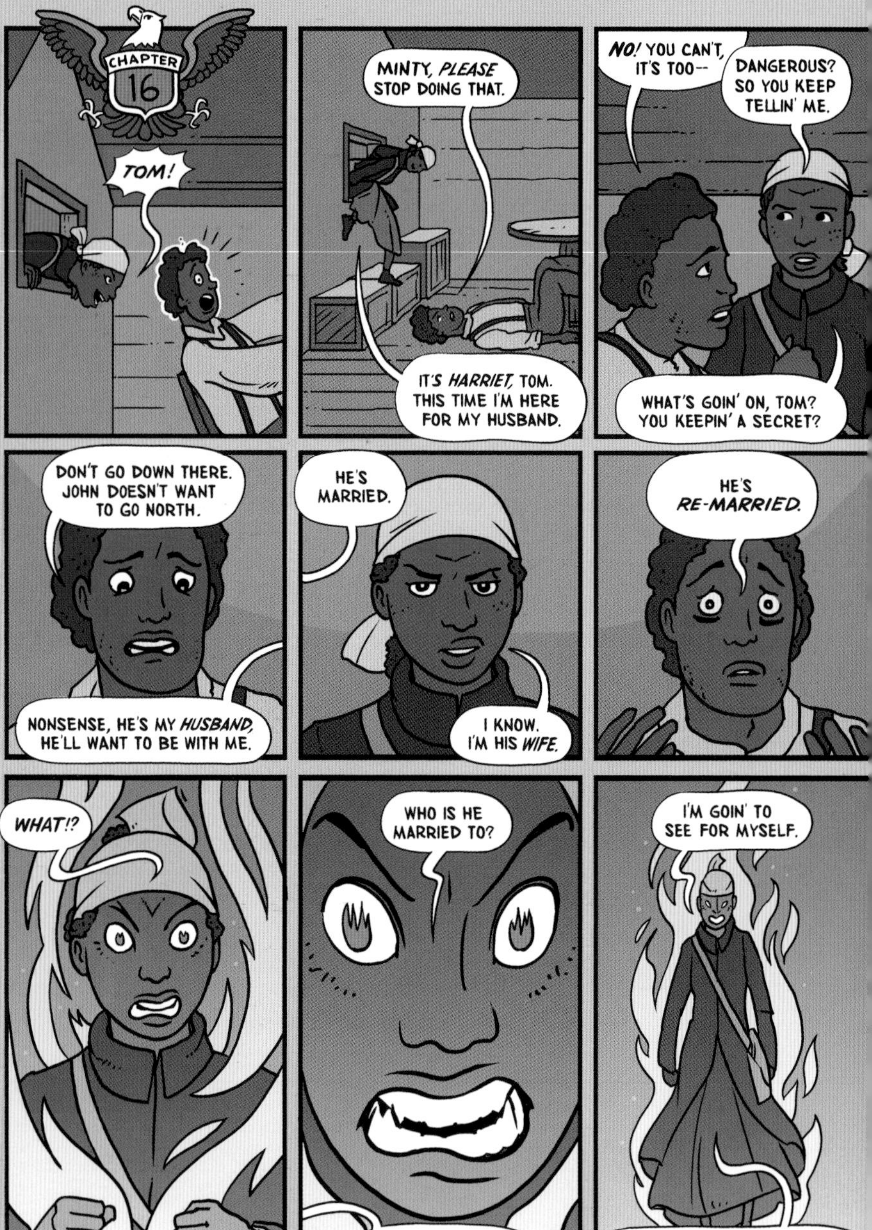
CHAPTER 16
TOM!
MINTY, PLEASE STOP DOING THAT.
IT'S HARRIET, TOM. THIS TIME I'M HERE FOR MY HUSBAND.
NO! YOU CAN'T, IT'S TOO--
DANGEROUS? SO YOU KEEP TELLIN' ME.
WHAT'S GOIN' ON, TOM? YOU KEEPIN' A SECRET?
DON'T GO DOWN THERE. JOHN DOESN'T WANT TO GO NORTH.
NONSENSE, HE'S MY HUSBAND, HE'LL WANT TO BE WITH ME.
HE'S MARRIED.
I KNOW. I'M HIS WIFE.
HE'S RE-MARRIED.
WHAT!?
WHO IS HE MARRIED TO?
A FREE WOMAN, NAME OF CAROLINE.
I'M GOIN' TO SEE FOR MYSELF.
I'M GOIN' RIGHT IN AND MAKIN' ALL THE TROUBLE I CAN!

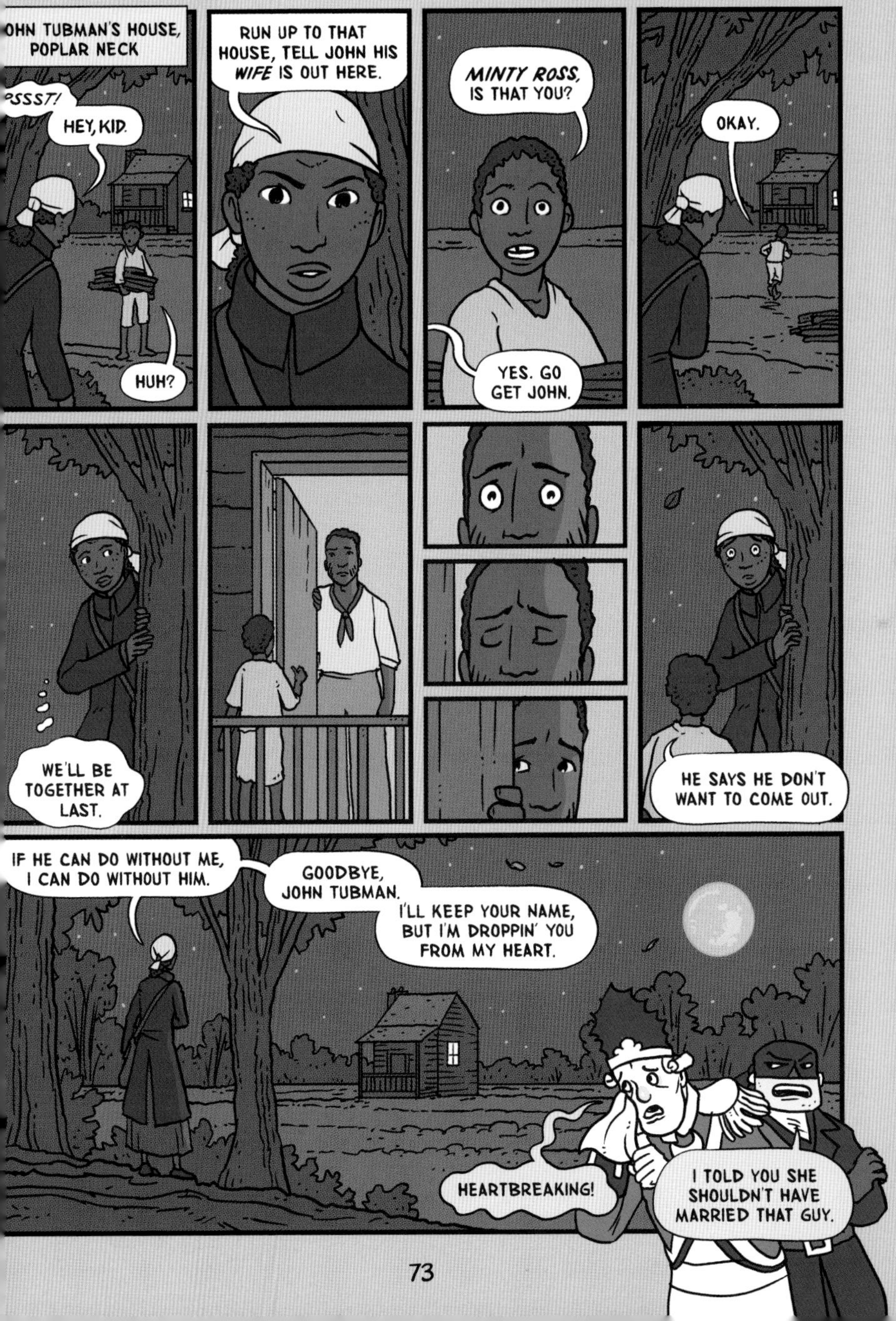

OHN TUBMAN'S HOUSE, POPLAR NECK
PSSST!
HEY, KID.
HUH?
RUN UP TO THAT HOUSE, TELL JOHN HIS *WIFE* IS OUT HERE.
MINTY ROSS, IS THAT YOU?
YES. GO GET JOHN.
OKAY.
WE'LL BE TOGETHER AT LAST.
HE SAYS HE DON'T WANT TO COME OUT.
IF HE CAN DO WITHOUT ME, I CAN DO WITHOUT HIM.
GOODBYE, JOHN TUBMAN.
I'LL KEEP YOUR NAME, BUT I'M DROPPIN' YOU FROM MY HEART.
HEARTBREAKING!
I TOLD YOU SHE SHOULDN'T HAVE MARRIED THAT GUY.

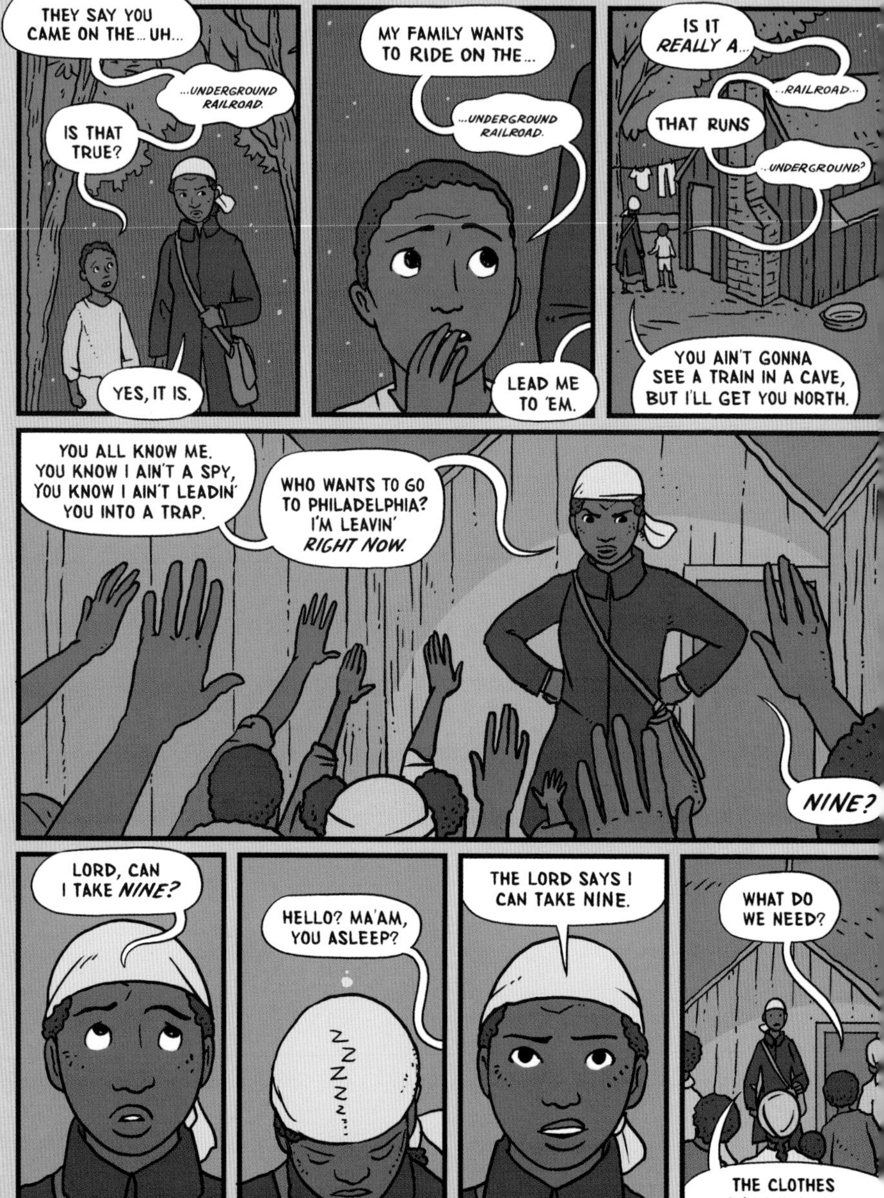
THEY SAY YOU CAME ON THE... UH...
...UNDERGROUND RAILROAD.
IS THAT TRUE?
YES, IT IS.
MY FAMILY WANTS TO RIDE ON THE...
...UNDERGROUND RAILROAD.
LEAD ME TO 'EM.
IS IT *REALLY* A...
...RAILROAD...
THAT RUNS
...UNDERGROUND?
YOU AIN'T GONNA SEE A TRAIN IN A CAVE, BUT I'LL GET YOU NORTH.
YOU ALL KNOW ME. YOU KNOW I AIN'T A SPY, YOU KNOW I AIN'T LEADIN' YOU INTO A TRAP.
WHO WANTS TO GO TO PHILADELPHIA? I'M LEAVIN' *RIGHT NOW.*
NINE?
LORD, CAN I TAKE *NINE?*
HELLO? MA'AM, YOU ASLEEP?
ZZZZz...
THE LORD SAYS I CAN TAKE NINE.
WHAT DO WE NEED?
THE CLOTHES ON YOUR BACK-- AND ANY FOOD YOU CAN CARRY.

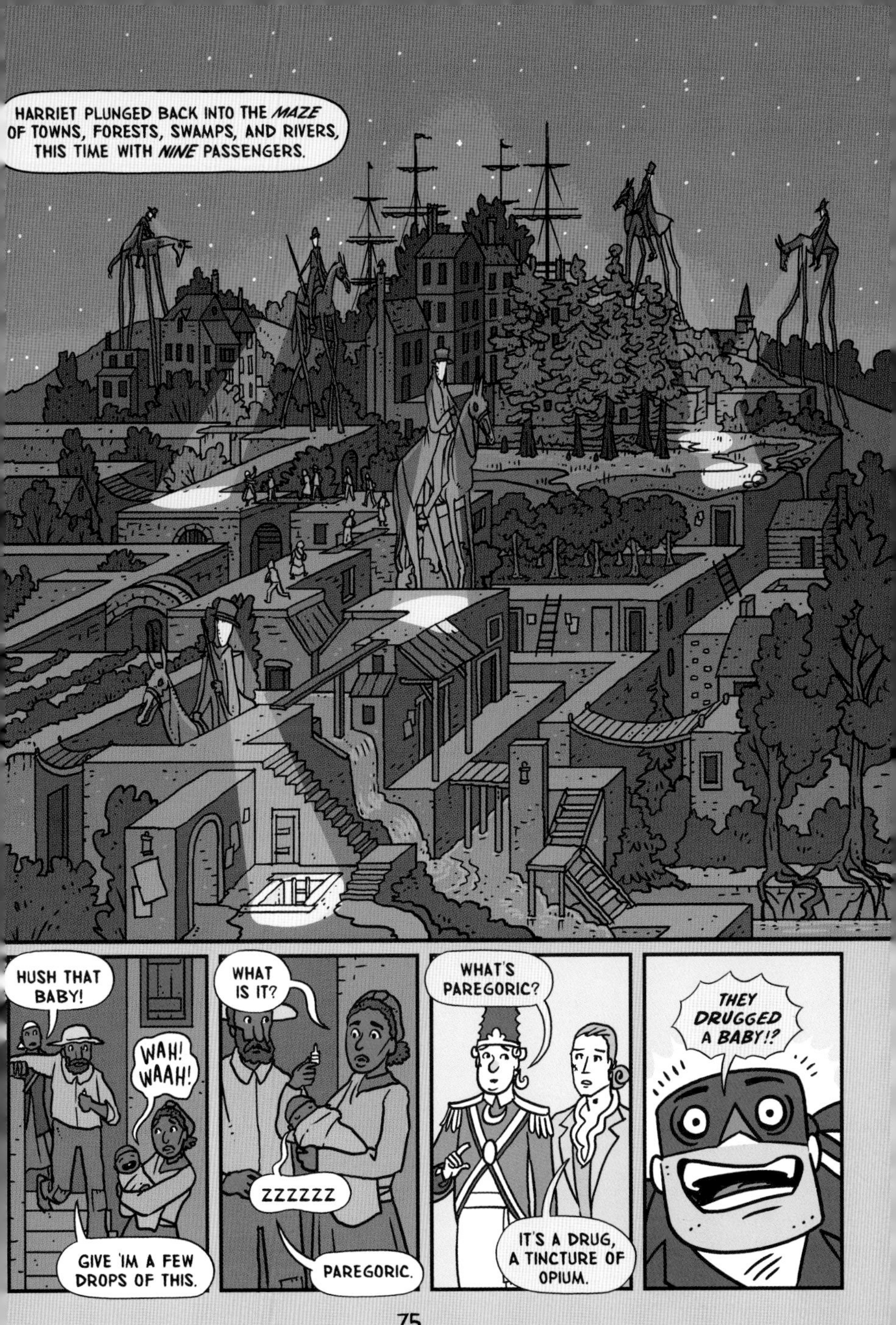
HARRIET PLUNGED BACK INTO THE *MAZE* OF TOWNS, FORESTS, SWAMPS, AND RIVERS, THIS TIME WITH *NINE* PASSENGERS.
HUSH THAT BABY!
WAH! WAAH!
GIVE 'IM A FEW DROPS OF THIS.
WHAT IS IT?
ZZZZZZ
PAREGORIC.
WHAT'S PAREGORIC?
IT'S A DRUG, A TINCTURE OF OPIUM.
THEY DRUGGED A BABY!?

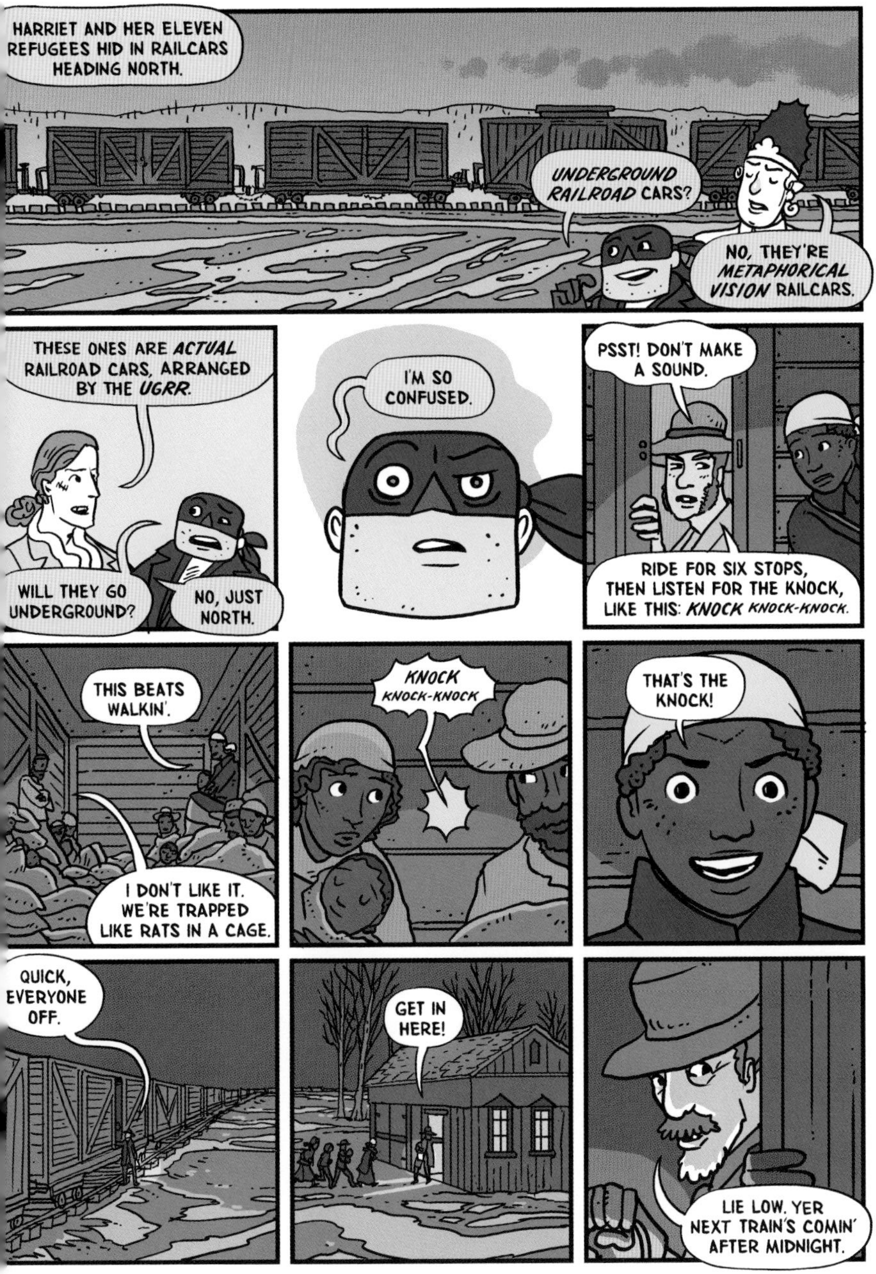
HARRIET AND HER ELEVEN REFUGEES HID IN RAILCARS HEADING NORTH.
UNDERGROUND RAILROAD CARS?
NO, THEY'RE METAPHORICAL VISION RAILCARS.
THESE ONES ARE ACTUAL RAILROAD CARS, ARRANGED BY THE UGRR.
WILL THEY GO UNDERGROUND?
NO, JUST NORTH.
I'M SO CONFUSED.
PSST! DON'T MAKE A SOUND.
RIDE FOR SIX STOPS, THEN LISTEN FOR THE KNOCK, LIKE THIS: KNOCK KNOCK-KNOCK.
THIS BEATS WALKIN'.
I DON'T LIKE IT. WE'RE TRAPPED LIKE RATS IN A CAGE.
KNOCK KNOCK-KNOCK
THAT'S THE KNOCK!
QUICK, EVERYONE OFF.
GET IN HERE!
LIE LOW. YER NEXT TRAIN'S COMIN' AFTER MIDNIGHT.

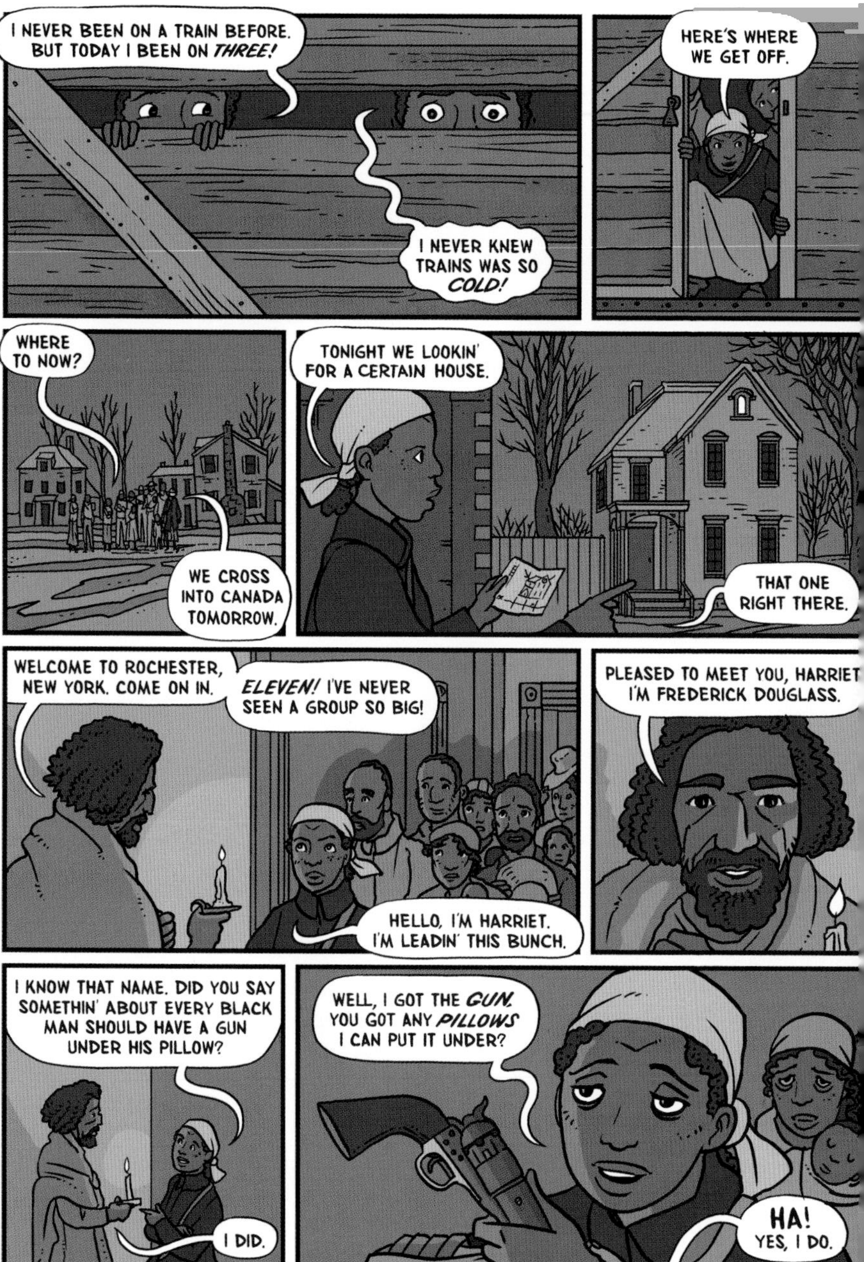
I NEVER BEEN ON A TRAIN BEFORE. BUT TODAY I BEEN ON *THREE!*
I NEVER KNEW TRAINS WAS SO *COLD!*
HERE'S WHERE WE GET OFF.
WHERE TO NOW?
WE CROSS INTO CANADA TOMORROW.
TONIGHT WE LOOKIN' FOR A CERTAIN HOUSE.
THAT ONE RIGHT THERE.
WELCOME TO ROCHESTER, NEW YORK. COME ON IN.
ELEVEN! I'VE NEVER SEEN A GROUP SO BIG!
HELLO, I'M HARRIET. I'M LEADIN' THIS BUNCH.
PLEASED TO MEET YOU, HARRIET. I'M FREDERICK DOUGLASS.
I KNOW THAT NAME. DID YOU SAY SOMETHIN' ABOUT EVERY BLACK MAN SHOULD HAVE A GUN UNDER HIS PILLOW?
I DID.
WELL, I GOT THE *GUN.* YOU GOT ANY *PILLOWS* I CAN PUT IT UNDER?
HA! YES, I DO.

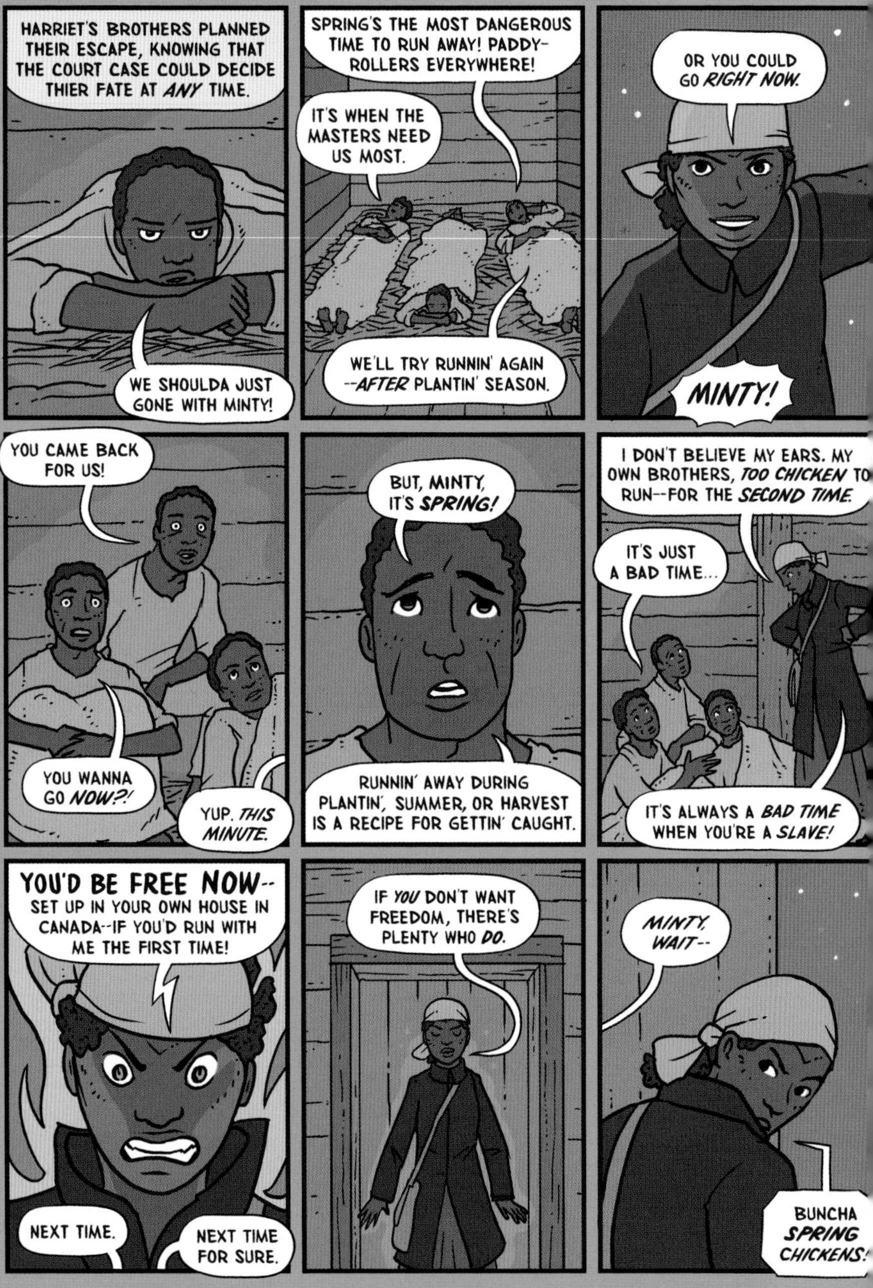
HARRIET'S BROTHERS PLANNED THEIR ESCAPE, KNOWING THAT THE COURT CASE COULD DECIDE THIER FATE AT *ANY* TIME.
WE SHOULDA JUST GONE WITH MINTY!
SPRING'S THE MOST DANGEROUS TIME TO RUN AWAY! PADDY-ROLLERS EVERYWHERE!
IT'S WHEN THE MASTERS NEED US MOST.
WE'LL TRY RUNNIN' AGAIN --*AFTER* PLANTIN' SEASON.
OR YOU COULD GO *RIGHT NOW.*
MINTY!
YOU CAME BACK FOR US!
YOU WANNA GO *NOW?!*
YUP. *THIS MINUTE.*
BUT, MINTY, IT'S *SPRING!*
RUNNIN' AWAY DURING PLANTIN', SUMMER, OR HARVEST IS A RECIPE FOR GETTIN' CAUGHT.
I DON'T BELIEVE MY EARS. MY OWN BROTHERS, *TOO CHICKEN* TO RUN--FOR THE *SECOND TIME.*
IT'S JUST A BAD TIME...
IT'S ALWAYS A *BAD TIME* WHEN YOU'RE A *SLAVE!*
YOU'D BE FREE NOW-- SET UP IN YOUR OWN HOUSE IN CANADA--IF YOU'D RUN WITH ME THE FIRST TIME!
NEXT TIME.
NEXT TIME FOR SURE.
IF *YOU* DON'T WANT FREEDOM, THERE'S PLENTY WHO *DO.*
MINTY, WAIT--
BUNCHA *SPRING CHICKENS!*

87

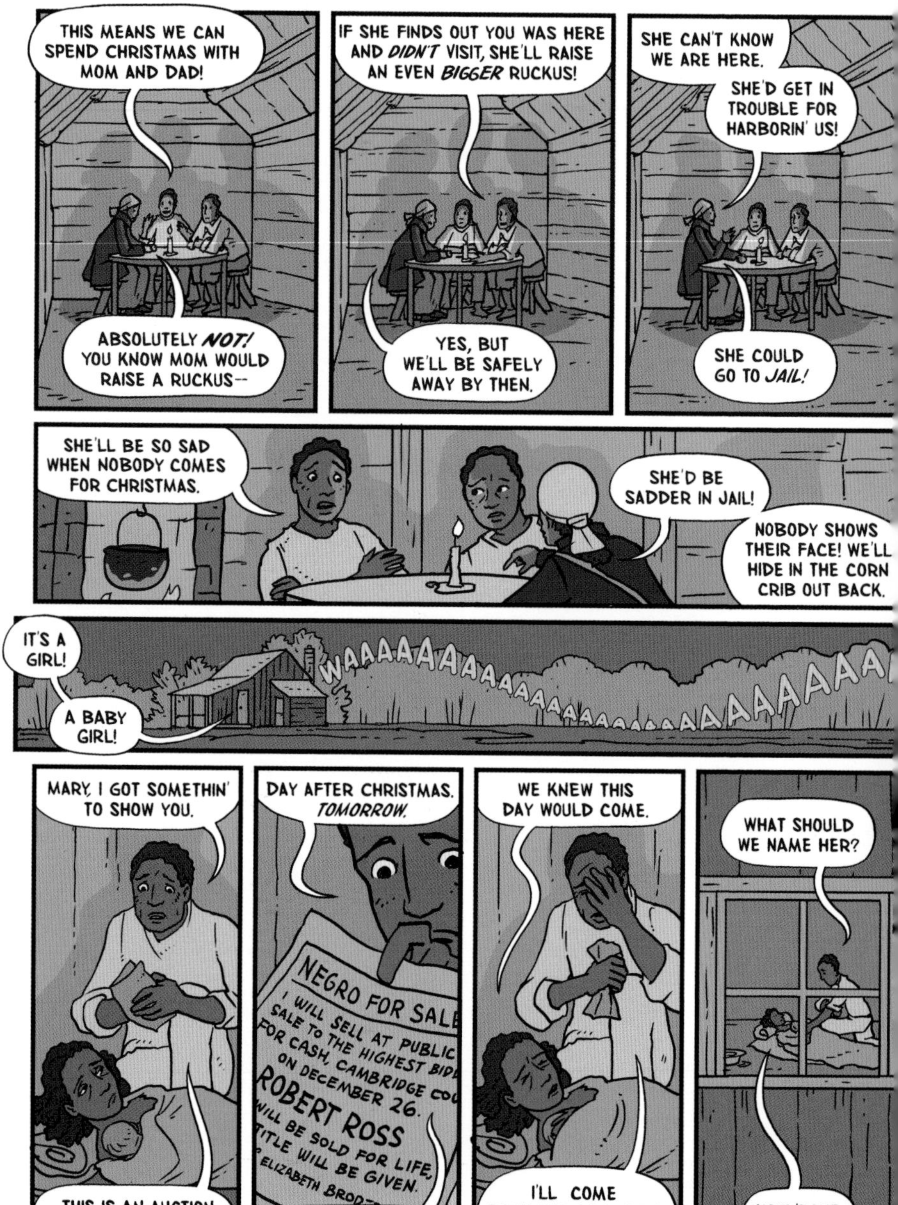
THIS MEANS WE CAN SPEND CHRISTMAS WITH MOM AND DAD!
ABSOLUTELY *NOT!* YOU KNOW MOM WOULD RAISE A RUCKUS--
IF SHE FINDS OUT YOU WAS HERE AND *DIDN'T* VISIT, SHE'LL RAISE AN EVEN *BIGGER* RUCKUS!
YES, BUT WE'LL BE SAFELY AWAY BY THEN.
SHE CAN'T KNOW WE ARE HERE.
SHE'D GET IN TROUBLE FOR HARBORIN' US!
SHE COULD GO TO *JAIL!*
SHE'LL BE SO SAD WHEN NOBODY COMES FOR CHRISTMAS.
SHE'D BE SADDER IN JAIL!
NOBODY SHOWS THEIR FACE! WE'LL HIDE IN THE CORN CRIB OUT BACK.
IT'S A GIRL!
A BABY GIRL!
WAAAAAAAAAAAAAAAAAAAAAAAAAAAAAAAA!
MARY, I GOT SOMETHIN' TO SHOW YOU.
THIS IS AN AUCTION NOTICE. MRS. BRODESS GONNA SELL ME AT LAST.
DAY AFTER CHRISTMAS. *TOMORROW.*
NEGRO FOR SALE
I WILL SELL AT PUBLIC SALE TO THE HIGHEST BIDD FOR CASH, CAMBRIDGE CO ON DECEMBER 26.
ROBERT ROSS
WILL BE SOLD FOR LIFE, TITLE WILL BE GIVEN.
ELIZABETH BROD-
WE GOT NO CHOICE. I GOT TO RUN AWAY.
WE KNEW THIS DAY WOULD COME.
I'LL COME BACK FOR YOU WHEN THE BABY'S OLD ENOUGH.
WHAT SHOULD WE NAME HER?
HOW 'BOUT HARRIET?

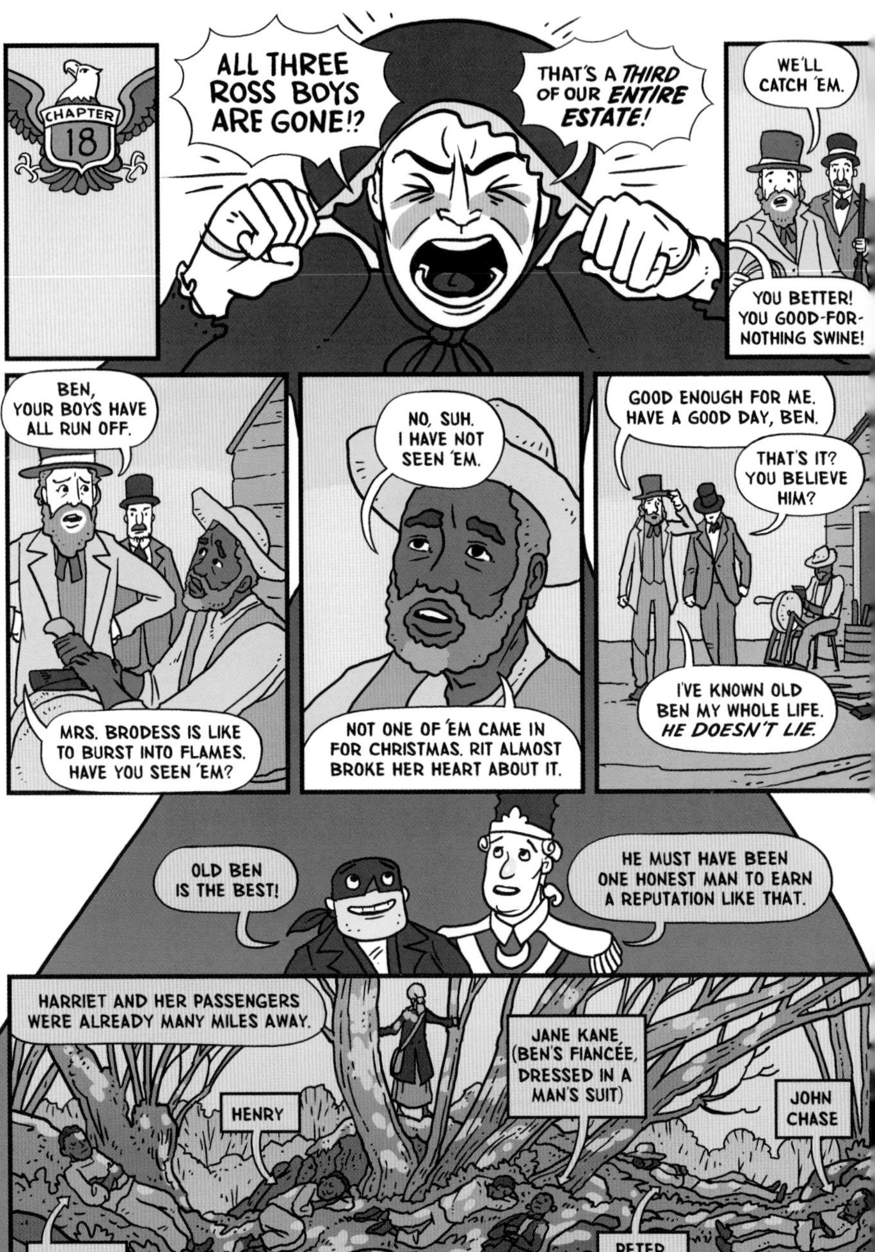
CHAPTER 18
ALL THREE ROSS BOYS ARE GONE!?
THAT'S A *THIRD* OF OUR *ENTIRE ESTATE!*
WE'LL CATCH 'EM.
YOU BETTER! YOU GOOD-FOR-NOTHING SWINE!
BEN, YOUR BOYS HAVE ALL RUN OFF.
MRS. BRODESS IS LIKE TO BURST INTO FLAMES. HAVE YOU SEEN 'EM?
NO, SUH. I HAVE NOT SEEN 'EM.
NOT ONE OF 'EM CAME IN FOR CHRISTMAS. RIT ALMOST BROKE HER HEART ABOUT IT.
GOOD ENOUGH FOR ME. HAVE A GOOD DAY, BEN.
THAT'S IT? YOU BELIEVE HIM?
I'VE KNOWN OLD BEN MY WHOLE LIFE. *HE DOESN'T LIE.*
OLD BEN IS THE BEST!
HE MUST HAVE BEEN ONE HONEST MAN TO EARN A REPUTATION LIKE THAT.
HARRIET AND HER PASSENGERS WERE ALREADY MANY MILES AWAY.
HENRY
JANE KANE (BEN'S FIANCÉE, DRESSED IN A MAN'S SUIT)
JOHN CHASE
ROBERT
BEN
PETER JACKSON

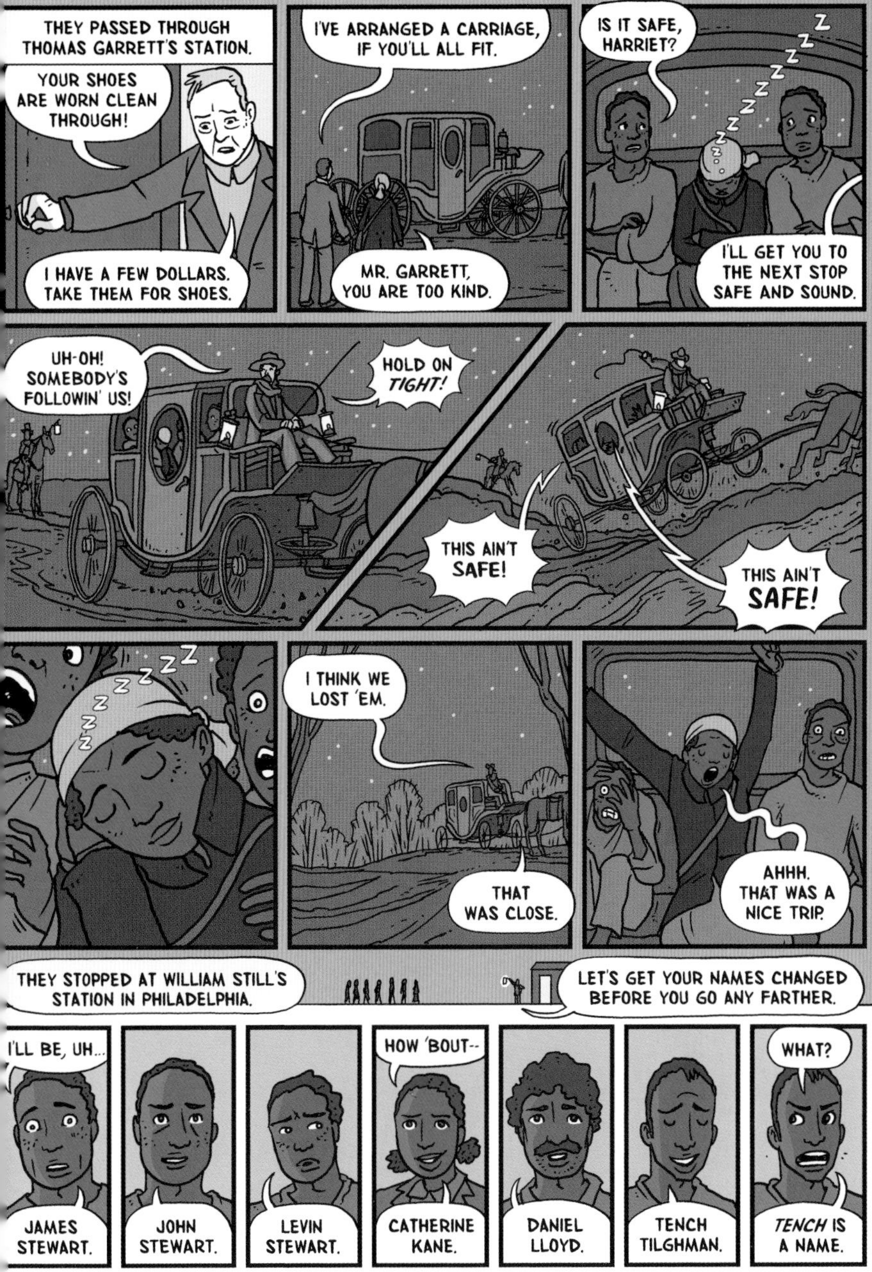
THEY PASSED THROUGH THOMAS GARRETT'S STATION.
YOUR SHOES ARE WORN CLEAN THROUGH!
I HAVE A FEW DOLLARS. TAKE THEM FOR SHOES.
I'VE ARRANGED A CARRIAGE, IF YOU'LL ALL FIT.
MR. GARRETT, YOU ARE TOO KIND.
IS IT SAFE, HARRIET?
Z Z Z Z Z Z Z Z Z
I'LL GET YOU TO THE NEXT STOP SAFE AND SOUND.
UH-OH! SOMEBODY'S FOLLOWIN' US!
HOLD ON *TIGHT!*
THIS AIN'T SAFE!
THIS AIN'T **SAFE!**
Z Z Z Z Z Z Z
I THINK WE LOST 'EM.
THAT WAS CLOSE.
AHHH. THAT WAS A NICE TRIP.
THEY STOPPED AT WILLIAM STILL'S STATION IN PHILADELPHIA.
LET'S GET YOUR NAMES CHANGED BEFORE YOU GO ANY FARTHER.
I'LL BE, UH...
JAMES STEWART.
JOHN STEWART.
LEVIN STEWART.
HOW 'BOUT--
CATHERINE KANE.
DANIEL LLOYD.
TENCH TILGHMAN.
WHAT?
TENCH IS A NAME.

92

93

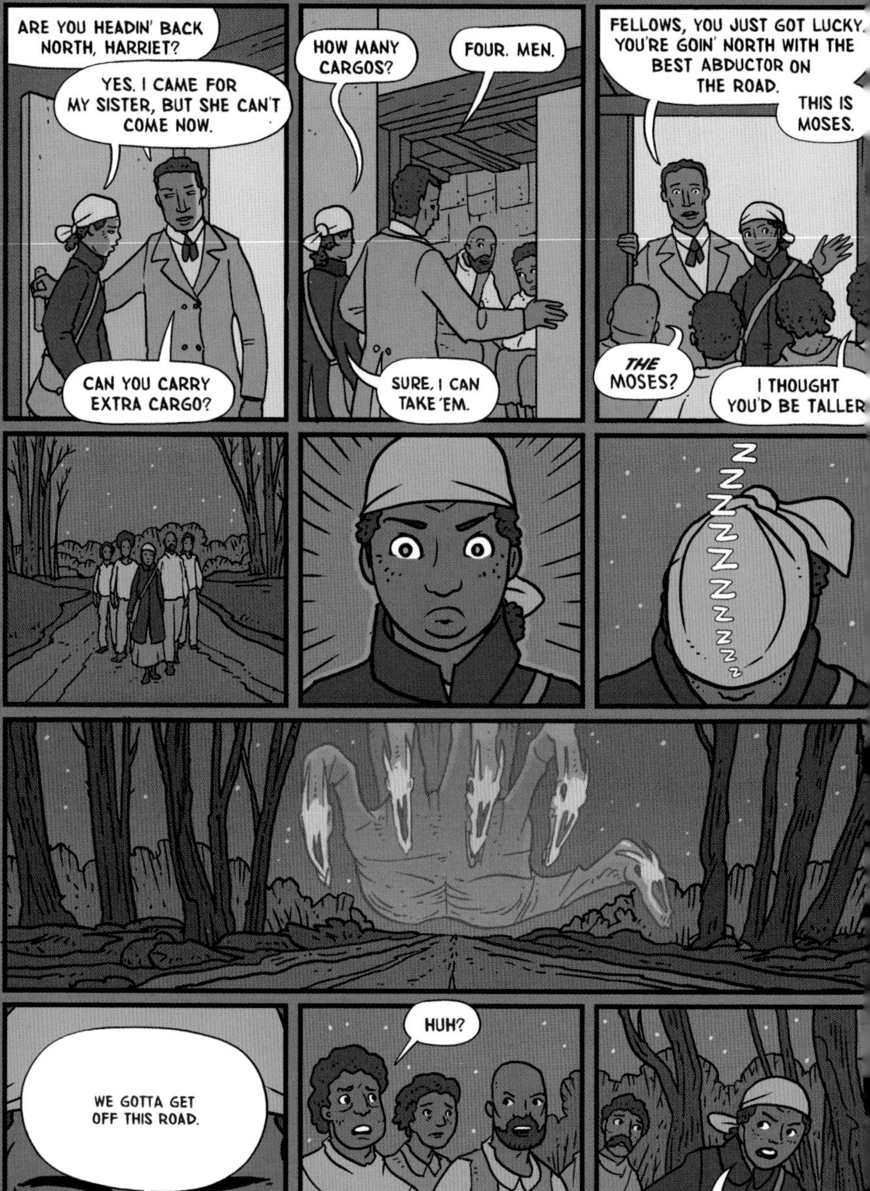
ARE YOU HEADIN' BACK NORTH, HARRIET?
YES. I CAME FOR MY SISTER, BUT SHE CAN'T COME NOW.
CAN YOU CARRY EXTRA CARGO?
HOW MANY CARGOS?
FOUR. MEN.
SURE, I CAN TAKE 'EM.
FELLOWS, YOU JUST GOT LUCKY. YOU'RE GOIN' NORTH WITH THE BEST ABDUCTOR ON THE ROAD.
THIS IS MOSES.
THE MOSES?
I THOUGHT YOU'D BE TALLER
ZZZZZZZZZZ
WE GOTTA GET OFF THIS ROAD.
HUH?
MOSES KNOWS WHEN TROUBLE'S COMIN'.
RIGHT NOW! EVERYONE OFF!

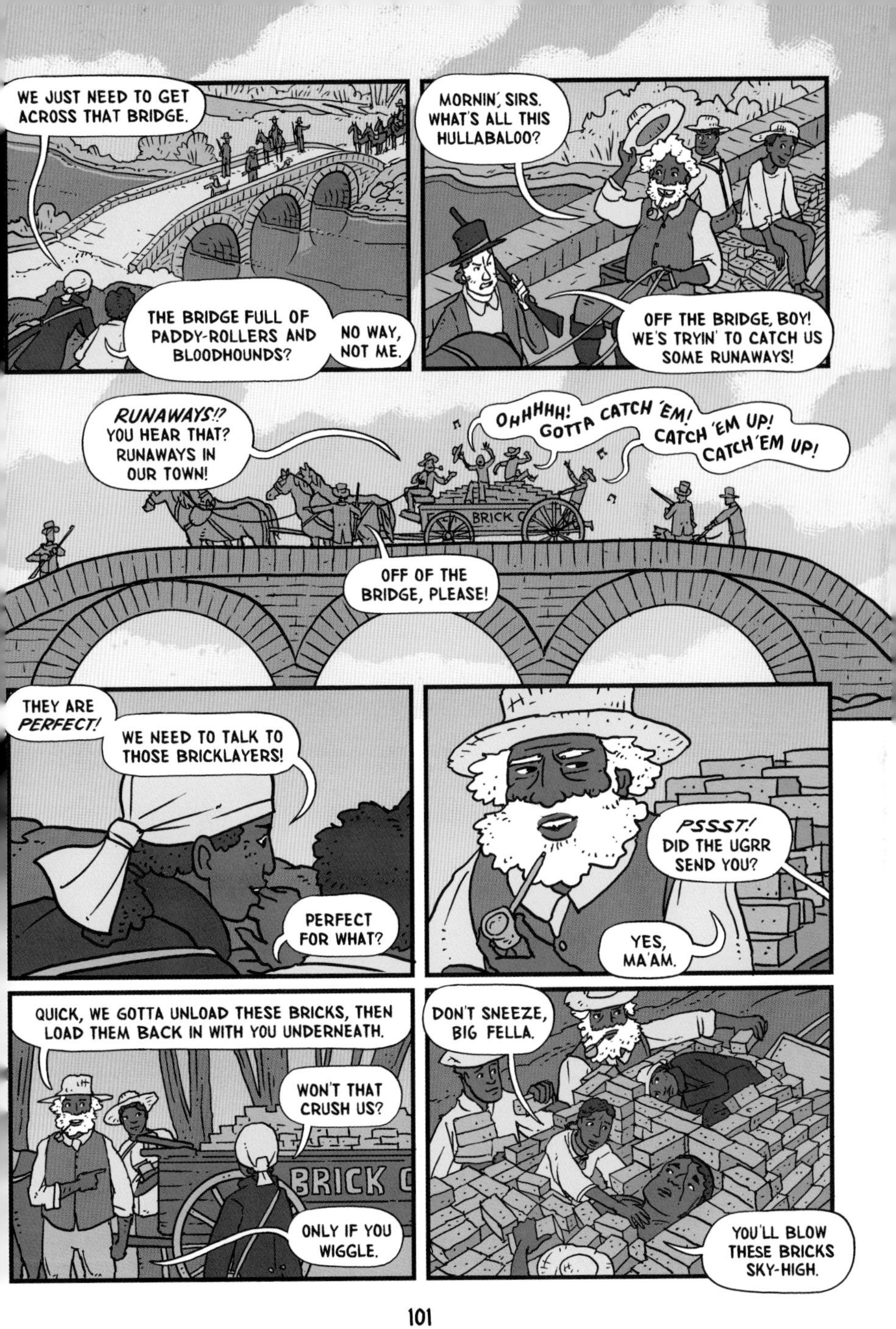
WE JUST NEED TO GET ACROSS THAT BRIDGE.
THE BRIDGE FULL OF PADDY-ROLLERS AND BLOODHOUNDS?
NO WAY, NOT ME.
MORNIN', SIRS. WHAT'S ALL THIS HULLABALOO?
OFF THE BRIDGE, BOY! WE'S TRYIN' TO CATCH US SOME RUNAWAYS!
RUNAWAYS!? YOU HEAR THAT? RUNAWAYS IN OUR TOWN!
OHHHHH! GOTTA CATCH 'EM!
CATCH 'EM UP! CATCH 'EM UP!
BRICK C
OFF OF THE BRIDGE, PLEASE!
THEY ARE PERFECT!
WE NEED TO TALK TO THOSE BRICKLAYERS!
PERFECT FOR WHAT?
PSSST! DID THE UGRR SEND YOU?
YES, MA'AM.
QUICK, WE GOTTA UNLOAD THESE BRICKS, THEN LOAD THEM BACK IN WITH YOU UNDERNEATH.
WON'T THAT CRUSH US?
BRICK C
ONLY IF YOU WIGGLE.
DON'T SNEEZE, BIG FELLA.
YOU'LL BLOW THESE BRICKS SKY-HIGH.

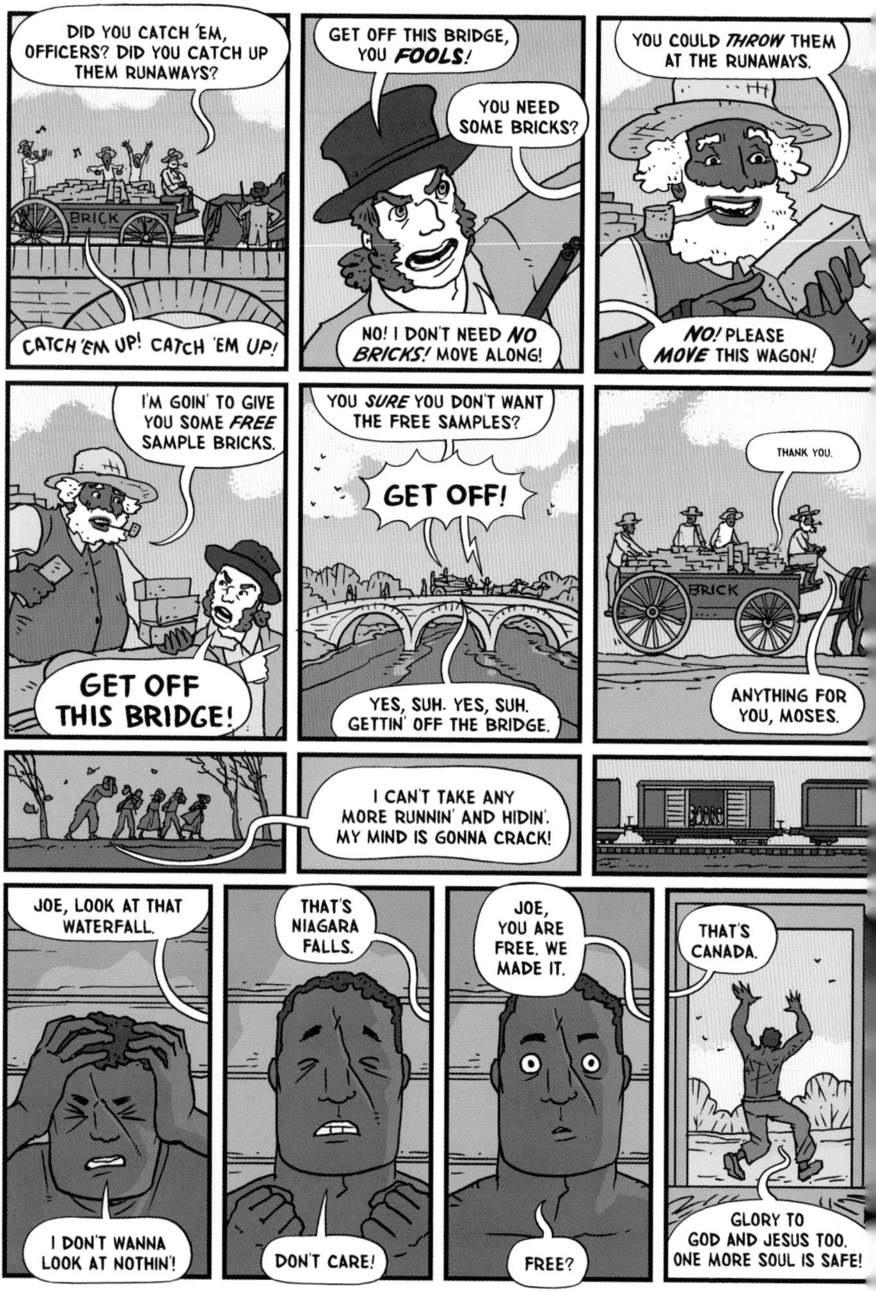
DID YOU CATCH 'EM, OFFICERS? DID YOU CATCH UP THEM RUNAWAYS?
BRICK
CATCH 'EM UP! CATCH 'EM UP!
GET OFF THIS BRIDGE, YOU FOOLS!
YOU NEED SOME BRICKS?
NO! I DON'T NEED NO BRICKS! MOVE ALONG!
YOU COULD THROW THEM AT THE RUNAWAYS.
NO! PLEASE MOVE THIS WAGON!
I'M GOIN' TO GIVE YOU SOME FREE SAMPLE BRICKS.
GET OFF THIS BRIDGE!
YOU SURE YOU DON'T WANT THE FREE SAMPLES?
GET OFF!
YES, SUH. YES, SUH. GETTIN' OFF THE BRIDGE.
THANK YOU.
BRICK
ANYTHING FOR YOU, MOSES.
I CAN'T TAKE ANY MORE RUNNIN' AND HIDIN'. MY MIND IS GONNA CRACK!
JOE, LOOK AT THAT WATERFALL.
I DON'T WANNA LOOK AT NOTHIN'!
THAT'S NIAGARA FALLS.
DON'T CARE!
JOE, YOU ARE FREE. WE MADE IT.
FREE?
THAT'S CANADA.
GLORY TO GOD AND JESUS TOO. ONE MORE SOUL IS SAFE!

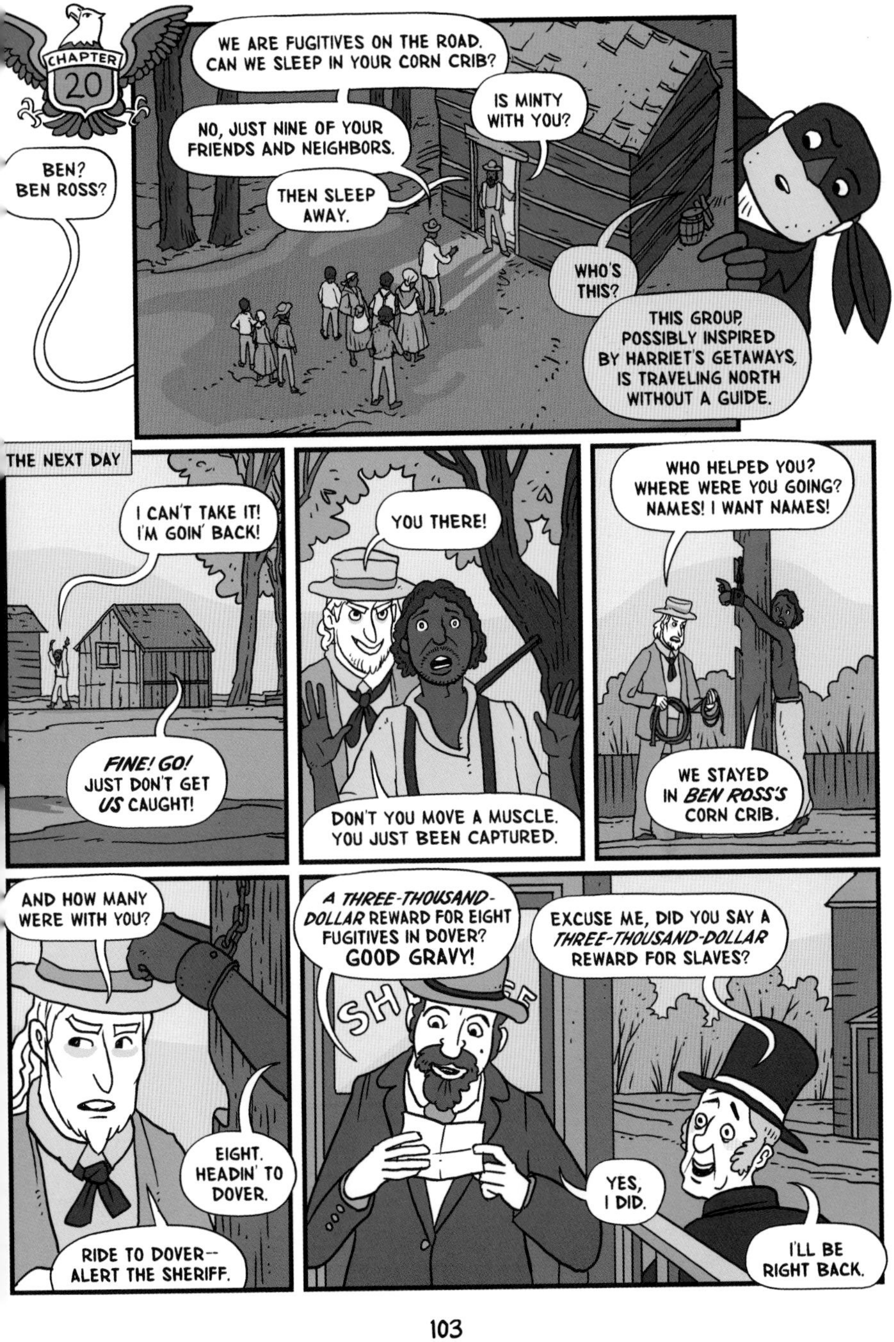
CHAPTER
20
BEN?
BEN ROSS?
WE ARE FUGITIVES ON THE ROAD.
CAN WE SLEEP IN YOUR CORN CRIB?
IS MINTY
WITH YOU?
NO, JUST NINE OF YOUR
FRIENDS AND NEIGHBORS.
THEN SLEEP
AWAY.
WHO'S
THIS?
THIS GROUP,
POSSIBLY INSPIRED
BY HARRIET'S GETAWAYS,
IS TRAVELING NORTH
WITHOUT A GUIDE.
THE NEXT DAY
I CAN'T TAKE IT!
I'M GOIN' BACK!
FINE! GO!
JUST DON'T GET
US CAUGHT!
YOU THERE!
DON'T YOU MOVE A MUSCLE.
YOU JUST BEEN CAPTURED.
WHO HELPED YOU?
WHERE WERE YOU GOING?
NAMES! I WANT NAMES!
WE STAYED
IN *BEN ROSS'S*
CORN CRIB.
AND HOW MANY
WERE WITH YOU?
EIGHT.
HEADIN' TO
DOVER.
RIDE TO DOVER--
ALERT THE SHERIFF.
A THREE-THOUSAND-DOLLAR REWARD FOR EIGHT
FUGITIVES IN DOVER?
GOOD GRAVY!
EXCUSE ME, DID YOU SAY A
THREE-THOUSAND-DOLLAR
REWARD FOR SLAVES?
YES,
I DID.
I'LL BE
RIGHT BACK.

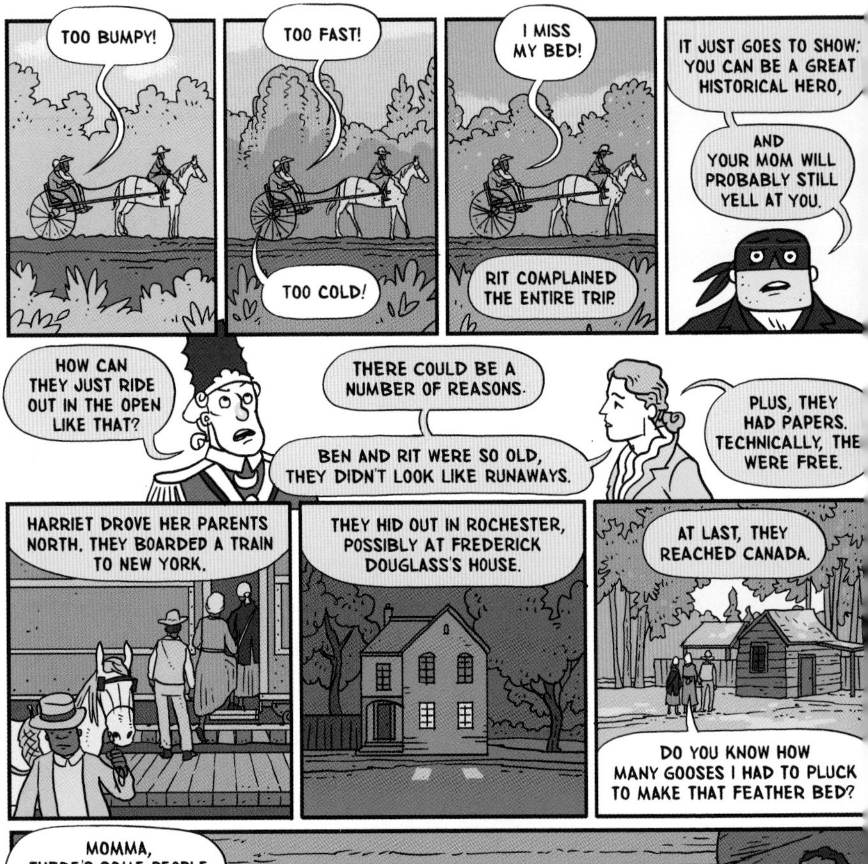
TOO BUMPY!
TOO FAST!
TOO COLD!
I MISS MY BED!
RIT COMPLAINED THE ENTIRE TRIP.
IT JUST GOES TO SHOW: YOU CAN BE A GREAT HISTORICAL HERO,
AND YOUR MOM WILL PROBABLY STILL YELL AT YOU.
HOW CAN THEY JUST RIDE OUT IN THE OPEN LIKE THAT?
THERE COULD BE A NUMBER OF REASONS.
BEN AND RIT WERE SO OLD, THEY DIDN'T LOOK LIKE RUNAWAYS.
PLUS, THEY HAD PAPERS. TECHNICALLY, THE WERE FREE.
HARRIET DROVE HER PARENTS NORTH. THEY BOARDED A TRAIN TO NEW YORK.
THEY HID OUT IN ROCHESTER, POSSIBLY AT FREDERICK DOUGLASS'S HOUSE.
AT LAST, THEY REACHED CANADA.
DO YOU KNOW HOW MANY GOOSES I HAD TO PLUCK TO MAKE THAT FEATHER BED?
MOMMA, THERE'S SOME PEOPLE HERE TO SEE YOU.
OH MY GOODNESS.
MOMMA!
MOM!
GRANDMA!

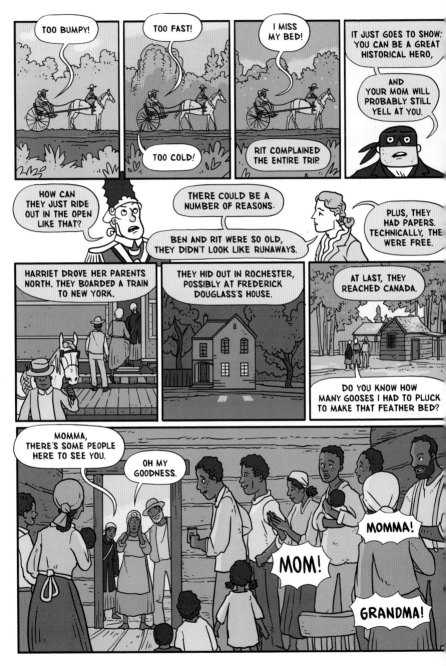

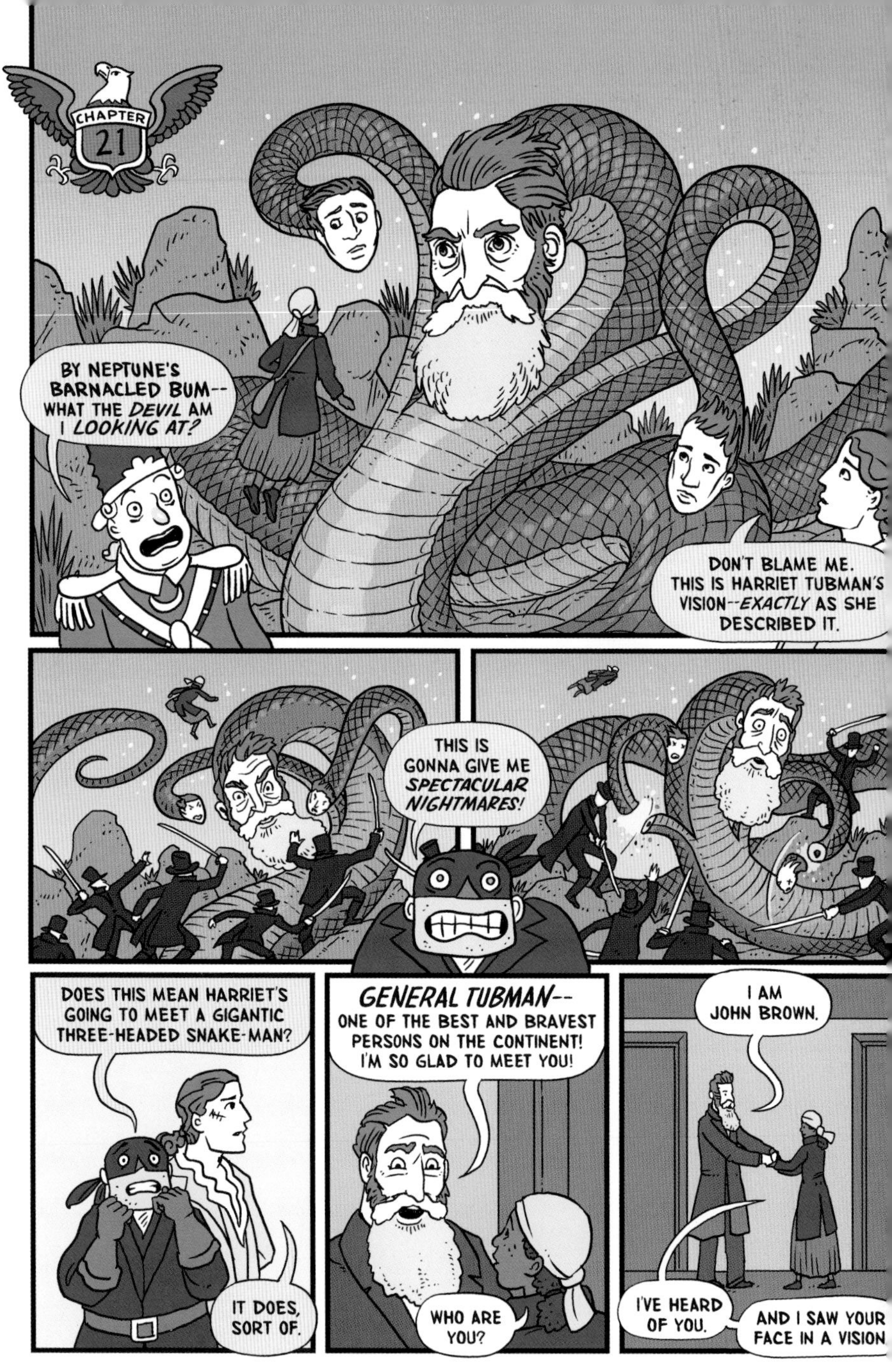
CHAPTER 21
BY NEPTUNE'S BARNACLED BUM--WHAT THE *DEVIL* AM I *LOOKING AT?*
DON'T BLAME ME. THIS IS HARRIET TUBMAN'S VISION--*EXACTLY* AS SHE DESCRIBED IT.
THIS IS GONNA GIVE ME *SPECTACULAR NIGHTMARES!*
DOES THIS MEAN HARRIET'S GOING TO MEET A GIGANTIC THREE-HEADED SNAKE-MAN?
IT DOES, SORT OF.
GENERAL TUBMAN-- ONE OF THE BEST AND BRAVEST PERSONS ON THE CONTINENT! I'M SO GLAD TO MEET YOU!
WHO ARE YOU?
I AM JOHN BROWN.
I'VE HEARD OF YOU.
AND I SAW YOUR FACE IN A VISION

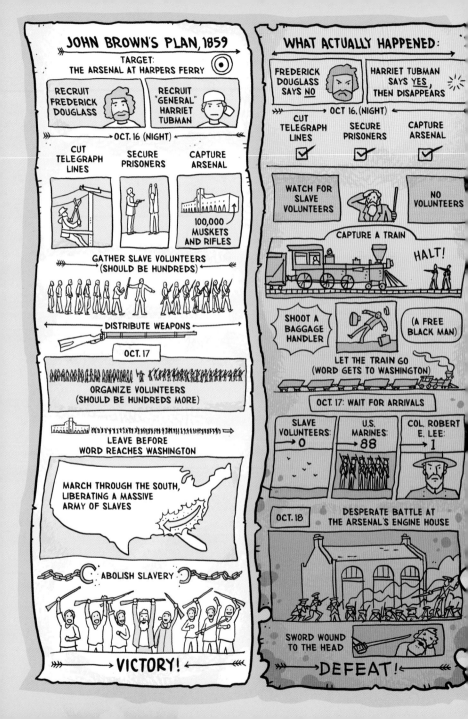

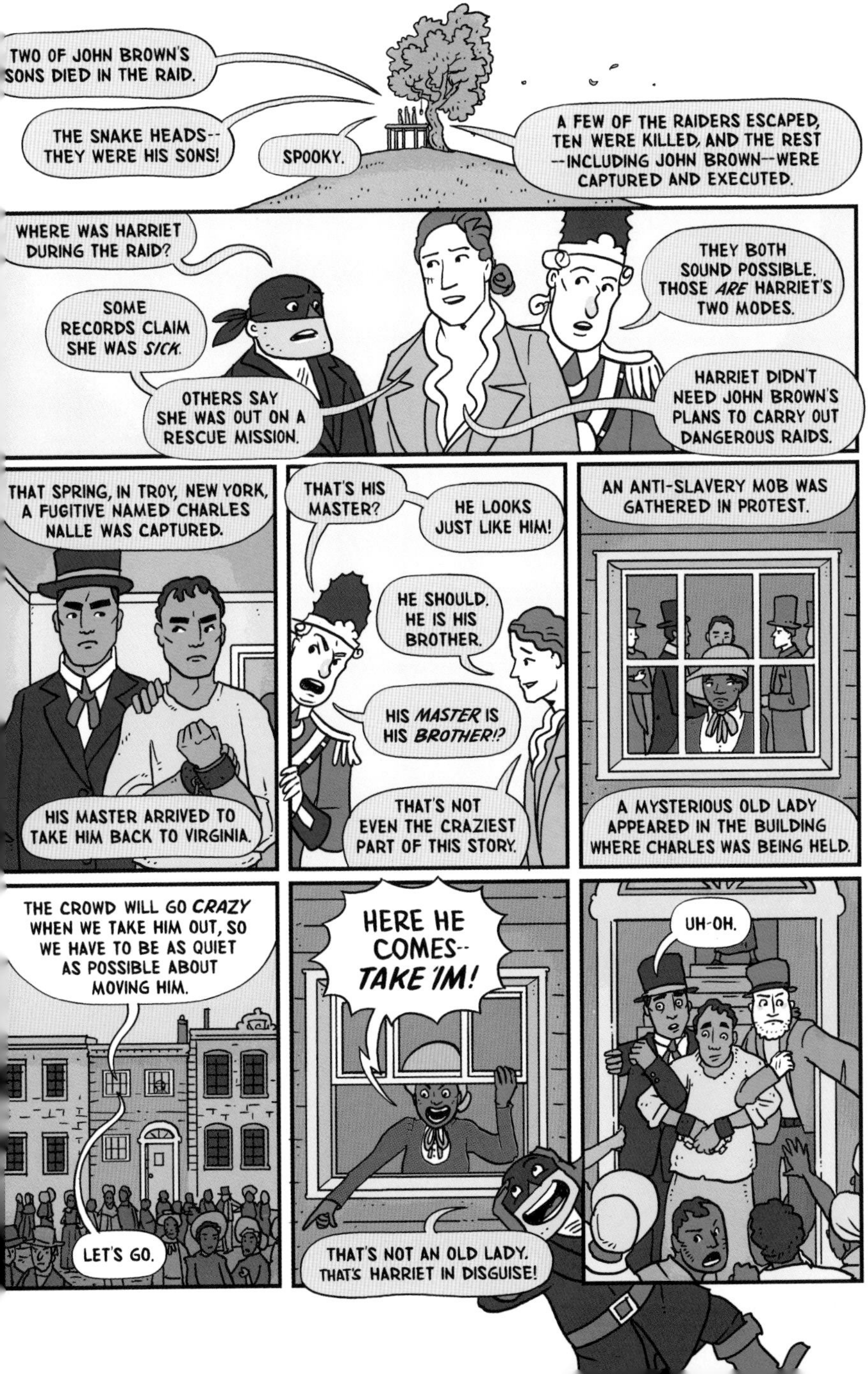
TWO OF JOHN BROWN'S SONS DIED IN THE RAID.
THE SNAKE HEADS-- THEY WERE HIS SONS!
SPOOKY.
A FEW OF THE RAIDERS ESCAPED, TEN WERE KILLED, AND THE REST --INCLUDING JOHN BROWN--WERE CAPTURED AND EXECUTED.
WHERE WAS HARRIET DURING THE RAID?
SOME RECORDS CLAIM SHE WAS *SICK*.
OTHERS SAY SHE WAS OUT ON A RESCUE MISSION.
THEY BOTH SOUND POSSIBLE. THOSE *ARE* HARRIET'S TWO MODES.
HARRIET DIDN'T NEED JOHN BROWN'S PLANS TO CARRY OUT DANGEROUS RAIDS.
THAT SPRING, IN TROY, NEW YORK, A FUGITIVE NAMED CHARLES NALLE WAS CAPTURED.
HIS MASTER ARRIVED TO TAKE HIM BACK TO VIRGINIA.
THAT'S HIS MASTER?
HE LOOKS JUST LIKE HIM!
HE SHOULD. HE IS HIS BROTHER.
HIS *MASTER* IS HIS *BROTHER!?*
THAT'S NOT EVEN THE CRAZIEST PART OF THIS STORY.
AN ANTI-SLAVERY MOB WAS GATHERED IN PROTEST.
A MYSTERIOUS OLD LADY APPEARED IN THE BUILDING WHERE CHARLES WAS BEING HELD.
THE CROWD WILL GO *CRAZY* WHEN WE TAKE HIM OUT, SO WE HAVE TO BE AS QUIET AS POSSIBLE ABOUT MOVING HIM.
LET'S GO.
HERE HE COMES-- *TAKE 'IM!*
THAT'S NOT AN OLD LADY. THAT'S HARRIET IN DISGUISE!
UH-OH.

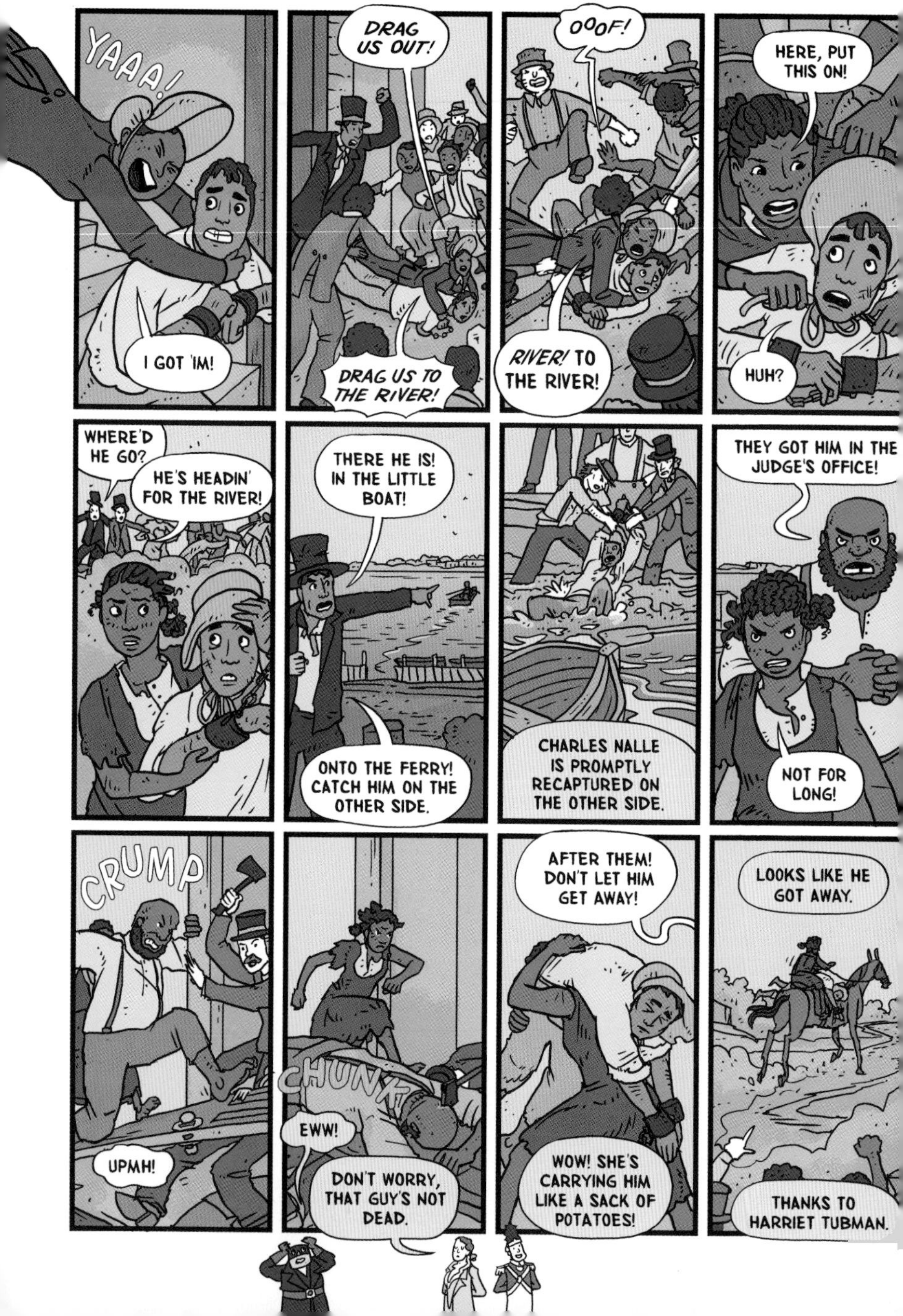
YAAAA!
I GOT 'IM!
DRAG US OUT!
DRAG US TO THE RIVER!
OOOF!
RIVER! TO THE RIVER!
HERE, PUT THIS ON!
HUH?
WHERE'D HE GO?
HE'S HEADIN' FOR THE RIVER!
THERE HE IS! IN THE LITTLE BOAT!
ONTO THE FERRY! CATCH HIM ON THE OTHER SIDE.
CHARLES NALLE IS PROMPTLY RECAPTURED ON THE OTHER SIDE.
THEY GOT HIM IN THE JUDGE'S OFFICE!
NOT FOR LONG!
CRUMP
UPMH!
CHUNK
EWW!
DON'T WORRY, THAT GUY'S NOT DEAD.
AFTER THEM! DON'T LET HIM GET AWAY!
WOW! SHE'S CARRYING HIM LIKE A SACK OF POTATOES!
LOOKS LIKE HE GOT AWAY.
THANKS TO HARRIET TUBMAN.

114

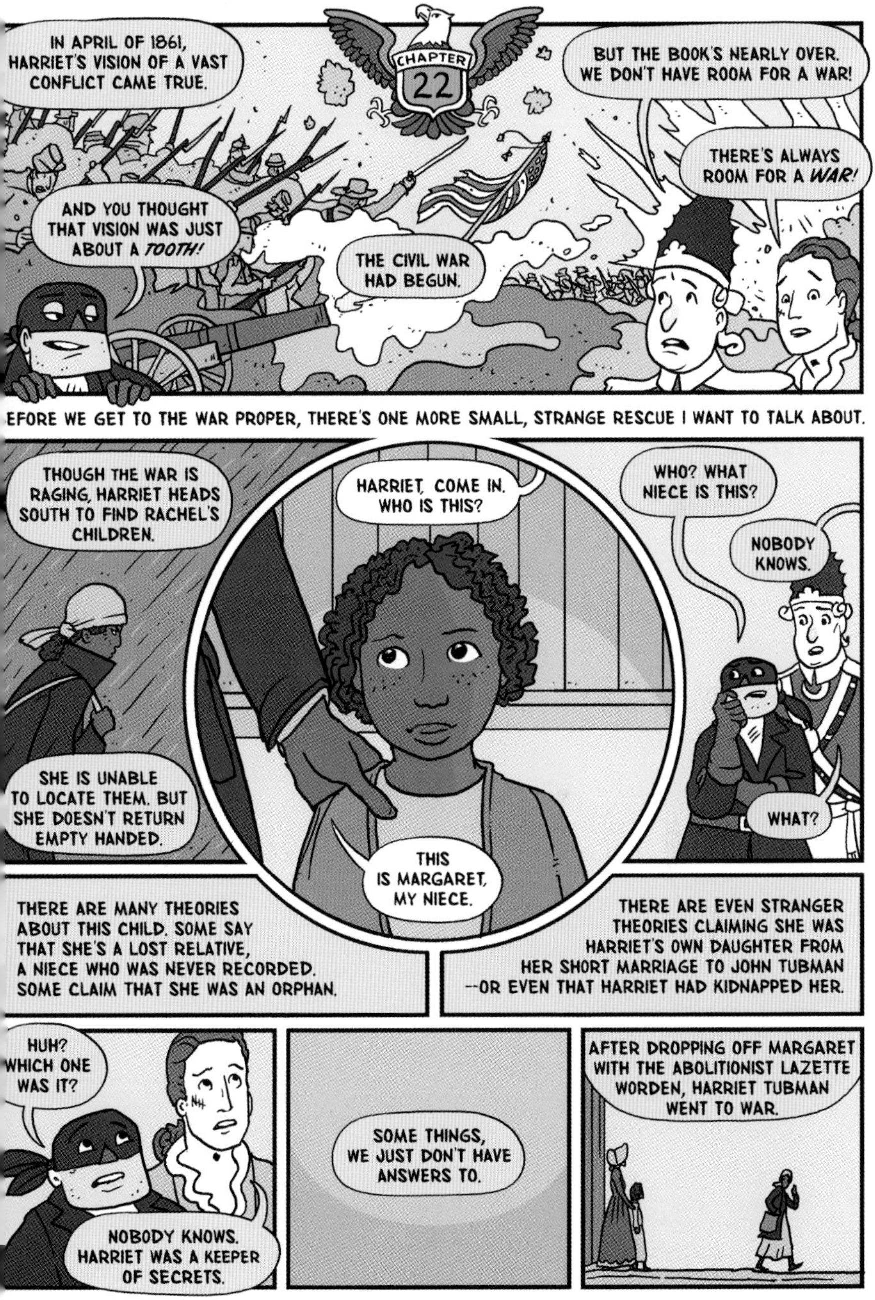
CHAPTER 22
IN APRIL OF 1861, HARRIET'S VISION OF A VAST CONFLICT CAME TRUE.
BUT THE BOOK'S NEARLY OVER. WE DON'T HAVE ROOM FOR A WAR!
THERE'S ALWAYS ROOM FOR A *WAR!*
AND YOU THOUGHT THAT VISION WAS JUST ABOUT A *TOOTH!*
THE CIVIL WAR HAD BEGUN.
EFORE WE GET TO THE WAR PROPER, THERE'S ONE MORE SMALL, STRANGE RESCUE I WANT TO TALK ABOUT.
THOUGH THE WAR IS RAGING, HARRIET HEADS SOUTH TO FIND RACHEL'S CHILDREN.
SHE IS UNABLE TO LOCATE THEM. BUT SHE DOESN'T RETURN EMPTY HANDED.
HARRIET, COME IN. WHO IS THIS?
THIS IS MARGARET, MY NIECE.
WHO? WHAT NIECE IS THIS?
NOBODY KNOWS.
WHAT?
THERE ARE MANY THEORIES ABOUT THIS CHILD. SOME SAY THAT SHE'S A LOST RELATIVE, A NIECE WHO WAS NEVER RECORDED. SOME CLAIM THAT SHE WAS AN ORPHAN.
THERE ARE EVEN STRANGER THEORIES CLAIMING SHE WAS HARRIET'S OWN DAUGHTER FROM HER SHORT MARRIAGE TO JOHN TUBMAN --OR EVEN THAT HARRIET HAD KIDNAPPED HER.
HUH? WHICH ONE WAS IT?
NOBODY KNOWS. HARRIET WAS A KEEPER OF SECRETS.
SOME THINGS, WE JUST DON'T HAVE ANSWERS TO.
AFTER DROPPING OFF MARGARET WITH THE ABOLITIONIST LAZETTE WORDEN, HARRIET TUBMAN WENT TO WAR.

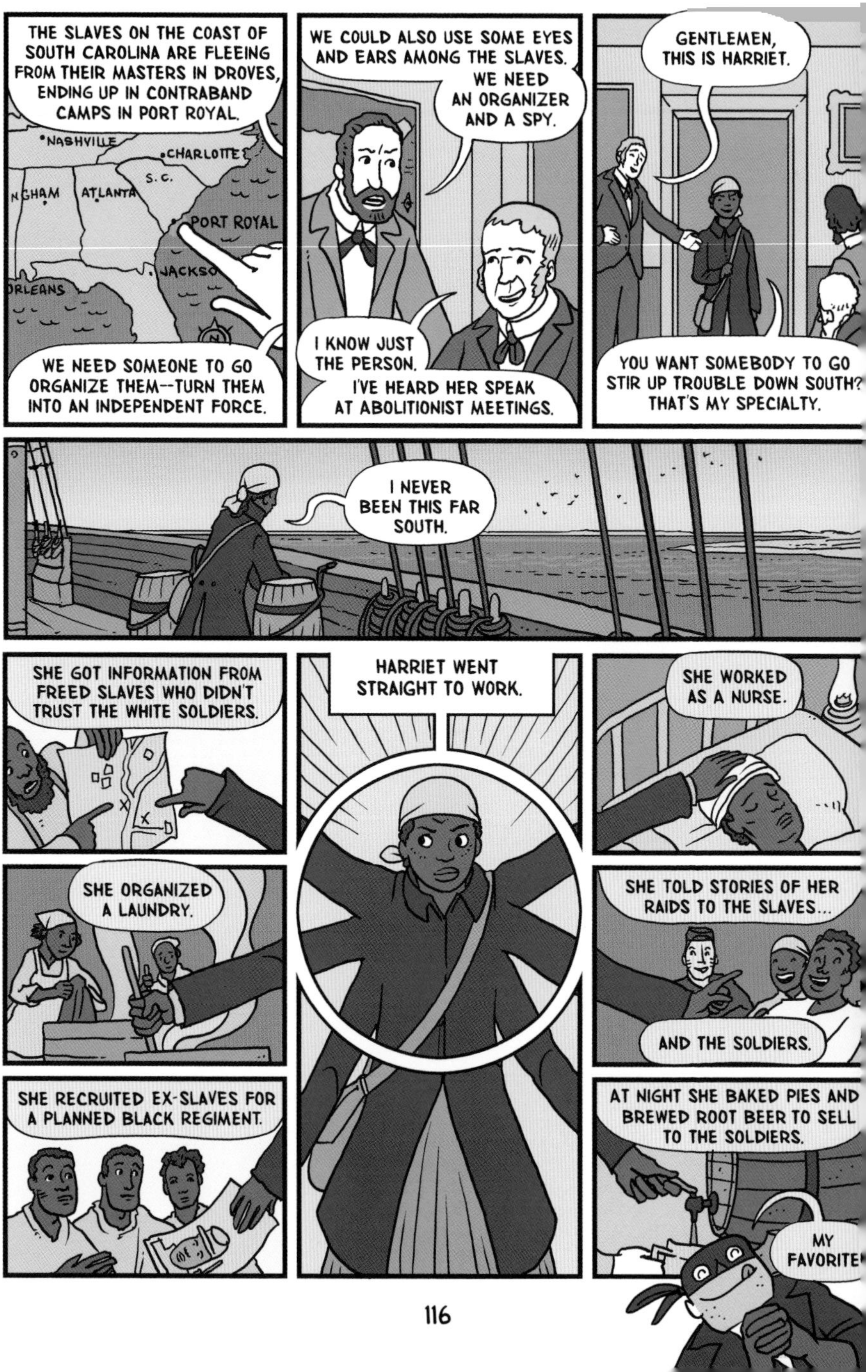
THE SLAVES ON THE COAST OF SOUTH CAROLINA ARE FLEEING FROM THEIR MASTERS IN DROVES, ENDING UP IN CONTRABAND CAMPS IN PORT ROYAL.
NASHVILLE
CHARLOTTE
S.C.
ATLANTA
PORT ROYAL
WE NEED SOMEONE TO GO ORGANIZE THEM--TURN THEM INTO AN INDEPENDENT FORCE.
WE COULD ALSO USE SOME EYES AND EARS AMONG THE SLAVES.
WE NEED AN ORGANIZER AND A SPY.
I KNOW JUST THE PERSON.
I'VE HEARD HER SPEAK AT ABOLITIONIST MEETINGS.
GENTLEMEN, THIS IS HARRIET.
YOU WANT SOMEBODY TO GO STIR UP TROUBLE DOWN SOUTH? THAT'S MY SPECIALTY.
I NEVER BEEN THIS FAR SOUTH.
SHE GOT INFORMATION FROM FREED SLAVES WHO DIDN'T TRUST THE WHITE SOLDIERS.
HARRIET WENT STRAIGHT TO WORK.
SHE WORKED AS A NURSE.
SHE ORGANIZED A LAUNDRY.
SHE TOLD STORIES OF HER RAIDS TO THE SLAVES...
AND THE SOLDIERS.
SHE RECRUITED EX-SLAVES FOR A PLANNED BLACK REGIMENT.
AT NIGHT SHE BAKED PIES AND BREWED ROOT BEER TO SELL TO THE SOLDIERS.
MY FAVORITE

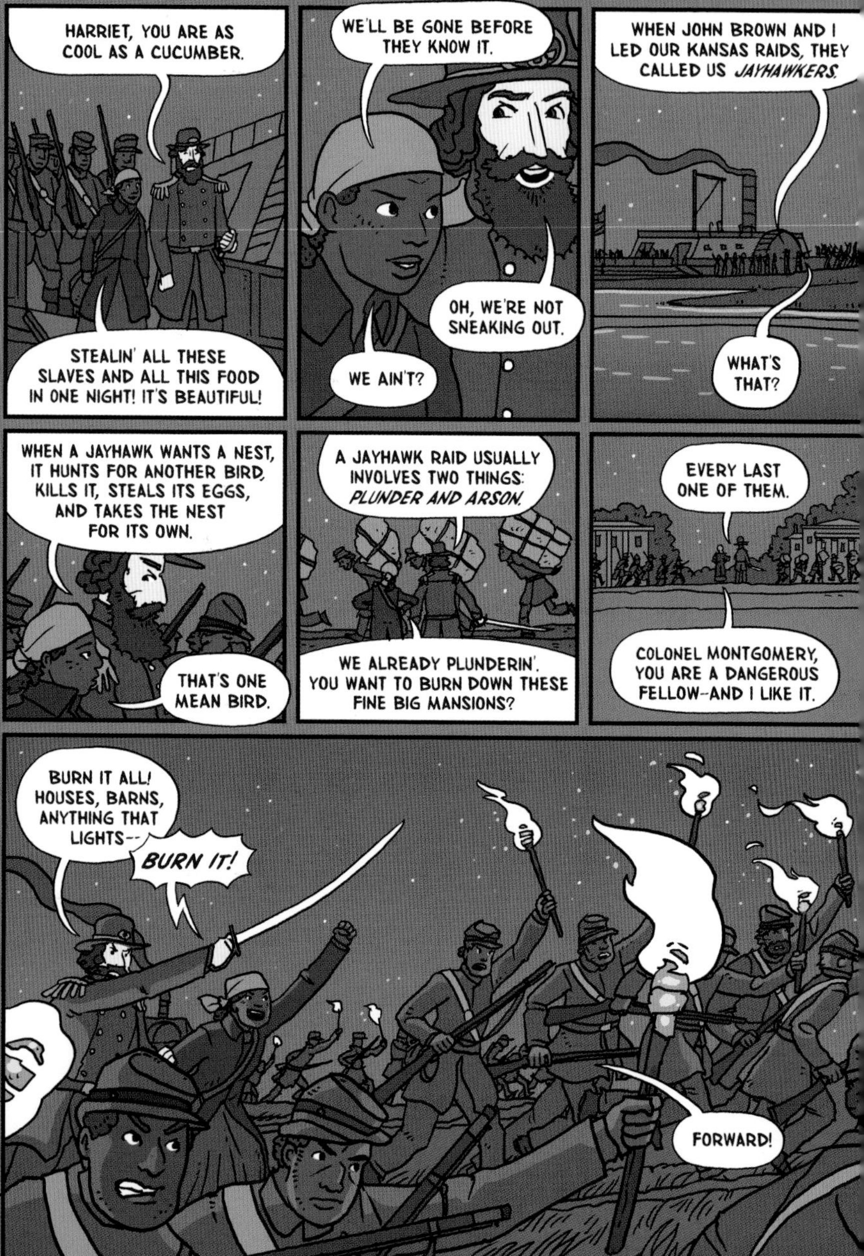
HARRIET, YOU ARE AS COOL AS A CUCUMBER.
STEALIN' ALL THESE SLAVES AND ALL THIS FOOD IN ONE NIGHT! IT'S BEAUTIFUL!
WE'LL BE GONE BEFORE THEY KNOW IT.
OH, WE'RE NOT SNEAKING OUT.
WE AIN'T?
WHEN JOHN BROWN AND I LED OUR KANSAS RAIDS, THEY CALLED US *JAYHAWKERS.*
WHAT'S THAT?
WHEN A JAYHAWK WANTS A NEST, IT HUNTS FOR ANOTHER BIRD, KILLS IT, STEALS ITS EGGS, AND TAKES THE NEST FOR ITS OWN.
THAT'S ONE MEAN BIRD.
A JAYHAWK RAID USUALLY INVOLVES TWO THINGS: *PLUNDER AND ARSON.*
WE ALREADY PLUNDERIN'. YOU WANT TO BURN DOWN THESE FINE BIG MANSIONS?
EVERY LAST ONE OF THEM.
COLONEL MONTGOMERY, YOU ARE A DANGEROUS FELLOW--AND I LIKE IT.
BURN IT ALL! HOUSES, BARNS, ANYTHING THAT LIGHTS--
BURN IT!
FORWARD!

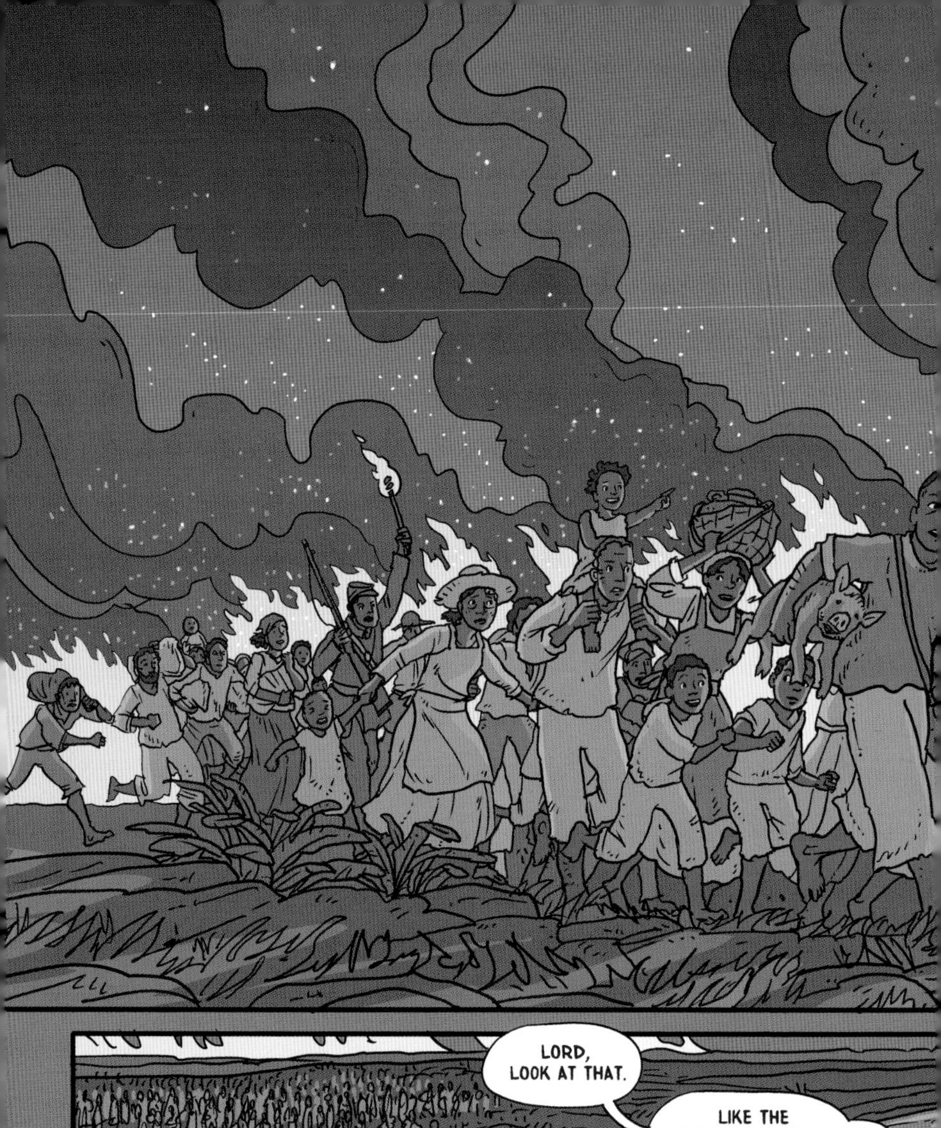

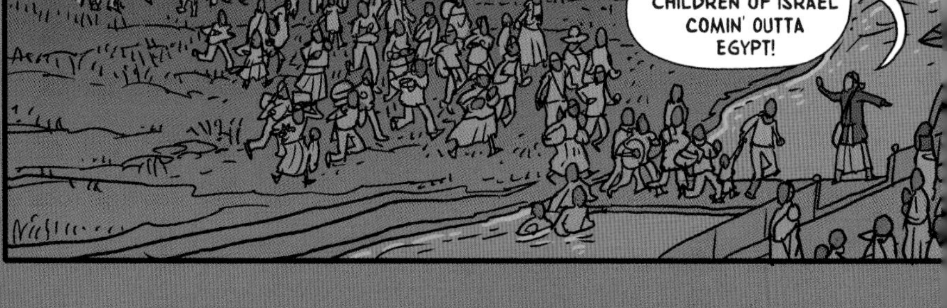
LORD, LOOK AT THAT.
LIKE THE CHILDREN OF ISRAEL COMIN' OUTTA EGYPT!

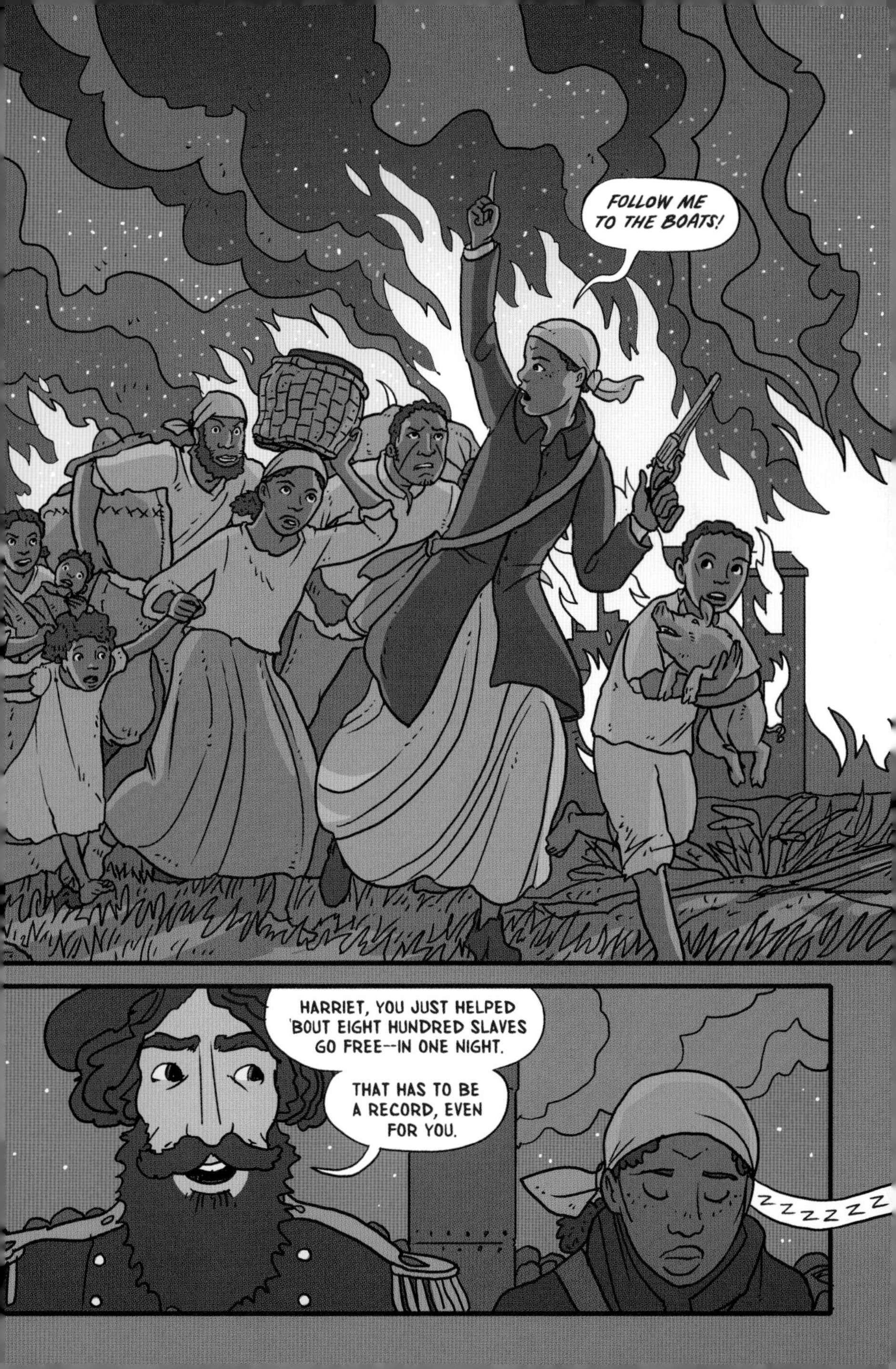
FOLLOW ME TO THE BOATS!
HARRIET, YOU JUST HELPED 'BOUT EIGHT HUNDRED SLAVES GO FREE--IN ONE NIGHT.
THAT HAS TO BE A RECORD, EVEN FOR YOU.
ZZZZZZZ

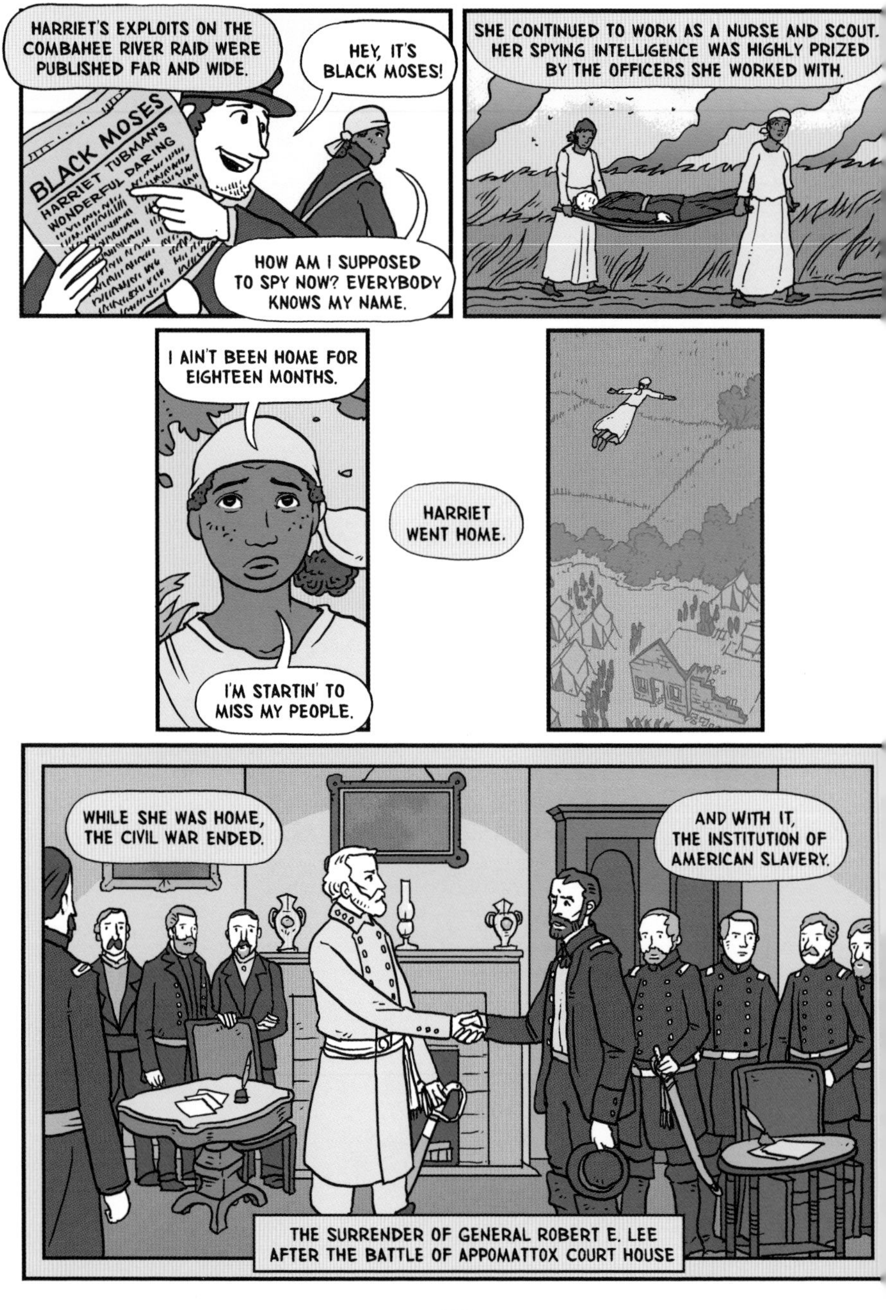
HARRIET'S EXPLOITS ON THE COMBAHEE RIVER RAID WERE PUBLISHED FAR AND WIDE.
HEY, IT'S BLACK MOSES!
BLACK MOSES
HARRIET TUBMAN'S WONDERFUL DARING
HOW AM I SUPPOSED TO SPY NOW? EVERYBODY KNOWS MY NAME.
SHE CONTINUED TO WORK AS A NURSE AND SCOUT. HER SPYING INTELLIGENCE WAS HIGHLY PRIZED BY THE OFFICERS SHE WORKED WITH.
I AIN'T BEEN HOME FOR EIGHTEEN MONTHS.
I'M STARTIN' TO MISS MY PEOPLE.
HARRIET WENT HOME.
WHILE SHE WAS HOME, THE CIVIL WAR ENDED.
AND WITH IT, THE INSTITUTION OF AMERICAN SLAVERY.
THE SURRENDER OF GENERAL ROBERT E. LEE AFTER THE BATTLE OF APPOMATTOX COURT HOUSE

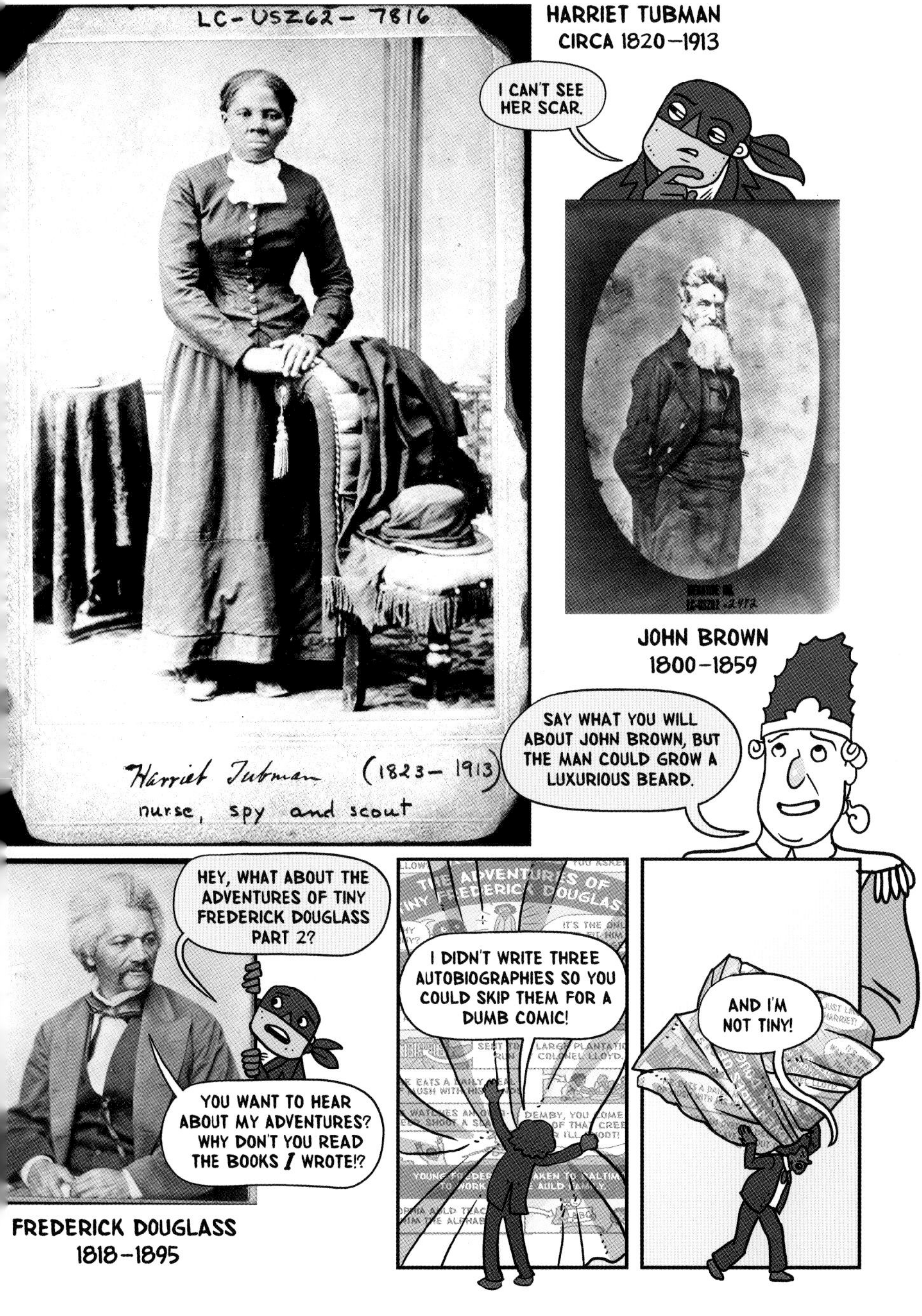
LC-USZ62- 7816
Harriet Tubman (1823- 1913)
nurse, spy and scout
HARRIET TUBMAN
CIRCA 1820–1913
I CAN'T SEE HER SCAR.
JOHN BROWN
1800–1859
SAY WHAT YOU WILL ABOUT JOHN BROWN, BUT THE MAN COULD GROW A LUXURIOUS BEARD.
HEY, WHAT ABOUT THE ADVENTURES OF TINY FREDERICK DOUGLASS PART 2?
YOU WANT TO HEAR ABOUT MY ADVENTURES? WHY DON'T YOU READ THE BOOKS *I* WROTE!?
FREDERICK DOUGLASS
1818–1895
I DIDN'T WRITE THREE AUTOBIOGRAPHIES SO YOU COULD SKIP THEM FOR A DUMB COMIC!
AND I'M NOT TINY!

WHO WOULD WIN IN A FIGHT BETWEEN

HENRY KNOX, THE SPECTER OF DEATH, GUSTAVUS FOX, AND THE 1916 GOD OF WAR

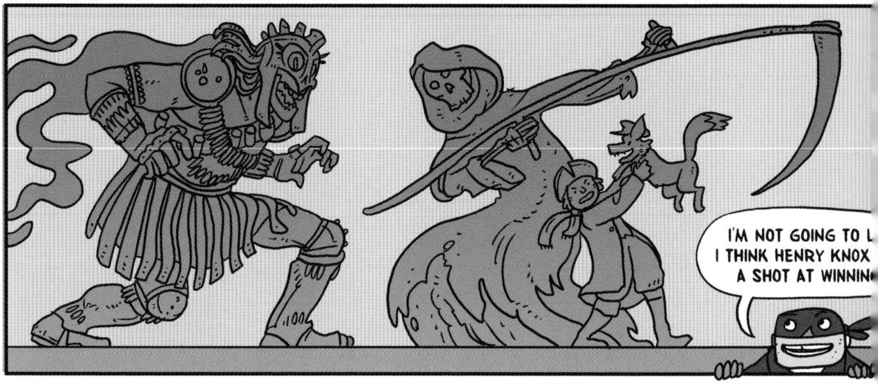

I'M NOT GOING TO L
I THINK HENRY KNOX
A SHOT AT WINNIN

THERE IS ONLY ONE WAY TO DECIDE: READ THE HAZARDOUS TALES SERIES!

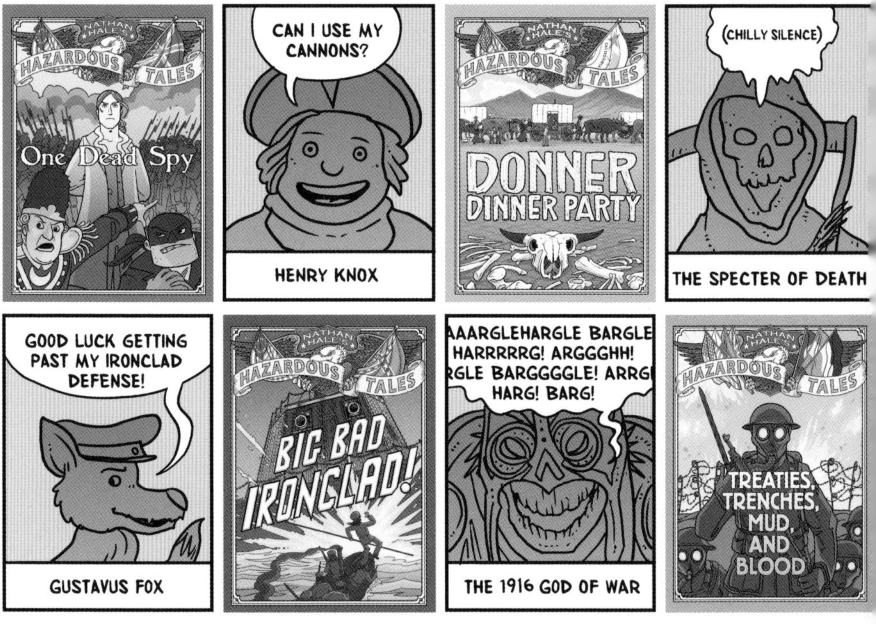

NATHAN HALE'S HAZARDOUS TALES
One Dead Spy
CAN I USE MY CANNONS?
HENRY KNOX
NATHAN HALE'S HAZARDOUS TALES
DONNER DINNER PARTY
(CHILLY SILENCE)
THE SPECTER OF DEATH
GOOD LUCK GETTING PAST MY IRONCLAD DEFENSE!
GUSTAVUS FOX
NATHAN HALE'S HAZARDOUS TALES
BIG BAD IRONCLAD!
AAARGLEHARGLE BARGLE HARRRRRG! ARGGGHH! RGLE BARGGGGLE! ARRG HARG! BARG!
THE 1916 GOD OF WAR
NATHAN HALE'S HAZARDOUS TALES
TREATIES, TRENCHES, MUD, AND BLOOD

NATHAN HALE (THE AUTHOR, NOT THE SPY) HAS ILLUSTRATED SEVEN GRAPHIC NOVELS, INCLUDING THE HAZARDO TALES BOOKS, *RAPUNZEL'S REVENGE,* AND ITS SEQUEL, *CALAMITY JACK.* HE ALSO ILLUSTRATED A FEW SILLY BOO ABOUT FRANKENSTEIN UNDER THE PEN NAME LUDWORST BEMONSTER.

BEFORE THE HAZARDOUS TALES SERIES, HE WAS HEALTHY AND RAN EIGHT MARATHONS (BEST TIME: 3:48:31). NOW HE SPENDS SO MUCH TIME RESEARCHING, WRITING, AND DRAWING, HE IS PUDGY, JOWLY, AND SLOW. HE IS WRECKING HIS HEALTH FOR THE LOVE OF HISTORY COMICS. MR. HALE LIVES IN UTAH. FOR MORE, VISIT WWW.HAZARDOUSTALES.COM

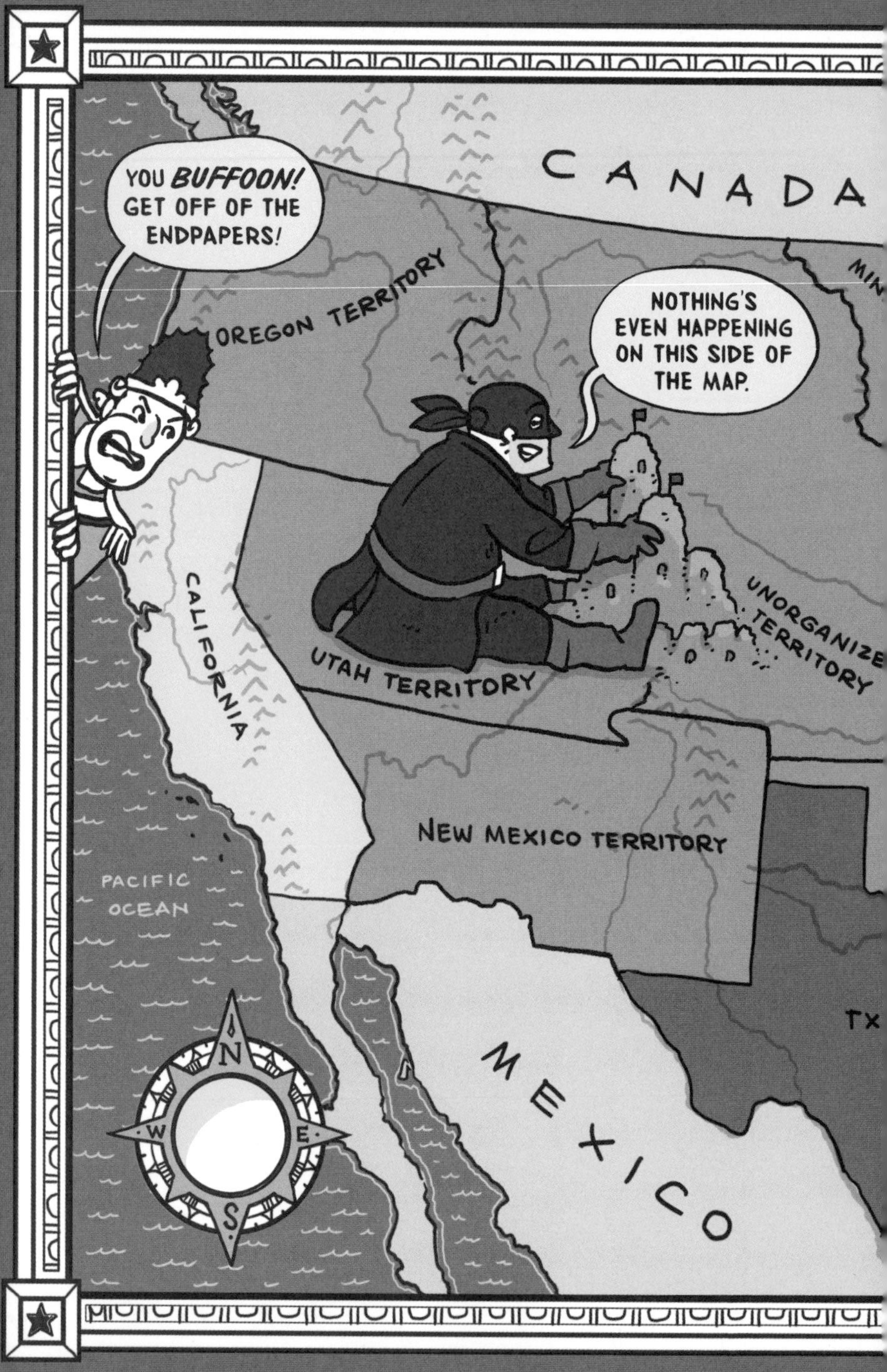
YOU *BUFFOON!* GET OFF OF THE ENDPAPERS!
CANADA
OREGON TERRITORY
NOTHING'S EVEN HAPPENING ON THIS SIDE OF THE MAP.
CALIFORNIA
UTAH TERRITORY
UNORGANIZE
TERRITORY
NEW MEXICO TERRITORY
PACIFIC OCEAN
MEXICO
TX
N
W
E
S